Re-framing Literacy

Imaginative and attractive, cutting edge in its conception, this text explicates a model for the integration of language arts and literacy education based on the notion of framing. Framing as a unifying principle derives from the frames used in the visual and performing arts, and is also a concept that has been used in sociology. The act of framing – not frames in themselves – provides a creative and critical approach to English as a subject.

Re-framing Literacy

- Offers an authoritative, clear guide to a complex field
- Breaks new ground in the language arts/literacy field, integrating arts-based and sociologically based conceptions of the subject
- Is internationally relevant – the concept of framing does not align itself to a particular culture or language but is generally applicable to thinking about communication arts in a number of languages and cultures.

The theory of rhetoric described in this book and which provides its overarching theory for framing is dialogic, political and liberating. Pedagogically, the text works inductively, from examples up toward theory: starting with visuals and moving back and forth between text and image; exploring multimodality; and engaging in the transformations of text and image that are at the heart of learning in English and the language arts.

Structured like a teaching course, designed to excite and involve readers and lead them towards high-level and useful theory in the field, *Re-framing Literacy* is widely appropriate for pre-service and in-service courses globally in English and languages arts education.

Richard Andrews is Professor in English at the Institute of Education, University of London.

Language, Culture, and Teaching
Sonia Nieto, Series Editor

Visit **www.routledge.com/education** for additional information on titles in the Language, Culture, and Teaching series.

Re-framing Literacy

Teaching and Learning in English and the Language Arts

Richard Andrews

 Routledge
Taylor & Francis Group

NEW YORK AND LONDON

First published 2011
by Routledge
270 Madison Avenue, New York, NY 10016

Simultaneously published in the UK
by Routledge
2 Park Square, Milton Park, Abingdon, Oxon OX14 4RN

Routledge is an imprint of the Taylor & Francis Group, an informa business

© 2011 Taylor & Francis

Typeset in Minion by Glyph International

Printed and bound in the United States of America on acid-free paper by Edwards Brothers, Inc.

Library of Congress Cataloging in Publication Data
Andrews, Richard, 1953 Apr. 1–
Re-framing literacy : teaching and learning in english and the language arts / Richard Andrews.
    p. cm. – (Language, culture, and teaching)
Includes bibliographical references.
1. Literacy. 2. Language awareness in children.
3. Language arts (Early childhood) I. Title.
LC149.A64 2010
371.33'44678–dc22   2010020904

ISBN 13: 978-0-415-99552-8 (hbk)
ISBN 13: 978-0-415-99553-5 (pbk)
ISBN 13: 978-0-203-85312-2 (ebk)

For David, Zoë and Grace
and in recognition of the work of Howard Hodgkin

Foreword

Sonia Nieto

So much in education today is dry, unfeeling and predictable. This is particularly true of the language arts, a field suffering from an excess of rubrics and templates and "best practices" but short on innovation and hope. Richard Andrews's *Re-framing Literacy* provides a welcome antidote to this context. Both exciting and energizing, the ideas in this book give teachers and scholars other ways of viewing literacy and the language arts by *re-framing* them. While many schools and classrooms are consumed with test scores and with quick schemes to raise them, Andrews focuses instead on creativity, interpretation, critical thought, and the fluid nature of language and, indeed, of teaching and learning.

The books in the Language, Culture, and Teaching Series ask you to rethink your assumptions about the language arts and to recognize that teaching and learning are always immersed in a particular context, and that all students come to school with specific sociocultural realities. *Re-framing Literacy* powerfully reflects these ideas. Based on the idea of the frame not only as "enclosing" content but also as "disclosing" it, for Andrews, re-framing is not so much a theory as it is an action. In this way, frames help us transgress the limits of static forms. Rather than a static theory, his "re-framing" is dynamic, on the move. It is also inevitably concerned with power and politics, because in Andrews's words, "English as a school subject is fraught with political baggage" (p. 165). The idea that the language arts are concerned with power is challenging for some teachers to accept, but the author describes many ways in which this is true. Andrews's ideas are also provocative, as in his suggestion that the very term "English" is no longer appropriate for what needs to happen in classrooms.

A unique feature of this book is the juxtaposition of the language arts and the arts in general. The arts have unfortunately been drained out of much of education, but Andrews has placed them squarely with the language arts, considering not only texts of various kinds, but also the visual and performing arts, and even sports. In this book, the verbal arts are considered a true art, and writing itself is re-framed as a multimodal art. By shining a spotlight on the arts in education, Andrews links them naturally and elegantly. The interconnections among the arts are explored, not only in words but also in the many images interspersed throughout the text. This is another valuable contribution of the book.

Through the extended metaphor of framing throughout the text, the author encourages teachers to think critically and act creatively. At the same time, re-framing assumes that teachers may work in contexts that do not support reflection, joy, and creativity. Given these times where standardization and accountability reign supreme in many school systems around the world, teachers need support and encouragement to think differently and with courage about their work. This book will provide some of that support.

Through his ideas of "re-framing", Andrews invites you to envision a different kind of language arts, one imbued with artistic possibility and energy, not simply rote and ritual, as is so often the case today. With far-reaching and intriguing examples in everything from soccer to technology, and from Shakespeare's plays to Van Gogh's letters, he suggests implications for pedagogy and curriculum. The great value of this book is that it can help all language and literacy teachers bridge the gap between the grim reality that exists in many schools and the hopeful and visionary schools in which they would like to work. It is my hope that, after you have read it, you too will come to think of the language arts more expansively and imaginatively than you had before.

Preface

During the 1970s and 80s, English as a school subject began to form into different camps. The unsatisfactory nature of the situation in the 1990s brought about a desire to find a unifying theory for the subject: one which would provide the basis for a solution to the split between fiction and non-fiction, 'personal growth' and a skills-based curriculum, heritage and the international dimension of literature.

It is in order to strengthen the theoretical foundation for English as a school subject, particularly at a time when electronic communication and multimodality offer new opportunities and challenges to the nature of the subject, that this book was conceived. I present a case for the potency of the idea of framing as a way of helping the reading and writing of texts, as well as speaking and listening; its appropriateness as texts are increasingly being framed on computer and hand-held screens; the simplicity of the notion of framing; the fact that communication is re-framed, especially to suit purposes in education; and its social and political significance. I argue and demonstrate that re-framing and transformation are at the heart of effective practice in language arts and English teaching and link them to framing theory and to everyday classroom practice and possibility.

I argue, at both theoretical and practical levels, that the only body of theoretical knowledge about language use able to account for the range of communication necessary for the 1990s and first part of the twenty-first century is contemporary rhetoric. Not only does rhetoric have a history of 2,500 years, thus providing continuity throughout history; it also is flexible enough as a body of approaches to adapt itself to present-day needs. Essentially, the rhetoric described in the book and which provides its overarching theory is dialogic, political and liberating. In short, rhetoric is the art of discourse. Under the canopy of rhetoric, framing – the way language is shaped to particular situations, taking into account generic context, function, intention and audience – is the principal working activity by which the English curriculum can operate and hold its own in a fast-changing educational world. Framing also allows an exploration of the relationships between the verbal, visual and performing arts, especially in the light of electronic communication.

This book is for teachers, undergraduate and postgraduate students, and lecturers who are looking for an authoritative, clear guide to a complex field; and particularly pre-service and in-service teachers in English education and language arts education. This is also a book with its feet on the ground. I am aware, through work with the Department of Children, Schools and Families in the UK Government, that standards in writing and literacy generally have to improve yet further, for *all* socio-economic groups. Target setting alone, as in No Child Left Behind or Every Child Matters (the UK version), will not in itself achieve such improvement: there has to be engagement, transformation and consolidation of the learning process. That's why this book will also resonate with policy-makers and curriculum-designers.

Pedagogical Approach

Pedagogically, this book works inductively and deductively, from examples up towards theory and back again. It engages students and lecturers/professors through exemplars and other examples; starting with visuals and moving back and forth between text and image; exploring multimodality; and engaging in the transformations of text and image that are at the heart of learning in English and the language arts. My intent is to excite and engage you, the reader, and lead you towards high-level and useful theory in the field. The work of others is incorporated, with all due permissions, to diversify the voices used. In this vein, I also draw on sources and student voices from across a range of cultures worldwide.

Overview

Chapter 1, "What's in a Frame?", begins with some key examples of how messages are framed. It traces the evolution of framing theory from its use in psychology and sociology in the 1940s to its adoption by discourse analysts in the early 1990s as a useful and interesting level at which to look at language use and the teaching/learning of language. The origin of the metaphor of framing in painting is discussed, with references to visual framing and the changing nature of frames within art. The place of framing within a wider theory of rhetoric is also set out in this chapter. The context for framing is important (and the final chapter completes the framing of the present book) in the effort to work towards a new theory for English and the language arts.

Having established the power of framing as both a practical device and a metaphor for understanding composition and interpretation in oral and written language, in Chapter 2, "Framing in the Visual Arts", I take a closer look at framing in the visual world. Several questions are asked. Why are pictures and photographs 'framed'? How is it done, and what kinds of framing are at play? To what degree is the reaction against formal framing just another kind of framing device? Is it indeed possible not to frame in the visual arts? This chapter proceeds inductively via a series of examples or cases. It suggests that frames are there to be re-framed, broken or transgressed as well as to contain and define. Practically, frames were also originally devised to allow paintings to be preserved and *moved*. In literacy, frames allow the creation of common contexts that allow the 'transportation' of ideas between people.

Chapter 3, "Framing in the Performance Arts", addresses the common notion of a stage for the performance of dance, theatre and other performance arts. Works are performed on stages, which are highly framed spaces; works also take place in time within these spaces. And yet many art forms break the frame by engaging directly with the audience: both by bringing the audience on stage and by the actors or dancers exploring and peopling the spaces beyond the stage. The stage-space itself can also be transformed. A *New York Times* music review in September 2007 carried the headline 'Before erasing borders you first traverse them'. This principle can hold true for the verbal arts as well as the visual and performing ones. It is a principle that also operates in the photographic images as well as in film and animation, where timing, rhythm and sequencing are key elements; and where the act of editing is central to the creative process. Film itself is not explored much in the present book, but the principle of framing and re-framing is one that has been explored by the British Film Institute in its attempts to link film to literacy and thus to making moving image a more central part of the school curriculum.

Chapter 4, "Visual and Verbal Frames", looks at the problem not so much from a visual arts perspective as from a verbal arts viewpoint (by which I mean the oral and written arts). So rather than consider with a group of artists how the verbal is included in or mediates their visual work, the chapter, in keeping with the argument of the book as a whole and its focus on literacy, considers various aspects of printed written material: how writing itself is a visual art; how writing relates to other graphic arts; how writing, in combination with more purely visual forms, shapes its messages; and what exciting contiguities are emerging between written language and the visual from the perspective of multimodality? The relationship between the verbal and visual has developed throughout history; in the last 20 years or so, it has been foregrounded again as the computer screen has brought the two modes (and sound) together.

In Chapter 5, "Frames of Reference: Framing in Relation to a Theory of Multimodality", I explore a number of questions. What implications do theories of multimodality have for a framing approach to composition? What place does framing have within such theories? This chapter suggests that the two sit well with each other, with rhetoric as the overarching theory, multimodality as a range of possibilities in shaping and communicating with others from a social semiotic point of view and framing as the creative and critical act which can bring such communication into being/action. The chapter suggests that 1980s and 1990s approaches to genres, which often saw them as static text-types and/ or recognizable patterns of social action, need to be updated to allow for rhetorical, multimodal and framing perspectives – and to provide a way in which

Acknowledgements

My greatest intellectual debt is to Ian Bentley, Carey Jewitt, Gunther Kress, Richard Lanham, Gale Maclachlan, Peter Medway, Ian Reid, Michael Simons and Richard Sterling, all of whom in different ways have helped to shape and challenge my ideas about framing.

Much of the inspiration for my work on framing has come from my work at Middlesex University, London, in the 1990s. I continue to work with Stephen Boyd Davis, Howard Hollands, Usha Agarwal-Hollands, Magnus Moar, Karen Raney, Vivienne Reiss (then of the Arts Council), Victoria de Rijke, Rebecca Sinker and others on the interface of the visual and verbal. At the Institute of Education, London, collaboration with Gillian Anderson, Jeff Bezemer, Andrew Burn, David Buckingham, Caroline Daly, Anton Franks, John Hardcastle, Chris Husbands, Mary Irwin, Adam Lefstein, Morlette Lindsay, Di Mavers, Pam Meecham, Caroline Pelletier, Sue Rogers, Anne Turvey, Rebekah Willett and John Yandell on literacy, the visual arts, drama, media and English development provides a rich intellectual context in which to work, not only in the Centre for Multimodal Research and the Department for Learning, Curriculum and Communication, but in the Faculty of Culture and Pedagogy and across the Institute more widely.

Faculty and students at New York University's Steinhardt School of Culture, Education and Human Development have been instrumental in making me think about framing in drama and with regard to multimodality, especially Sarah Beck, Mary Brabeck, Myrrh Domingo, Jim Fraser, Glynda Hull, David Kirkland, Joe McDonald, Rebecca Packer, Gordon Pradl, Joe Salvatore and Anna Smith.

Other colleagues who have inspired me in thinking about English and literacy are Carla Asher, Catherine Beavis, Panayiota Charalambous, Stephen Clarke, Caroline Coffin, Teresa Cremin, Sophia Diamantopoulou, Carol Fox, Andy Goodwyn, Eve Gregory, Colin Harrison, Hilary Janks, the late and much missed Jenny Leach, Terry Locke, Janet Maybin, Sally Mitchell, Wendy Morgan, Gemma Moss, Debbie Myhill, Rebecca Packer, Robert Protherough, Wayne Sawyer, Ilana Snyder, Brian Street and Dominic Wyse. I have been inspired by the work of the National Writing Project in the USA, and by the efforts of

Simon Wrigley and Jeni Smith to launch a seminal version in the UK; and by the work of Cary Bazalgette and Mark Reid at BFI (British Film Institute) Education, whose report 'Reframing literacy: film education for all?' prefigures the title of the present book.

I am particularly grateful to Naomi Silverman at Routledge for her belief in the book and her helpful ideas in its evolution; and to Sonia Nieto for her support from the very beginning of the project.

Part of Chapter 1 was first given as an inaugural lecture at Middlesex University, London in 1996 and has since been unpublished. Part of Chapter 4 first appeared in an earlier version as 'The nature of "visual literacy": problems and possibilities for the classroom' in *Literacy Learning: Secondary Thoughts*, 6:2, 8–16, June 1998 (now called *Literacy Learning: the Middle Years*) and is here reworked courtesy of Marion Meiers and the Australian Literacy Educators' Association. A section from Chapter 6 first appeared as 'The base of a small iceberg: mark-making in the work of a four year old' in *Image Text Persuasion* Adelaide, University of South Australia, 1998, 5–22. I am grateful to the editors of *Literacy Learning: the Middle Years* and to Claire Woods of the University of South Australia for permission to revise and reprint those pieces.

I wish to acknowledge the insights, inspiration and support given to me by my family during the writing of this book, including the many visits to art galleries, museums, theatres and 'real world spaces': Dodi Beardshaw, David, Zoë and Grace. In particular, to David for introducing me to the Building Centre in London, and for structural designs for buildings; to Zoë and Grace for all things theatrical. I dedicate this book to our children, in thanks to them for inspiring me in different ways of looking at framing; and to encourage them in framing and re-framing their own lives. The book also recognizes the contribution of Howard Hodgkin to notions of framing and re-framing in the visual arts.

Chapter 1

What's in a Frame?

This chapter starts with some key examples of how messages are framed. It traces the evolution of framing theory from its use in sociology to its adoption by discourse analysts in the early 1990s as the most useful and interesting level at which to look at language use and the teaching/learning of language. The origin of the metaphor of framing in painting will also be used, with references to visual framing and the changing nature of frames within art. The place of framing within a wider theory of rhetoric will also be set out in this chapter.

Introduction

At its simplest, a frame is rectangular, in a square, 'portrait' or 'landscape' shape.

The rectangular nature of most frames is for literal and practical reasons: wooden or steel frames (or frames constructed in most materials) are more easily made if they are rectangular, because of the straightness of the material and the way it can be joined at the corners. Rectangularity, however, is not the principal feature of frames that is most salient for the purposes of this book. Rather, it is a number of other features. First, that frames both exclude and include: there is space outside the frame and space inside the frame, and the demarcation is significant. Second, the frame in the language arts world is largely invisible: it may be there in some form or other, as in the boundaries of the page of a book, or the assumed white space around a poem, but it is rarely

Figure 1.1 Rectangular frames.

to the language arts – and especially those arts as taught in schools, colleges and universities.

What is significant about the rise of interest in framing at the beginning of the 1990s in the field of discourse studies and interpretation is the *level* at which framing applies to the language arts. The previous 45 years or so had seen intense focus, through the discipline of linguistics, on units of language below the level of the whole text: phonetics, phonemics, grapho-phonemics, morphology, lexicology, syntax; and, to a lesser extent, sub-units of whole texts such as paragraphs, stanzas etc. From a literary point of view, the field of stylistics applied this linguistic interest to fiction, plays and poetry. In linguistic systems, the tendency has been to move to 'higher' levels of analysis for two reasons: first, that a meta-level of understanding is necessary in order to make sense of the level below (a fact that has not always been recognized by those that are wedded to a bottom-up approach, from smaller units to bigger ones, in the analysis of language); and, second, that once a particular level of language is heavily analysed and (to all intents and purposes) fairly well understood, there is a need to move on to a higher level of analysis in order to maintain momentum and motivation in the field as a whole. This is not to say that the previous levels of interest become redundant. On the contrary, new understanding and perspectives at the higher levels require re-analysis of the lower levels.

Framing, therefore, comes to the fore in the early 1990s as the level at which language use became interested (again) in the relationship between whole texts and their contexts. Rhetorical perspectives suggest that when there is an occasion for communication between two parties, a genre has to be chosen as the vehicle for the communication. This genre can be 'off-the-shelf' or a hybrid or a newly made-up genre to suit the purposes of the communication. The 'context' is made up of the social situation of the two parties, the motivation for the communication, the particularities of the occasion and the available means at disposal for communication (technological, generic) and the particular slant the speaker/writer (in rhetoric, the 'rhetor') wishes to give. It is because the act of framing delineates and defines what is expressed/communicated/read that it is a crucial mediator between context and text, between speaker and listener/writer and reader.

Tannen's book *Framing in Discourse* (1993) includes a key chapter entitled 'What's in a frame? Surface evidence for underlying expectations' in which she sets out some of the main theories in the field. Underlying notions of schemata, frames, scripts are, she suggests, 'structures of expectation' that enable us to bring pattern and sense to memory (cf. Bartlett 1932) and to present interactions of an oral or written kind. It is not so much the structures of *expectation* that are relevant to the present book, but the *act of framing* as a basic principle of composition, with an emphasis on writing and speech in a multimodal world. That is why 'framing' is the preferred term for the present project rather than 'schemata' or 'scripts', which suggest something more static. Such emphasis on action is consonant with the work of Gumperz (1977) or Frake (1977), both of whom take an anthropological/sociological concentrate perspective on *activity* rather than focusing on entities like scripts or schemata. To quote Tannen (1993, p.19):

> Frake (1977) ends his paper with the extended metaphor of people as mapmakers whose "culture does not provide a cognitive map, but rather a set of principles for mapmaking and navigation" resulting in "a whole chart case of rough, improvised, continually revised sketch maps".
>
> (pp.6–7)

A different, though more focused perspective, is taken by MacLachlan and Reid in *Framing and Interpretation* (1994). Their emphasis is clearly on framing in the Bateson tradition, but on the interpretive side of the activity rather than the compositional side. They distinguish between *extratextual framing* where interpretation depends on outside information, "unspecified by the text but felt to be presupposed by it" (p.3); *intratextual framing* where "subdivisional and other internal framing devices" are used; *intertextual framing* which relate one text or text-type to another; and *circumtextual* features like book titles, imprint pages, references etc. which indicate that the main body of the text in a book is to be considered as a particular type of text, and thus read with a particular type of approach. MacLachlan and Reid suggest that the power of framing as an interpretive device is that it both separates the making of meaning in semiotics from other such creations, but at the same time relates the making of new meaning to existing patterns and knowledge: "Framing is thus the process of demarcating phenomena in a double-edged way that is simultaneously inclusive and exclusive" (p.16).

In *Framing and Interpretation*, MacLachlan and Reid (1994) quote Frow (1986) who suggests that a frame

> can be anything that acts as a sign of qualitative difference, a sign of the boundary between a marked and an unmarked place.
>
> (p.17)

They go on to say that in the case of literary texts, fictional space is thus set off from reality by the use of various framing devices like titles, subtitles and prefaces and specific locations in bookshops and libraries. We have come to think of fiction as looking like a book of a certain size and colour, just as art is conventionally conceived as being in a gallery:

> the aesthetic space of a painting is bordered by the frame, setting it off from the extra-aesthetic space of the wall, which in turn may be part of a room within a gallery.
>
> (p.13)

The acts of framing – the term MacLachlan and Reid prefer to use to 'frame' because of its very inscription of action and flexibility – seems a more useful one than 'genre' (when used to mean 'text-type'), in that it describes *acts* rather than *phenomena*; it is flexible, as frames can be adapted and changed according to the needs of the participants within the frame. Metaphors of framing can indicate that "in order to perceive and understand anything we must provisionally distinguish it from other things while also relating it to them".

Like MacLachlan and Reid, the present book prefers the term 'framing' because it suggests an activity involving an agent. 'Frames' are reserved for those products that are the result of framing; and 'frameworks' are larger-scale "superordinate set[s] of frames" or overarching structures. These frameworks and frames are largely invisible, but are invoked when transparency and clarity are required as to the nature and origin of a particular act of communication.

The theatre director Peter Brook's perception about words from his book *The Empty Space* (1972) can serve to develop the argument further:

> A word does not start as a word – it is an end product which begins as an impulse, situated by attitude and behaviour which dictates the need for expression ... for the actor the word is a small visible portion of a gigantic unseen formation.

> (p.15)

What implications does this statement have for language-based views of communication? First, it is liberating – "A word does not start as a word". Liberating, because it puts words in their place. All too often, we see words as opaque, as some form of reification of the world, as having real active presence in the world. In speech act theory and practice, they do have action and consequences. They are transactional; they make things, thoughts and feelings happen. Even a written contract is like this, and so is a spoken one, as instanced in the words "I do" in a marriage ceremony, or the declaration "Not guilty" in a trial: writing is, as Vygotsky (1978) calls it, a 'second order symbolic system', based on speech, a 'first order symbolic system'. Part of the problem with the prevailing notion in the latter part of the twentieth century of how language worked in education was that language was either transactional or 'poetic', or somewhere on a spectrum between the two. That is to say, it *either* made things happen, was transparent; *or* it was opaque, meant to be looked at for itself, meant to be the object of pleasure and spectatorship. This is a rather static view of what language does; just as the notion of genres as text-types is static. But if it is static, you can teach it – so some thinking goes. Soon, it becomes stale, imposed, authoritative in a negative way. Children do not like it, and before you know where you are, you have a National Curriculum or a set of national standards, strategies and targets with prescribed genres, prescibed texts, prescribed authors.

This book argues that all language – including poetic language – is transactional, and that the framing that goes on both separates and distinguishes different kinds of language from the everyday discourse of the world, and also places it in relation to the everyday world of discourse. The frames both enclose and, because they are metaphorical and not made of wood, *disclose*.

Second, however, Peter Brook's perception only goes half way. He talks about a word being an 'end-product'. He is thinking here about the word as produced by the actor on stage. Yes, it is a product, a 'mouthful of air', vibrations *shaped* in the air between the actor and the audience. But it is not the end, because the audience, by definition, is not a collection of cardboard cut-outs. It is a group which listens and which interprets in its myriad ways, each according to the life-history he/she brings to the framed moment in the theatre or in the framed space that stands for a theatre. Communication, then, is not one-way: it is rhetorical, dynamic, dialogic, dramatic – even if only one person is speaking – and it takes place within frames of different sizes and natures. So the 'gigantic unseen formation' informing the word is one example of an invisible frame, just as the stage is a more tangible one. And, of course, some works assume gigantic and multiple frames, like *Hamlet*. Others are not so large or potentially ambiguous, like the note to the milkman, 'Two pints today please'. Within a larger frame, however, the phrase 'Two pints today please' could assume greater significance: as the last line in a play, it could signify the start of a beautiful new relationship (for the last 20 years, the order has been one pint) or the end of one (it used to be three pints). And so on.

The intention in citing Brook at the start of this exploration of framing as a metaphor for education in the language arts is to set out the backcloth for an exploration about language. It offers the following: i) the 'empty space', the arena in which words operate, very like a frame; ii) the reinforced notion that words are transactional; and iii) a chance to go beyond Brook and suggest that there is more to consider beyond the limits of the stage, that communication is always two-way, always rhetorical, always situated.

Why the term 'framing' rather than 'genre' to talk about language at the macro-level? Our understanding of how language works and is learnt has developed considerably over the last 30 years. In the 1950s, linguists were refining theories about phonology, the sound components in words. They then moved on to morphology, the science of how bits of words – like prefixes, roots and suffixes, i.e. grammatically meaningful micro-units of language. The logical next step was to study whole words – lexicography – and then came Chomsky, suggesting that syntax, or the ways words were put together in strings, was the key, not only to understanding language, but also to understanding the way the human mind works. After syntax, the focus shifted to the whole sentence, then to strings of sentences, paragraphs, stanzas and so on and notions of cohesion and coherence in text; thence to study of the 'whole text' and consequently, a fascination with different types of text, or 'genres'. Now, at the start of the second decade of the twenty-first century, we can see that texts are so flexible, varied, more and more mixed-mode and mixed-media (see Kress and van Leeuwen 2001) in their composition, and dependent upon their context for full comprehension. The interface between the text and its context is the area that linguists and educationalists are concerned with now, and hence the need for a closer look at framing. Framing both defines the text – think of the white space around a poem – and gives it 'position' in relation to other texts and less formal language. Framing, crucially, is responsive to context; whereas genre theory, at least in some extreme versions, is not.

But, just as a word does not start as a word, so too, a genre does not start as a genre, which is why framing is important in the creation of theatre spaces, dance spaces, boardrooms, conversations around café tables, classrooms and, less obviously, to invisible frameworks that operate in speech and, more obviously though more ambiguously, in print.

We know that a single phrase like "No no no no" can be spoken, heard and read in many different ways: Lear enchained with Cordelia at the end of *King Lear*; Mrs Thatcher on Europe (there were in fact five 'no's); de Gaulle's earlier position ('non'); Richard Huelsenbeck in a Dada manifesto of 1918: "Have expressionists fulfilled our expectations of an art that burns the essence of life into our flesh? No! no! no!"; in terror, in sympathy, with arrogance, as straightforward denial, as first words and, perhaps concurrently, as the beginnings of notions of identity. How we interpret the phrase depends on its immediate linguistic context – which words surround it – and on whether there are any non-linguistic cues, either in body language, tone, visual or musical accompaniment. Who is saying it to whom, when and why are other factors to consider. Language is inescapably rhetorical. There are clearly a number of frames to take into account, even around the simplest word.

As suggested earlier in this chapter, the concept of framing as applied to language in interaction is not new. Its first use of this kind in recent times is in Bateson's *A Theory of Play and Fantasy* (Bateson 1954) where it is suggested that "no communicative move, whether verbal or non-verbal [can] be understood" without reference to the frame of interpretation being applied to it (Tannen 1993, p.3). As Tannen suggests, notions of framing have been taken up by researchers in communication, psychology, anthropology and sociology (especially in Goffman's *Frame Analysis*, 1974).

Framing is a metaphor from the visual arts, and so is an associated term 'shaping', a term to be added to the emerging field in language education. Shaping is a useful addition to the metaphorical repertoire in the field of composition in that, on the one hand, it helps to describe the processes by which situations are shaped (and thus framed), processes in which power relations play a part. We are *shaped* by history, by circumstance and by those more powerful than ourselves. On the other hand, participants within the frame have the power to shape the course of the discussion or exchange to varying degrees. Furthermore, shaping links the process of *making* talk or writing or multi-channel communication with the other creative arts. In a way, if framing as a metaphor is two-dimensional, then shaping is three-dimensional (its products in the art world would be dances, sculptures, jewellery, buildings or furniture, for example; though the shaping, composing activity is also common to the largely two-dimensional arts like photography and painting).

As far as poetry goes, it is now well accepted that the same words that constitute a non-fictional text like a newspaper article, for instance, can also constitute, with some re-framing, a poem.

Certainly, it is no longer possible to hold the position that established itself towards the end of the eighteenth century, which Donald Davie (1952) has characterized in *The Purity of Diction in English Verse*, when there was a diction for poetry which was a selection from the language.

But there are still critics who see intrinsic textual features as defining a genre, and one of these is Barbara Herrnstein Smith. MacLachlan and Reid (1994) take her to task for suggesting that metre – some more organized, musical dimension to a poem than is there in everyday life and discourse – might be the distinguishing feature. *They* privilege the reader's role, suggesting that it is the frame brought to the words by the reader which determines the marks on the page, the sound in the air as poetry.

Smith (1968) refers to a number of different ways in which a poem might end (her book is called *Poetic Closure*) – repetition of a refrain, by picking up a rhyme from earlier in the poem, with a concluding statement – but as MacLachlan and Reid (1994) say, there is no considered theory of framing to emerge from her work: all the focus is on the internal dynamics of the poem.

What is particularly significant for the argument here is that formalist notions of literary identity (i.e. one equation for poetry, one for short story, one for the novel etc.) "ignore the paradoxical status of the frame itself ... and refuse to make the frame work except as a barrier between literature and its contexts" (Carroll 1987, p.145). That is to say, formalist approaches do not recognize the two-way traffic that a frame sets up, nor the invigorating nature of that two-way traffic. Frames as barriers set up hierarchical relationships between literature and other kinds of language, between poetry and non-poetic language (whatever that is) and between fiction and non-fiction.

In the history of framing in art, the period between 1870 and 1914 is pivotal. Whistler's painting of Mrs Frederick R. Leyland which hangs in the Frick Collection, New York, uses the frame as part of the painting: it is flat, etched, gold, picking up the colours and textures of the painting itself. Chaplin (1994, p.271) notes that "from 1887 onwards, Seurat would sometimes paint the frame surrounding the canvas using the same pointillist techniques that he used on the canvas itself". But according to Staniszewski (1995, p.206), "Around 1913, at the very moment that artists were experimenting with abstraction, others began to see the cultural contingency of Art – that is to say, they began to see the institutional limitations of Art. Artists literally began to look beyond the limits of a painting's frame".

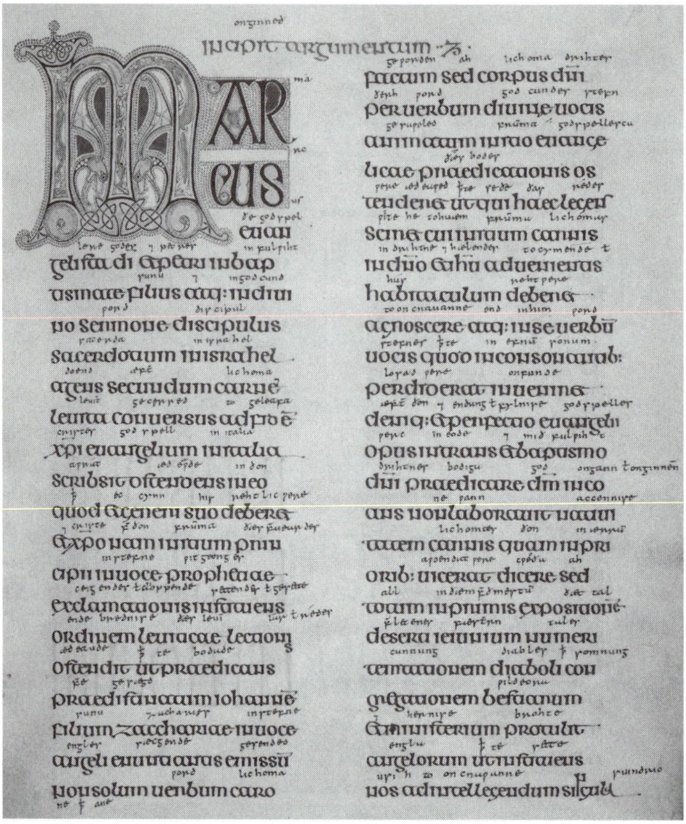

Figure 1.4 Glossed gospels, Mark, with commentary.

Finally, Figure 1.7, from Roberts' (2005) *Guide to Scripts used in English Writings up to 1500,* is a page from an Anglo-Saxon translation of Genesis which combines verbal text and images within the frame of the page. This early example of multimodality at work is from a manuscript that contains "a cycle of some four hundred illustrations" (p.78). In this particular case, the illustration is to be 'read' from the bottom upwards and includes commentary both within the frame of the illustration, and added in the top margin, as well as in the main text at the head of the page.

The main points to be made here are: that framing of text has been going on since the inception of text itself; that there are always frames that are borne in mind and which shape the actual script, whether they are carved in stone or inscribed on vellum or paper; that the relationship between what is inside and outside the frame is important; and, furthermore, that there is

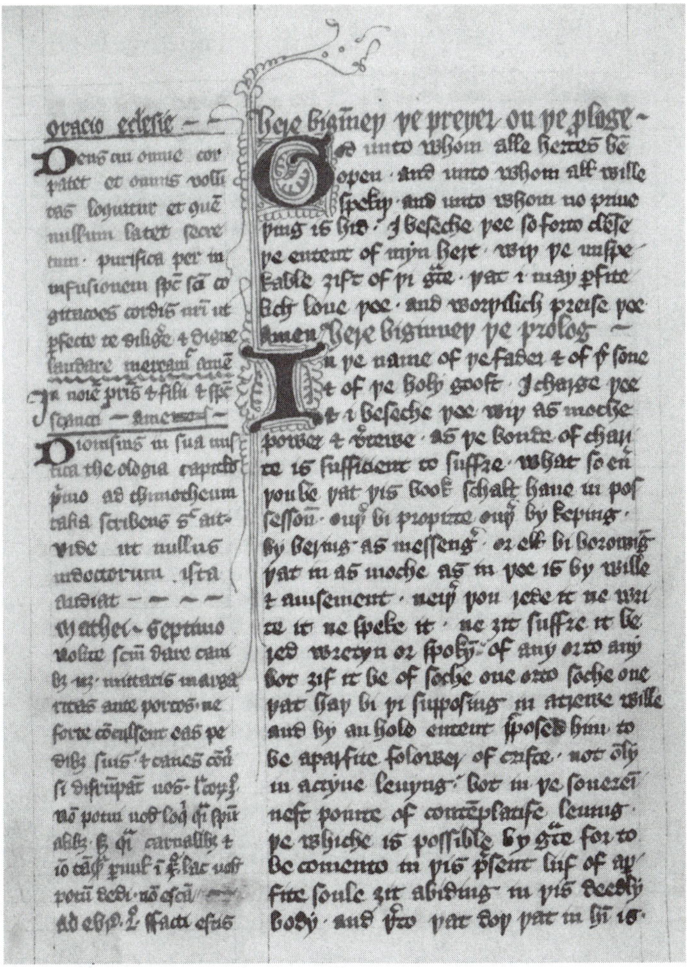

Figure 1.5 The Cloud of Unknowing, with continuous marginal gloss in Latin.

room for variation between kinds of text or between text and image within the frame.

It is not difficult to conceive of an unbroken tradition in composition, from the past to the present, of artists who combine word and image in the same frame (e.g. Lichtenstein, Kruger), and to contemporary use of word-processing programs and web 2.0 affordances like collective commentary on a shared text, or the 'comment' device in Word. That unbroken tradition is also evident in storytelling, from the scrolls of Indian storytellers to the scrolling that is contiguity and collage between image and text, and the pedagogical imperatives implied in such a new world of composition.

Lanham suggests that:

> the digitalization now common to letters and shapes creates a mixed text of icons and words ... Texts have long had illustrations ... but that relationship was fixed, and it seldom favoured the illustrations ... We now have to do with a relationship, both more balanced and radically dynamic, between two very different kinds of signal.
>
> (1993, p.77)

Lanham draws on Susanne Langer:

> Visual forms – lines, colours, proportions etc. – are just as capable of *articulation*, i.e. of complex combination, as words. But the laws that govern this sort of articulation are altogether different from the laws of syntax that govern language. The most radical difference is that *visual forms are not discursive*. They do not present their constituents successively, but simultaneously, so the relations determining a visual structure are grasped in one act of vision.[1]

To put this another way, and at another level of language description, visual forms are not intrinsically narrative. But neither, for that matter, are verbal ones, despite the strength of narrative theory in the 1980s. The new relationship worth exploring is between the various elements in multi-panelled works: the kind of polyptical contiguity present in comics, triptychs and newspapers and which are seen most dramatically in contemporary multi-panelled works like Imants Tillers' *Izkliede* (1994) (Diaspora), 292 panels of visual/verbal overlay,[2] and in a 1990 exhibition at the Louvre called *Polyptiques*.

Polyptiques are 'multi-panelled works'. An example is seen in Figure 1.8: a triptych of the Virgin and child enthroned with angels and saints, from the fourteenth century; and in multi-panelled work by the video artist Gary Hill. The distinctive aspect of *polyptiques* is that they are an arrangements of frames, not just a grid on which or via which a range of images is arrayed.

Whereas a single frame sets up a relationship between what is outside and inside the frame, with possible further exploration of different modes and/or different kinds of text within (and occasionally, outside) the frame, the polyptique sets up a dynamic between the two or more frames in the composition. So, in the case of the Byzantine triptych, the Virgin and child take centre stage in the middle of the three panels, with the crucifixion of Christ at the top; and in the side panels, which are clearly subsidiary to the main one, angels, saints, legendary and other figures that are accessory to the central iconic character and story are depicted. Triptychs have a symbolic but also a practical function, in that they can stand on altars and in other places without support.

Figure 1.8 Triptych with Virgin and child enthroned with angels and saints.
© The National Trust. Used with permission.

The panels are related to each other in a hierarchical pattern, both vertically and laterally.

In Gary Hill's work, *House of Cards* (which is not shown in this book) the bank of five screens suggests the possibility of combining any two or three at a time in your mind's eye, while aware of other tracks, other events going on at the same time. In the actual exhibition of the work, all five screens froze their images momentarily at times, as if catching a moment of cohesion.

In teaching terms, the analogy is with the use of a number of photographs that students can move around to compose their own narratives. The number of possible sequences, even with five still photographs, is huge. Composing and viewing the video screens become almost the same act, given that you have to make the connections between the screens/images at any one time.

room – find learning in these spaces unsatisfactory. They do not wish to play that particular game. At the same time, the really exciting action in classrooms is when the frames are open to the urgency and rhythms of the language of the world.

Writing and communication that moves beyond the essentially fictional (which is, after all, bound by the book or film) is a threat to the classroom, and to the institutional nature of schooling, because it breaks down the walls of the classroom. It cannot be contained.

In summary:

- framing is helpful to the language arts, coming as it does from sociological theory, because: i) it takes us beyond the sterile debate on genre; ii) it is flexible, dynamic, rhetorical and keyed in to people; and iii) it links English again with the other arts – dance, theatre, music, art, design, architecture etc.
- what goes on inside frames is in urgent need of study and research, particularly the contiguity of the verbal and visual
- what frames do when they come up against each other is also interesting. This phenomenon suggests a non-narrative kind of communication, linking composition to reading/reception in a more collage-like way than we have been used to
- framing also helps us to see what we do now, and the shortcomings of it. The overemphasis on teaching fiction in English classrooms, or, to put in another way, the misunderstanding of the relationship between fiction and documentary, has blinkered us as English teachers to the possibilities and importance of argument/dialogue, and the importance of going beyond the classroom if we are to educate children fully in language
- framing is an important element in a rhetorical theory of communication, privileging neither the visual nor the verbal, but accepting that they complement each other in the making of meaning
- as far as the subject 'English' in concerned in schools, the New Zealanders are right in suggesting that [teaching] "in visual language should be planned so as to strengthen students' oral and written language, as they analyse examples, form critical judgements, and carry out reading, discussion and research". (New Zealand Ministry of Education 1993, p.16)

Where does an approach to language education through framing *sit* in relation to theory about language use, language development and learning? The most potent theory that will provide a foundation for the book as a whole, and to which we will return in the last chapter, is contemporary rhetoric. This is not the place to engage in a history of rhetoric, but an assumption will be made in the present book that the arguments for rhetoric have been won; that the negative connotations of the term 'rhetoric' can be discounted in the present discussion; and that it provides an overarching or underpinning theory for communication. More precisely, rhetoric can be seen as *the arts of* discourse. To put it very simply, a key rhetorical question is: given the available resources in terms of media and modes of communication, what is the best choice in communicating something of substance from one person (or persons) to another (or other persons)? In other words, rhetoric deals with the arts, politics and economics of communication. It is concerned with the *how* of communication in particular contexts.

Framing sits within an overarching theory of rhetoric in that it sets up parameters within which the act of communication takes place. Such communication will be more effective and more fluent if both parties are using the same frames. Conversely, communication is likely to be less than perfect and possibly difficult or confusing if the frames do not align. In most cases, there is no need to make the framing explicit, as both parties will be operating within conventional frameworks that have been tried and tested. But in cases where there are very different sets of values or ideologies, there is the potential for mis-construal because the frames of communication are not well known to the other party. Words, gestures, whole sentences, tones and other features of communication are likely to be mis-interpreted.

Framing, therefore, is not a theory. It is an action that can be seen as the principal agent in a theory of contemporary rhetoric. It applies to composition as well as to interpretation. It operates in fields conventionally described and analysed by the disciplines of sociology, anthropology and psychology, while at the same time having application in the visual and performing arts as a means of demarcating a space in which something special happens, or within which the audience is asked to give a particular kind of attention. The quality of this attention is important, and is seen to be different from that employed in an unframed space. Within the framed space, the attention might be said to be heightened; sensitive to what is inside and outside the frame; looking for correspondences within the unity created inside the frame; and of a different order from the consciousness and attention that is present in everyday life. The very shift in attention is an educational act in itself, because it focuses the mind for the period of contemplation. Consciously or unconsciously, the mind is asked to be critical, to consider difference and to seek patterns of correspondence.

When applied to the English, literacy and the language arts, framing has a particularly pertinent function. It makes visible the often invisible boundaries that are at play in acts of communication, whether they are oral or written. It provides an explanation for genres and their history, and re-locates the definition of 'genre' as social action (Miller 1984) rather than a set of text-types. From a compositional or interpretive viewpoint, framing allows a double-edged vision of making and understanding, of inclusion within a frame and exclusion from it. It helps us to see that even with a seemingly monomodal stream of communication, as in a page of printed text, there is, first, more than one mode at play (print is visual as well as an alphabetic transcription of what could be said); second, in multimodal texts that have intratextual framing (see MacLachlan and Reid 1994, above), there is the possibility of considering how the different modes complement each other, and also how they stand in tension with one another (which, if any, is the dominant mode?); third, framing is mode-neutral, like rhetoric. It is not allied to a particular language or mode, so it can play across the modes and examine relations between them. Fourth, framing puts the language arts back on a par with the visual and performing arts so that the field of communication can be re-energized. Learning to speak and write fluently, in any number of languages, will cease to be a matter of learning specific language systems; but will include consideration of how verbal languages operate in relation to other visual, physical, musical and mathematical languages – and thus how the available resources of language, in the broadest sense, can be deployed for successful communication. That is why framing is a powerful concept in communication, and why it is the focus of the present book.

Chapter 2

Framing in the Visual Arts

Having established the power of framing as a metaphor for understanding composition and interpretation in oral and written language, the second chapter will take a closer look at framing in the visual world. Why are pictures and photographs 'framed'? How is it done, and what kinds of framing are at play? To what degree is the reaction against formal framing just another kind of framing device? Is it indeed possible not to frame in the visual arts? The chapter will proceed via a series of examples or cases. It will suggest that frames are there to be broken or transgressed as well as to contain and define.

Introduction

The picture frame's principal function is to allow a picture to be moved. Part of the function is protection of the artwork. But the practicalities of moving pictures are only the beginning of the significance of framing in the visual arts. There is also a visual and symbolic dimension to framing. First, the frame adds a visual element to a painting, and is then considered part of the work itself. Thus, the picture-framer's art is an important one, as an inappropriate frame can detract from, and even spoil, the effect of a painting. Second, the frame acts as a symbolic, separating device between the painting and, not only the wall on which it hangs, but the rest of the world from which it is distinguished. What is implied in this symbolic separation is a different way of looking: the frame is saying to the viewer 'what I frame is something you should look at with more consideration, more reflection and a heightened degree of attention'. It is also saying 'the painting that I frame operates by laws and conventions of the time in the visual arts, and you need to attend to these to appreciate fully what is different about what is *within* the frame from what is *outside* it'.

An early example of framing is the Bayeux Tapestry. Although the tapestry has not been moved much, it is moveable and transportable, like a painting. The narrative of the tapestry (Figure 2.1), here showing the death of Harold, hit by a Norman arrow with the inscription 'Harold:Rex:Interfectus:Est'; and in three separate images, each depicting a stage in his death (like a piece of early animation or filmic narrative), is further framed by friezes at top and bottom.

Figure 2.1 Tapisserie Bayeux: Harold dies, hit by a Norman arrow.
Detail from the Bayeux Tapestry – 11th century. By special permission of the City of Bayeux.

The top frieze depicts heraldic icons; the bottom, scenes from the Battle of Hastings. Thus the main panel tells the grand story, and the friezes convey the heraldic nobility of the occasion and a running backdrop of action across the battlefield.

An exhibition in 1996–7 at the National Portrait Gallery in London, *The Art of the Picture Frame*, was devoted to the stylistic development of frames from the sixteenth to the end of the twentieth century. Portrait painters in particular needed to give attention to the frames in which their portraits were set, especially if their clients' preferences needed to be taken into account. Status was often associated with the nature of the frame. Pictures might be framed or re-framed according to a particular setting. For example, "the portraits of Mary Shelley [the author of *Frankenstein*] and her parents Mary Wollstonecraft and William Godwin were reframed in the mid-nineteenth century in matching papier-mâché frames, apparently for the Shelley 'Sanctum' at Boscombe Manor, the home of Mary Shelley's son near Bournemouth" (exhibition brochure, p.3).

Re-framing, in this context, was often undertaken to give unity to a series of portraits, or because the original frame was weak or out of fashion. There is an important principle at stake behind re-framing: it provides a new interface between the portrait and the particular historical period in which it finds itself, so that the new frame acts as an interpretive mediator between the audience and the painting.

Below are three examples of frames, from the eighteenth to the late-nineteenth century:

The first (Figure 2.2), of Handel, is an elaborate rococo frame with inserts of musical scores and instruments, indicating key attributes and talents of its subject. The second (Figure 2.3), of the actress Ellen Terry, is a plainer gilt frame with a wide central frieze and raised inner and outer mouldings. This style became so popular in the late-nineteenth century that one critic at the

Figure 2.2 George Frederic Handel, by Thomas Hudson, 1756.
© National Portrait Gallery, London. Used with permission.

Figure 2.3 Dame Ellen Terry, by George Frederic Watts, c.1864.
© National Portrait Gallery, London. Used with permission.

Royal Academy claimed a third of exhibits were so framed. But the portrait of Coventry Patmore (Figure 2.4), from the end of the century, marks a yet plainer style, though still weighty and imposing.

Frames within Frames

Both in fine art and in graphic, applied art, framing and re-framing can mean frames within frames as well as a complete re-structuring of a work of art. In fine art, William Scott's *Orange, black and white composition* (Figure 2.5) from 1953 is a good example of frames within frames.

There are key differences between this mid-twentieth century painting and those discussed in the previous section. First, the work is oil on a canvas that has no frame, in the conventional sense. It is typical of contemporary abstract art that is painted to be seen on a plain white wall of a gallery. In a sense, then,

Figure 2.4 Coventry Patmore, by John Singer Sargent, 1894.
© National Portrait Gallery, London. Used with permission.

the painting frames itself against its background. Second, however, it also paints its own frame in grey, on to the canvas itself. This frame is conventional insofar as it is fairly regular and gives rectangular definition to the work; but it is also irregular, of inconsistent width and in one place (the top left-hand corner) transgressed upon by the block of bright, deep orange colour. It is as if the painter has decided to use the visual and symbolic aspects of framing – and thus draw more attention to them – without the decorative and practical aspects. Third, the dynamic of the artwork, within the frame, is in the relationship between the blocks and shapes of colour: each 'framed' block of colour is composed – as is also the case in the work of Sean Scully – in relation to the others.

Figure 2.5 Orange, black and white composition, by William Scott, 1953.
© William Scott Foundation Ltd and Tate, London 2008. Used with permission.

The principle of frames within frames is an important one for the purposes of the development of ideas in the present book, as it is rarely the case that a single frame is operating. For the moment, the idea is pursued visually in order to achieve a clear sense of what such multiple framing *looks* like. To pan out for a moment, in order to get a wider perspective on this issue, paintings are usually housed in rooms with other paintings ('galleries') inside galleries or museums, which themselves are framed institutional spaces within society. These museums vary in character according to their collections and purpose. For example, a small specialist gallery like the Musée Picasso is different in nature from a private gallery (e.g. the Anthony d'Offay Gallery in London, open by private appointment only) or from a major public institution like the National Gallery in London or its equivalent in any other city. Size, type of funding, period of art, specialism, character (e.g. the Whitechapel Gallery in east London is noted for its ground-breaking collections and exhibitions) and location all bear upon the expectations of visitors as they cross the threshold from the real world to the gallery spaces. There are cultural expectations and frameworks at work, so no single viewing of a painting is framed in quite the same way: seeing a new Howard Hodgkin in the Ingleby Gallery in Edinburgh, where there are only two small exhibition rooms in a house on a Georgian terrace, is different from an exhibition of his work in the Gagosian Gallery in Brittania Street near King's Cross in London in a larger converted warehouse space; yet again, as Berger pointed out a generation or more ago in *Ways of Seeing* (1972), holding a postcard of the same painting in the hand is different from seeing it in a book like this one, or in a coffee-table book on his work. Many of these differences are a result of the social and cultural framing of perception.

Two examples of how frames within frames operate in graphic art are seen in Figures 2.6 and 2.7.

These are both based not only on the 'polyptique' or multi-panelled principle that was discussed briefly in Chapter 1, but also on a simple and regular grid. The *NMC Songbook* takes single letters from differently embedded contexts and arrays them to spell out 'The NMC Songbook', advertising both a series of concerts at Kings Place, London and a boxset of CDs. *In the Mix* advertises an exhibition at Kings Place. Whereas the first of these *polyptiques* creates a sequence of letters to make up a message, the second not only arrays the types of art on show at the exhibition, but also invites the viewer/reader to make connections, e.g. between the spiky figure in the top row and the pointed sculpture and spiky rubber suit in the second; between the smoother sculptural forms across the selection; and so on. The combination of similarity and difference

Figure 2.6 The NMC Songbook.
© NMC Recordings Ltd. CD Cat NMC D150. Used with permission.

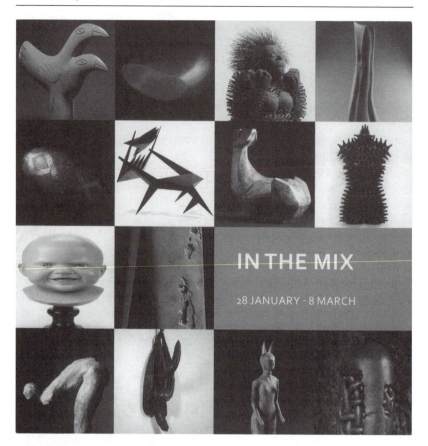

Figure 2.7 In the Mix.
© Pangolin London. Used with permission.

across the set of images is enhanced by the grid-like framing of the images in a set. These two invitations operate at the edges of the art world, as invitations to enter it; at the same time, they have the status of art objects themselves as card-sized polyptical objects in their own right.

Polyptiques have a particular connection with literary and other linguistic compositions, and with other forms of composition in music, architecture, garden design etc. The polyptical principle can work in a series or sequence; it can also, at the same time, work spatially so that connections between panels can be made. Whereas in the spatial arts, those connections can be made relatively freely by those experiencing the building, garden or artwork, in the time-based arts like film, music and writing, the sequence is less adaptable, more prescribed. If we take poems that work on polyptical principles, like Wallace Stevens' 'Thirteen ways of looking at a blackbird' or any number by

Seamus Heaney (e.g. 'Elegy for a still-born child', 'Up the shore' from 'A Lough Neagh sequence' or 'The Tollund man') the sections in which they are written operate like chapters in a novel, or scenes in a play. This is not to say that there is not yet another level of framing in stanzas within poems; it is simply to say that basically the act of framing works on the same principle in poems as in polyptical artworks. No doubt, in the moments of composition, the artist or poet experiments with the arrangements of the panels, trying them in particular sequences or arrays until the one that best suits the intended expression is found. A practical exercise in reading such works is to imagine other sequences or arrays, for example (in reading a poem) by cutting a copy up into its constituent stanzas and sections, and then seeing if students can re-compose the piece. Their justifications for the arrangements they create, whether they match those of the writer or not, are grist for the critical mill. The process also suggests that reading and interpretation are an act of re-composition.

Finally, in this section on frames within frames, the principle of compositional framing is used in less arty contexts. In Figures 2.8 and 2.9, from a catering firm specializing in servicing the education market in the UK, a recipe for peach crumble with raspberry cream on the back of a postcard is fronted by an image of the crumble, with the chef and his signature in smaller boxes. In an interesting piece of design, then, the front is mirrored on the back as frames are used within frames to convey different aspects or elements of the message.

Each element of the recipe has its own framed space: the title, the introduction, the preliminary work, the two elements of the dessert and then the section on serving it. On the left of the recipe, the ingredients are listed in sections.

We can understand, from this small example of a message that is highly dependent on frames within frames, how the visual nature of the framing can apply not only to the reading of the text and images, but also to their composition. In this case, the arts of graphic design, informed as they are by fine art principles, meet the demands of a written genre such as the recipe, with its headings, stages and procedures. We can see, for example, that even short texts like recipes can be heavily framed; that within the genre of the recipe, there are headings and sub-headings, sections and sub-sections that aid the communication process. Similarly, in larger texts like novels or manuals, there are sections with different names ('chapters', 'stages' etc.) and that within those larger textual structures are paragraphs, stanzas and other sub-textual units.

Indeed, close examination of the genre of the recipe, as evidenced in this example, could lead to engaging work in school where: i) the recipe might be tried out and annotated to see how clear a piece of communication it is; and ii) new recipes might be composed/designed on the same principle, or with new original designs.

In a variation on the theme of frames within frames, consider the two examples on page 36 (Figure 2.10) of calligraphy used in programme notes to a performance by a Taiwanese dance company, Cloud Gate.

Figure 2.8 Peach crumble with raspberry cream.
© Recipe courtesy of Sodexho, Inc.

One, framed within the tight geometric grid used to teach Chinese characters as well as to write them, is in standard cursive script; the other shows 'wild cursive' where the individual characters transgress the boundaries of the grid. In this case, as the reading is from top to bottom and right to left, the script becomes increasingly 'wild' as it moves from the top right to the bottom left, mirroring the ethos and characters of the dance company itself. The comparison between a more formal, restricted and tightly framed composition and one which spills beyond the grid, is a theme which will form the basis of the next section in this chapter. Framing, then, is to be seen not as an act that constrains the composer, but one which provides an often invisible structure to work with, and one which can be transgressed according to the function of the

SIGNATURE DISHES
by

SERVES 4

1 kg fresh ripe peaches
50-75g sugar, depending on
sweetness of peaches
15g plain flour
grated zest of half a lemon
65g ground almonds
65g flaked almonds

For the crumble topping:
50g white caster sugar
50g light brown sugar
100g plain flour
100g unsalted butter, chilled
and diced
100g flaked porridge oats

For the raspberry cream:
200g raspberries, fresh or frozen
50g caster sugar
5ml lemon juice
150ml whipping cream

Peach Crumble with Raspberry Cream

Such a scrumptious aroma fills the whole house when
this dessert is baking in the oven! It's guaranteed to
woo all ages; almost any type of fruit can be used:
peaches or nectarines, plums or apples, or try tossing
in some blackberries.

Pre-heat the oven to 190°C/ 375°F/ gas 5.
Halve and peel the peaches. Slice each half into
8 wedges. Toss the peaches with the sugar, flour and
lemon zest, place peaches in a baking dish.

To Make the Topping
Work together the sugars, flour, oats and butter with your
fingertips until they are sticking together in rough bits
about pea-size consistency.
Generously sprinkle on the crumble topping about 1 cm
thick. Place in the pre-heated oven for about 30 minutes
until the top is golden and a knife will pierce the peach
flesh easily, remove from the oven.

To Make the Raspberry Cream
Puree the raspberries and sugar in a blender or food
processor. Pass the puree through a fine sieve to remove
the seeds. Add the lemon juice to the puree. Whip the
cream to soft peaks and fold in the puree.
Adjust sweetness if necessary by adding a tablespoon or
two more of sugar.

To Serve
Scoop a big spoonful of the peach crumble into a soup
plate or shallow bowl and top with a generous spoonful of
the raspberry cream. Serve at once, warm rather than hot.

Figure 2.9 Peach crumble with raspberry cream.
© Recipe courtesy of Sodexho, Inc.

communicative message that is conveyed. Issues about the performing arts,
like dance, theatre and opera, will be addressed in Chapter 3. As is clear from
the Wild Cursive performance, frames within frames are as important to the
creation and reception of the performing arts as they are to composition in
writing and in the broader contexts of multimodal composition.

The Frame as Part of the Picture

Ever since paintings were framed for protection and for transport, they have
been part of the picture. The close proximity of the frame to the painting; the
symbolic and visual addition of the frame to the artwork and the fact that the

of colour, texture etc. Each frame provides a context for further frames and panels within it, embedding these frames and panels, and, via a process of delineation, defining precisely the intended read-off.

The principle of using the frame as part of the work itself is seen most extensively, and with vibrant power, in the work of Howard Hodgkin. Two examples of many that could be used are *It can't be true* (Figure 2.12) and *Writing* (Figure 2.13).

It can't be true is painted on a series of frames-within-frames, just visible through the paint. Hodgkin's characteristic painting over the (often wooden) frames on which he works is given a particular twist in this painting by the skewed angle at which the painted frame sits in relation to its wooden base. The bold tigerish stripes of the painted frame lead into blocks of brighter colour at the heart of the picture. At the same time, the eye is led out again to the border, reversing the conventional movement from the outside to the centre. The skewed outer frame gives the impression of incompleteness, of a paradoxical

Figure 2.12 It can't be true, by Howard Hodgkin, 1987–90.

© Howard Hodgkin and Gagosian Gallery London. Used with permission.

Figure 2.13 Writing, by Howard Hodgkin, 1991–3.
© Howard Hodgkin and Gagosian Gallery London. Used with permission.

wish to present the painting as illusion and at the same time as a piece of material reality. It is as much a painting about painting as it is a painting of a remembered feeling.

Many of Hodgkin's paintings are created over a period of years, with completion coming with a sense of a memory and/or feeling being fully expressed and captured in the painting. In the following extract from Graham-Dixon's *Howard Hodgkin* (1994), the nature and use of framing in Hodgkin's work is explored:

> The paintings are both framed and unframed, since the artist treats the frame as integral to the support. His pictures start as blank panels of wood within frames and he paints on both elements, so frame and image are integrated … Sculptors have always understood the importance of edges, which define exactly how forms contains space. Painters, often content to let others frame their pictures for them, have infrequently understood this … Hodgkin knows that a painting's edge is its most valuable point. It is where the work of art ends and the world begins. It is where the painting completes itself, or, conversely, declares its incompletion. It is where the

present chapter, the exploration of framing in the visual arts is continued with a look at the breaking of frames.

First, it is important to note in an emerging theory of the field that rules are broken as well as observed. Any theory based on an unbreakable set of rules would soon be subject to objection and dis-proof. So a theory that both sets out the parameters within which it works and at the same time acknowledges that the rules may be broken and transgressed is a stronger theory. Indeed, the 'rules' are reinforced by breaking them; they become more evident, more central to explaining the varieties of behaviour within this particular set of frameworks and frames.

Breaking the frame can take various forms, but almost always concerns the questioning of the frame itself, and the reaching out to areas of meaning and significance beyond the frame. We have already seen in the work of Howard Hodgkin a transgressing of the line between the 'painting' and the frame, so that the frame becomes part of the work itself. Implied in such a move is a different take on the twentieth-century abstract expressionist tendency to leave large works 'unframed'. But conscious transgressing or breaking of a frame takes the statement a step further.

The French Regional American Museum Exchange advertisement (Figure 2.14) is from *The New York Review of Books*. In that particular issue (12–25 February 2009) all other text and images were tightly framed. Consequently, this small typographical transgression stands out. It is simply a logo in which the graphic artist has used a square block and drawn attention to

Figure 2.14 Advertisement for French Regional American Museum Exchange.
From *New York Review of Books*, p.22, Vol. LVI, no. 2, 12–25 February 2009.

Figure 2.15 New Wave Art: advertisement for Brooklyn Academy of Music.
Postcard ad for BAM 25th Next wave Festival, Oct 4–Dec 16, 2007.

the word 'Frame' by splitting it down the middle. Its black-on-grey as well as its size and frame-breaking make it stand out from the rest of the text, which is in white, smaller and conventionally framed (and also not blocked to its right-hand margin, so that it appears more like script).

In a more exuberant example (Figure 2.15), the advertisement for *Next Wave Art* at the Brooklyn Academy of Music (4 October–16 December 2007) overlays word upon word, but has them both bleeding off the page, thus suggesting that words have a more peripheral function in the exhibition, and a particular relationship to the box of white light that is given principal place on the advert. At the same time, the borders of the conventional advert are transgressed, with all the attendant implications for what the advert is saying about the exhibition.

Breaking frames and received expectations in this way is a practice in fine art and sculpture, installations and public art, as well as in the applied world of graphic design. The fourth plinth in London's Trafalgar Square is a good example of public art, where artists are invited to add something to a bare plinth (see http://www.london.gov.uk/fourthplinth). Recent installations have included work by Rachel Whiteread and Anthony Gormley.

The breaking of frames suggests a break with convention, a rebellion against the constraints of existing frameworks and frames. The implications for the verbal arts are clear: existing traditions and conventional forms can be transgressed and broken. Expression cannot be confined, despite Yeats' maxim that 'ancient salt is best packing'. New kinds of expression require new forms, and these new forms can only come into being if the old frames are broken. It is not difficult to see the same principle being applied to theatre, dance and the other performing arts. But the act is seen most graphically, and at its simplest, in the transgressing and breaking of frames within the visual arts. With such movement through and beyond frames, there is always a tension: that of the emerging shape of new forms in relation to the old ones. Such tension is seen in the verbal arts in the rhythmic variation in poems within phrases and sentences; in the tension between the spoken voice and the printed word; as well as in the large-scale counterpoints of prose escaping from its hide-bound genres.

Framing in Architecture and Interior Design

There is a risk of stating the obvious to say that architecture and interior design depend heavily on framing. Given that the subject of the previous section was the breaking of frames, it is fitting to start the present section with consideration of the interface between the *inside and the outside* of buildings, and the exploitation of the transitional spaces between inside and outside. To repeat the obvious again, buildings have an edge, a boundary, a limit; their framing depends on the delineation of distinct lines of separation between the outside of the building and the rest of the space around it. An exhibition in New York in 2007, *Inside/Out* was specifically devoted to this interface.

Figure 2.16 Architecture *Inside/Out.*
Center for Architecture, New York: 536 La Guardia Place, New York City, NY 10012.

First, a brief note on the poster and attendant publicity for the exhibition. The graphic solution to the *Inside/Out* theme is to reverse the word 'inside' so that reading the phrase becomes a challenge in comprehension and reading; the effect of this reversal is to suggest some of the themes of the exhibition itself. What is significant about the topic for the purposes of the present book is that the viewer is invited to look at the threshold between inside and outside by looking from both ways: from the inside out, and from the outside in. Thus the framing becomes a line across which we are invited to look, to gain different perspectives on the architectural and design 'problem' of the interface. The dividing line is not just one of architectural interest. Traditionally, the interior design and construction of a building is undertaken by different teams from the exterior design and construction. This particular exhibition looked at how to break down compartmentalization of this kind so that exterior and interior issues could be considered simultaneously. Issues that were at stake include eco-friendly practices, flexibility of use, the business of fabrication and use of materials; the issue of lighting; spatial considerations; and the more transcendent qualities of framed spaces that architecture (inside and out) tries, sometimes, to create.

In terms of interiors, framing need not be rectangular, but might consist in the re-shaping of part of a room. The example below (Figure 2.17) is from *The Architectural Journal*'s 2009 small projects award. It is an interesting case of

Figure 2.17 Lightwall, Turin, Italy.
"LightWall, Turin, Italy: Architect: ecoLogicStudio," In © *The Architects' Journal*, 22.1.09, p.32.

re-framing, as it "reinterprets the traditional massive Italian wall as a thick concrete sponge" to create a corner of a room where light can permeate the wall. The schematic drawing at the bottom of the page makes clear that the walls are constructed of framed blocks.

When looking in more detail at the construction of each block, it can be seen that these half-metre square units are conceived simply, with a skewed interior frame that admits light and is surrounded with insular material. Although the technical construction is complex, designed for maximum insularity and adequate strength, the overall concept of the 'building block' is a simple one. In Figure 2.18, we have a small-scale version of frames within frames, designed according to mathematical and engineering principles.

On a larger scale, and returning to framing principles, what is the basic framing activity in designing and putting up a building? From a structural engineer's point of view (rather than an architect's) consider the sequence opposite (Figures 2.19–24) in the design of a multi-floored building:

First, the footprint of the building is mapped out. For the purposes of these drawings, the building has been conceived of as a simple rectangular one (Figure 2.19). It may be that the actual building is going to take up just some of the ground space that has been allocated to it, so that transport access,

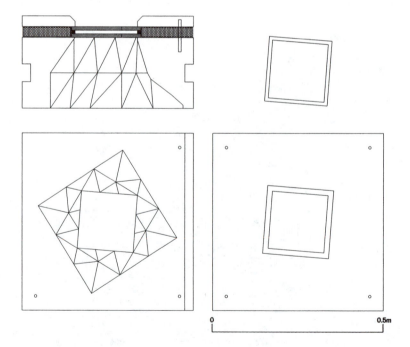

Figure 2.18 Detailed drawings of the concrete block, Lightwall, Turin, Italy.

"Concrete Block LightWall, Turin, Italy: Architect: ecoLogicStudio," In © *The Architects' Journal*, 22.1.09, p.3.

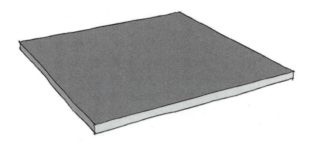

Figure 2.19 Building frame 1.
© David Andrews. Used with permission.

landscaped gardens, public plazas and other features outside the building can be accommodated; but in this schematic drawing, the rectangle can be considered to be the base of the building.

For functional purposes, in order to contain service features like lifts, water and power supplies, a central core is constructed (Figure 2.20). This core is already a frame within a frame. Sometimes it is constructed for the whole height of the building before the floors are added; at other times it is constructed floor by floor, ahead of the construction of the floors themselves.

In Figure 2.21, the supporting pillars are mapped out that will hold up the floors. These are positioned on the edge of the original frame of the proposed building, providing the vertical supports for the horizontal floors. In the remaining figures, it can be seen how the building is constructed stage by stage.

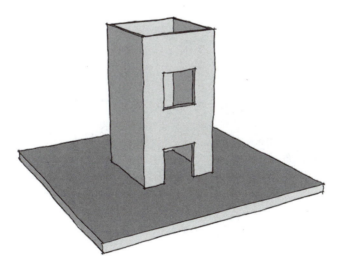

Figure 2.20 Building frame 2.
© David Andrews. Used with permission.

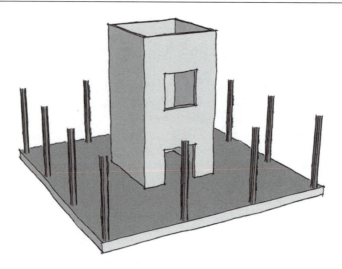

Figure 2.21 Building frame 3.
© David Andrews. Used with permission.

These figures show the practical engineering design necessary for the creation of a simple multi-floor building. Once the main framed structure is complete, individual rooms can be created inside the frame, thus creating the spaces in which people will operate. The building as a whole provides a frame for certain kinds of activity; it is separate from the rest of its immediate environment, and

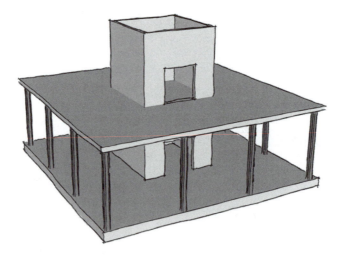

Figure 2.22 Building frame 4.
© David Andrews. Used with permission.

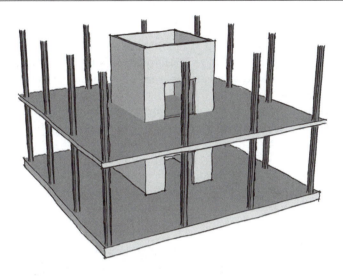

Figure 2.23 Building frame 5.
© David Andrews. Used with permission.

from the rest of the city and country in which it is located, defining a space that people enter and leave for particular purposes. Buildings thus are not only physical entities, constructed on engineering principles; but they are also framed spaces in which certain activities take place. The point is that they are highly framed, physically and sociologically.

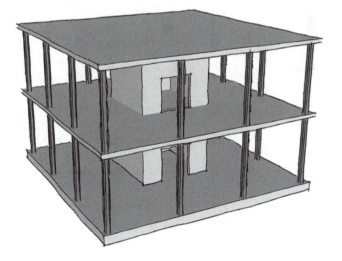

Figure 2.24 Building frame 6.
© David Andrews. Used with permission.

Framing in Other Visual/Spatial Fields

Not all frames are rectangular. It is important to remember that framing is an activity that, for economic and technical reasons, is usually rectangular, but could well be oval, round, triangular or in any other shape. For the purposes of this book and its emphasis on framing and re-framing in the language arts, frames are both literal and symbolic. Though grounded in the range of frames literally available, the symbolic framing can be more wide-ranging in its conception (at its extreme, the solar system is 'framed' within the universe; the positing of a deity is one way of framing the presence of consciousness and existence). Buildings like Gehry's Guggenheim Museum in Bilbao are designed and constructed on aerodynamic curvilinear principles. More modestly, the lapis lazuli icon of Christ and the Virgin from twelfth-century Constantinople (Figure 2.25) is shaped differently from the rectangular tradition:

Figure 2.25 Lapis lazuli icon with Christ and the Virgin, twelfth century.
© RMN/Daniel Arnaudet. Used with permission.

Here, the rounded top frames the lapis icon which is encrusted with gold, silver gilt, filigree, copper and wax resin. The framing is practical and elegant, and sets the icon apart from its surroundings, lending it resonance (as we will see later with poetry).

In garden design, to take another field in which framing is important, the overall layout of a garden can provide the basis for the overall effect once the plants grow and provide the colour, variety, sequencing and – crucially – the unpredictability of spilling over edges, haphazard seeding patterns etc. It is clear, in winter or early spring, what the exact layout of a garden is, before the organic growth begins to work towards the balance between the 'classical' emphasis on framing and the 'romantic' excesses of growth. In the case of Sissinghurst, in Kent, England, in a garden created by Vita Sackville-West and Harold Nicholson, the overall design of the garden used a moat that originally protected a castle on three sides, one side of which has been filled in to create a moat walk.

There are a number of framings at work in the garden. At the outside edges, the garden itself is separated from 'natural' landscape on one side and a country park on the other, with fences, gates etc. Within the garden, the house, on one side, and the moat and moat walk, on the other, provide an inner frame. Between the outer and inner frames are a number of specialist gardens, each with their own framing devices.

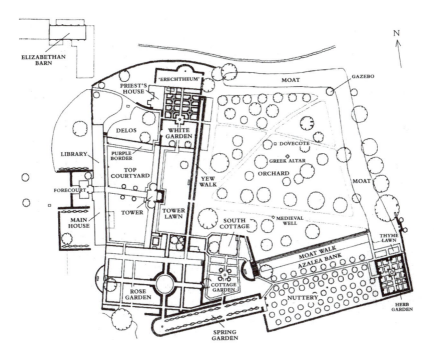

Figure 2.26 Map of Sissinghurst Garden, Kent.
© The National Trust. Used with permission.

In a telling quotation from Nicholson (2008), the gardener in charge of the mowing regime at Sissinghurst, Phil Norton, discusses the function of grass lawns within the framing conception:

> You don't notice the lawns when they are looking fantastic. If they are looking good, it makes everything else look good. They create the frame. And the garden wouldn't work without them. Very definite lines are Sissignghurst. They enhance the overflowingness of the rest. If you lose that edge, then you have lost the effect.
>
> (p.10)

In the terms in which framing is discussed in the present book, it is not the lawns that create the frame, but that rather work within the framing of the garden as 'panels' in a multi-panelled work to counterbalance the 'overflow-ingness'. The 'edge' to which Phil Norton refers is not only part of the grand design of definite lines and marked contrasts, but also the practical business of maintaining a fine edge to the lawn itself: such edges (the bane of many gardeners to maintain) accentuate the act of framing.

The Rhetoric of the Frame

At the end of Chapter 1, there was reference to an overarching theory – contemporary rhetoric – within which framing theory could be developed. Here, let us consider in more detail, and with regard to the visual arts, the issue of 'the rhetoric of the frame'.

The collection by Duro (1996), *The Rhetoric of the Frame: Essays on the Boundaries of the Artwork* is one of the most thorough explorations of the issue that the Introduction states as seeming to be "as unproblematic as it is marginal" (p.1). Rather, the book sees the frame in the visual arts as "creating a space that the work itself is incapable of furnishing" (ibid.). As a principle running through all the essays in the book, it sees the frame as indissociable from the work itself, whether that frame is material in nature or non-physical – Duro's book is recommended for that – but it should be noted that, for the purposes of the present book, a more nuanced account of framing in the visual arts is necessary before we apply framing theory to the language arts.

Duro discusses the first element of such an account in comparing Kant's notion that a frame is a non-essential element of an artwork, and that it is an "external complement" (Duro 1996, p.2) to the aesthetic work on the one hand, to Derrida's questioning of the notion of such an impenetrable boundary on the other. Derrida is more circumspect about the boundaries of art, seeing the work (or 'ergon') standing out by its 'parergon' or 'by-work' as a figure might from its ground. Derrida, then, posits a layer of framing between that of the 'work' and its material frame – almost like a 'mount' around a painting – that provides a further zone of compositional or interpretational buffering between the world and the work of art.

It has to be said that frames could proliferate, making the business of composition or interpretation almost impossible, and simply building an academic apparatus for its own sake. Instead of going down the road of proliferation, let us try to devise a simpler model for framing in the visual arts, derived from our discussion of the various arts that have been considered in this chapter, and which may be of use when we come to consider the verbal arts.

The first principle in designing such a model is one which applies to the whole of the present book: it concentrates on the act of framing rather than frames *per se.*

At the heart of this model is the work itself. By 'work' is meant the core artistic creation that is the focus and centre of the piece: a carved piece of lapis lazuli, the application of paint on a canvas, the space that constitutes a room in a building. Immediately framing that core work is the 'ground' which provides the basis for the material 'work'. In the case of a painting on canvas, it is the canvas itself; in the case of a painting on wood, the wood itself. These 'grounds' – not to be confused with the grounds in a Toulminian model of argumentation, meaning evidence in relation to a proposition – are, in turn, framed by the boundaries of the artwork, constituted in a number of ways: as a wooden frame, as a steel or aluminium frame, as 'no frame' (as in a borderless canvas abstract piece). The edges or boundaries of the work are important concepts in art theory, marking the dividing line between the area of aesthetic attention and the area beyond it; between the work of art in its most contained, object-like, curatorial state and the world beyond that object.

Behind the work of art as object is the wall, screen or other background against which the work is exhibited. In contemporary art galleries, these are almost always plain white walls – which allow, for example, a work to be 'framed' even though it has no material frame as such. In the case of slide shows or films, or any kind of projected image or set of images, a white screen usually forms the background. These backgrounds are, in turn, framed by material institutional spaces: private houses, cinemas, art galleries, museums. Such institutions are determined by financial, material and other economic factors (the issues that producers or executive directors or home owners deal with) that are not part of the artwork itself, but create the conditions in which the artwork can be supported, curated, exhibited and enjoyed. Finally, in more abstract mode and yet bearing upon the creation of museums, galleries and other publicly and privately framed spaces are a mix of ideological, personal, gendered, political and theoretical factors that shape composition and interpretation.

What appears to be at play in a highly framed model such as this is a successive interplay between the concrete tangibility of the artwork (represented by 'the work itself', the physical frame, the background and the institutional economic context in which the work finds itself); and the immaterial, represented

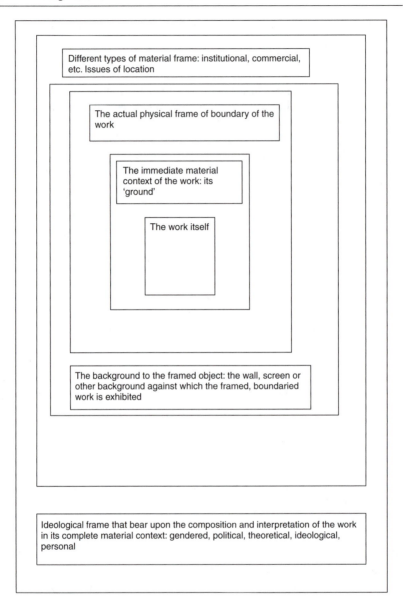

Figure 2.27 The 'work itself' within its frames.

by the 'ground' upon which the work is created, the background and the ideological, 'structures of feeling', personal framework which the viewer or creator brings to bear. And yet to characterize the dynamic polar movement as based on materiality or the immaterial is not quite to capture the accuracy of the relationship. Rather, it is one of relative foregrounding and backgrounding, the backgrounded features taking on the appearance of an abstract 'invisibility' in the light of the foregrounded concreteness of works and institutions.

Even if we accept a formalized model in which successive acts of framing operate in relation to each other, each informing the next frame in, the picture as a whole remains more complicated; but only so in a fairly simple way that can be easily incorporated into our emerging model of framing in the visual arts. That simple way is as follows: although the boundaries between each type of framing are theoretical categories (usually realized in actual works), there is scope for a blurring of the boundaries, or transgressing of boundaries, in the creation and reception of any particular work of art. A work in which the canvas (the ground) of a painting is deliberately exposed to show through its texture – even to the extent of presenting unpainted canvas in part of the created work – is blurring the boundary between the work of art and its ground. Similarly, if that same work remained unframed physically, relying on its background to set it off as a separate work in its own right, both the creator and the viewer are asking the question: where does this piece end, and where does it begin? Why does it deliberately blur the convention of the boundary of the artwork?

Finally, a reflection on the terms 'framing' and 'boundaries'. We have already established that the focus of the present book is on framing rather than frames, to emphasize the creative and critical *act* of determining the frames that form part of an artwork. Such an emphasis takes us away from an off-the-shelf pre-packaged approach to frames that might be adopted in order to help us avoid thinking about them. Rather, the term 'framing' makes us think about the frames as part of the artworks we are making and considering. But how different are these frames, and the act of framing, from boundaries and, by analogy, the act of boundary-making and policing? Part of the answer lies in the fact that framing is based on a verb (it's a gerund) and a boundary cannot easily be transformed into a verb; and part of the answer is that a boundary defines too clearly the 'edge' of a work. Such edges need 'policing'; they are the self-defining limits of the game (as in cricket), a *final* limit, a border, a termination. The term 'framing', on the other hand, has an active element to it. It supports as well as defines; it can be three-dimensional as well as two. It derives from the Old English *framian* meaning 'to be helpful', and is related to *fram*, meaning 'forward'. There is therefore an element of projection and possibility about it. The definition of the verb 'frame', in its transitive and intransitive forms, from the *Chambers Dictionary* will give an idea of its scope and range:

> *Vt* to form; to shape; to put together; to plan, adjust or adapt; to contrive, devise or concoct; to bring about; to articulate; to direct (one's) steps; to set about; to enclose in a frame or border; to make (someone) the victim of a frame-up *Vi* to make one's way; to resort; to pretend (*dialect*); to make a move; to give promise of success; to contrive (*Bible*).

I can take any empty space and call it a bare stage. A man walks across this empty space whilst someone else is watching him, and this is all that is needed for an act of theatre to be engaged. Yet when we talk about theatre this is not quite what we mean. Red curtains, spotlights, blank verse, laughter, darkness … box office, foyer, tip-up seats, footlights, scene changes, intervals, music, as though the theatre was by very definition these and little more.

(p.11)

The beginning of the book is part rhetorical counterpoint: the (Victorian) proscenium arch theatre, with all its trappings, is contrasted at the other end of the spectrum by the simplest of acts. At the institutionalized theatre end of the spectrum, we can identify a number of framings that distinguish 'theatre' from the outside world: first (not mentioned by Brook, but implied) a building on a street devoted to plays, performances etc. and going by a name of some sort: the Apollo, the Criterion, the People's Theatre. Then, as he points out, the box office which acts as the agent which allows the audience access to the theatre space itself, usually via payment; and the foyer, the intermediate space between the outside world and the theatre space. Foyers are interesting in that they are gathering spaces where people meet (the act of going to the theatre is usually a social experience), but they are also transition spaces which mark the change between operation in the outside world (most immediately the city/town, the pavement) and the usually hushed inner sanctum of the theatre space: a space in which a member of the audience becomes a willing participant in a social and cultural ritual. Foyers are often marked by bars or cafés, ushers and posters advertising other theatre experiences that can be bought. The transition is physical, emotional, imaginative: outside the frame one moves independently with a degree of choice; inside the frame there is a suspension of control, a willingness and a readiness to be transported.

Beyond the foyer are the elements that form another part of Brook's list: the red curtains, the tip-up seats, the spotlights and footlights, the darkness within the theatre space itself. These are the static or given elements of the inner sanctum. They remain to define the theatre space, whichever play is showing. As described above, there are particular qualities to this space, and certain expectations placed upon the audience which enters it. As theatre history would confirm, the inner sanctum is a version of a religious space: it is part-sanctuary, part-ritual space, part-holy. It signifies that experience will be at least reflective, if not moving and/or spiritual.

So far the framings have been physical, operating in time (theatres come and go) but relatively static compared to the plays that are performed and the actors that perform them. The further elements of framing inside the theatre space are more transitory. The stage will be designed in some way, from the barest of conceptions to a florid Italianate set. Then there is the play and its performance, indicated by "blank verse … scene changes, intervals, music".

Not all these elements are present in every play and performance, but they are indicative of the type of framing that takes place. *Scene changes*, not only in speech but also in set, indicate parts of a larger structure. Scenes in plays can be of various lengths, sometimes falling in clusters into 'acts', and sometimes taking up an entire play. *Intervals* are decided upon by the director of the play, and allow the actors and the audience to take a break, to relax their concentration, to mark a key break in the action, to create a rhythmic shape to the experience. *Blank verse* is clearly an option, as is *music*. The final element listed by Brook, *laughter*, depends on the play and its performance, and to an extent on the audience. Actors will testify that lines that are guaranteed laughter on one night, can fall completely flat on another; the audience itself can affect the actors, inspiring them or deflating them. Like the example from garden design in the previous chapter, the framework of the theatrical experience is defined and supported by a number of framings, some physical, some conceptual; but the growth of plants within that framework has a degree of unpredictability, just as each live performance is different.

At the other end of Brook's spectrum is the empty space: "I can take any empty space and call it a bare stage. A man walks across this empty space whilst someone else is watching him, and this is all that is needed for an act of theatre to be engaged." Brook's genius is partly realized in the inventiveness to call any empty space a stage: a warehouse, a naturally formed amphitheatre, a location in a desert. These spaces need not even be naturally framed by landscape or by people; they can simply be empty spaces anywhere (though emptiness is defined by other spaces that are 'filled' in some way). The key to empty space is that, as in the beginning of the book, it is counterpointed to 'traditional' proscenium-arch theatre. For the space to become a theatrical space, there are two ways of creating the theatre: a man walks across the space, defining it is 'space' through which he moves (there is a geometry of movement, a violation of empty space by a signature movement across it, the creation of presence against absence, etc.). The other way is via definition by the audience. In fact, as Beckett has shown us in *Breath* (1970), there does not even have to be an actor to define the space as theatre: this is a complex case, in which the trappings of theatre are used by Beckett to set up expectation, which is then transformed by a set consisting of miscellaneous rubbish, dim lighting and the interjection of recorded cries, inspiration and expiration. Just as someone watching a man walking across an empty space creates a theatrical moment, so too, in Beckett's play, it is the audience's perception and provision of a framing consciousness that creates the play. The audience is supported by the trappings of theatre, which suggest that what they will experience in the inner sanctum *is* theatre; and they fully cooperate in the fiction, so that they bring to the experience the expectation of theatre, the institutional and socially shaped framing that becomes inner framing.

Along the spectrum, from the empty space across which a man walks at one end, to the fully-fledged night-out-at-the-theatre experience at the other, is a range of types of theatrical experience: street theatre; 'talking heads'; small-scale one-act plays with one or a few actors; plays in theatres that are simple in their framing (sheds, warehouses, bare modernist and post-modernist spaces); simple unadorned theatres; 'naturally' constructed theatres like the Minack Theatre in Cornwall, or the amphiteatre at Epidavros in Greece. To give one example along the spectrum: in the 1990s, I attended a performance in an out-of-commission warehouse on the Amsterdam waterfront. The audience was gathered in advance of the performance just outside the warehouse. We were instructed that there was no 'theatre space' or auditorium as such, but that it would become clear to us as we entered the warehouse (the first frame) what to do as an audience. An audience of about 40 entered the vast semi-lit place, filled as it was with de-commissioned industrial machinery. At first it was not clear where to focus: there were signs of people (actors?) perched on bits of dusty machinery, but little action. Then a fire was lit at the far end of the warehouse (about three or four hundred yards away), and the audience moved towards it, attracted by the light and the compelling power of fire. Actors then appeared and danced. As that particular focus of attention faded, and our attention faded with it, another activity began to take place elsewhere in the warehouse. And so, by degrees, we were led (and appeared to lead ourselves) in a labyrinthine progress through the warehouse, in and out of the machinery, past vignettes of silent acting and posing, until we arrived at the heart of the scene: an enclosed space, more like a conventional theatre space, but simply a framed empty space in the middle of the warehouse, heavily framed by machinery and in which all the actors we had witnessed along the way gathered themselves for a choreographed finale.

Text, Script and Performance

Part of what is meant by framing and re-framing in this book can be illustrated by discussing the move from text to script to performance in the creation and production of a play. This section will take an edition and performances of *As You Like It* as a case in point.

As suggested in the previous section, one aspect of the framing that takes place in theatre is the actual play itself, often divided into sections and sub-sections: acts and scenes in Shakespeare's case. While knowing very little about the way in which Shakespeare composed (see Bryson 2007 for what we *do* know), we can assume that the five acts and 23 scenes of the play (at least in the New Cambridge edition) – even if that structure was super-imposed or brought to the surface by subsequent editors – represent a broad classical structure (the five acts) and the more pragmatic scene movement required by this particular play and its action. The original script, then, however open to improvisation and revision at the time of the first performances, is framed by a structure that gives it shape, momentum and dramatic identity. Shakespeare created his own version of the nature of five-act structure in tragedies and comedies, with the rhetorical development from scene-setting in Act I through development in Acts II and III, to contrapuntal complication in Act IV leading to resolution in Act V. But in terms of the next level down in structuring – that of scenes – the picture is more complicated. The Arden edition (Dusinberre 2006) of the play notes that plays for the public theatres in Shakespeare's time "were not divided into acts and scenes, although they were for children's performances at the private theatre at Blackfriars, where music was played between acts" (p.126), though the Folio text of 1623 divides the play into acts and scenes. The transition from the original working scripts to the Folio edition moved through "a fair-copy transcript based on a book-keeper's theatrical copy rather than on Shakespeare's original manuscripts" (p.127) and was probably prepared before 1606. This is not the place to rehearse the detailed progression from creation through various versions of the text to the first Folio edition, with all the attention to errors and textual variation. The point here, as far as the theme of the present book is concerned, is the hypothetical relationship between the framing and re-framing of the work. Whereas the suggestion of a movement from text to script to performance looks neat, the actual movement is probably one of continued interaction between text, script (in the hands of the playwright and actors) and performance, at least in the 20 years or so between the first performances and the first printed edition of the play in 1623.

What is the distinction between 'text' and 'script' being used here? The definition of 'text' is a relatively narrow one, referring to the printed version of the scripts that (in Shakespeare's case) preceded it, and as represented in the Folio (and subsequent printed) edition(s). 'Text' thus takes on a more static, more 'authoritative' character than 'script'. But 'script' refers not only to the early handwritten versions of the play in the hands of the playwright and actors; it also refers to a printed text in the hands of a director and actors. It is this latter sense that the Cambridge Schools Shakespeare was conceived by Rex Gibson, Keith Rose and others at Cambridge University Press in the early 1990s. The most recent edition of *As You Like It* (Andrews and Gibson 2009) in that series is an example of the 'text-as-script', implying a use in schools and by students of all ages that sees the play as being lifted off the page.

In framing terms, when a work moves from text to script or script to text, there is a re-framing taking place. The play as *text* is almost always printed. It sees the work as read by an individual or a class, potentially without any consideration of the work as a play to be performed. Its attention is on the words on the page, framed as they are by textual matters such as provenance, and textual apparatus such as glossaries, notes, introductions, illustrations etc. Its intention, mediated by editors, is to provide a frame via which the words on the page can be accessed by the mind of the individual and/or group *reader*. Such mediation can be crucial when it comes to treating the play as a script and in performance.

The play as *script* might be printed or it might not. The script implies provisionality in the hands of the author, actors and director. Crucially, the words on the page are there for translation (re-framing) into speech and action: from an (apparent) two-dimensional page into three- or four-dimensional space and time. Whereas words in a text are opaque and physical in their black-type-on-white-paper presence, words in a script are means to an end – transparent windows through which action and speech are seen and realized.

What about 'performance'? There are degrees of performance from a script, from the simple act of reading aloud or a pared-down mime version at one end of the spectrum (cf. the discussion of Peter Brook above) to a fully-fledged production with all the machinery of theatre at the other. In thinking about the fully-fledged performance of the text/script, the role of the director is central. Before discussing it in more detail, it is worth noting a comment from Dusinberre (2006) about the relationship between text and performance:

> One of the biggest changes in Shakespeare studies since the publication of the second Arden edition of *As You Like It* in 1975 has been the closing of the gap between text and performance, scholar and director/actors, the academy and the theatre.
>
> (pp.136–7)

In the hands of a director, the script can be cut, re-arranged (edited, re-framed) according to his/her conception of the play as a whole, and in relation to some of the pragmatics of putting on a production in a particular place and time, and for a particular audience. What appears in textual form is almost never what an audience exactly hears (and sees) on stage in a production.

In pedagogic terms, activities, commentary and other editorial apparatus for the 2009 edition of *As You Like It* were trialled in 2007 with graduate students at New York University's Steinhardt School of Culture, Education and Human Development. In a room that was not designed for drama or theatre, tables and chairs were moved back to create a space in which improvisation on themes of the play and actual sections of the text/script were used in experimental ways. An example of improvisation was the placing of two items of luggage in the middle of the floor. In small groups, students/actors were asked to decide which characters they would like to play, and then to improvise a scene in which the luggage played a part. The (unopened) luggage itself suggested travel, change of location – and, variously, excitement, weariness, squabbling, vision, difference, the movement between the past and present as well as between locations. The tension and difference in the play between the court and Arden, between the city and country, between corruption and an experienced view of innocence were all potential areas of exploration. In drama terms, a further dimension could be added by revealing the contents of the luggage, and factoring these contents into the developing improvisation and/or into an interpretation of the play itself. Thus the luggage acts as a frame within a frame: a device which encloses, and which has a significance even as a piece of unopened baggage within a space that has been designated as a space of drama within an unpromising room, and within the context of a course on dramatic approaches using *As You Like It*. But, like Chinese boxes, the luggage itself can be opened to reveal more possibilities of connection, in mime and/or in speech. Pedagogically, too, it is always possible to move outside the frame of an activity like this and reflect upon it in learning terms (for the individual participants) and in teaching terms as potential or practising teachers.

The text of the play itself was removed from its particular conventional framing within the confines of a book, and arranged in scenes and acts as continuous script on a wall of a separate room, so that students could: i) visit and revisit the play as a whole; ii) see, at a glance, how long the scenes and acts were in relation to each other; iii) annotate the script, drawing lines to connect one part with another; and iv) illustrate the script with additional material. The aims of re-framing the experience of reading in a number of ways, then, were to give the students different perspectives on the play; to provide a space for critical purchase on the play and to allow creative new connections to take place between the students' own lives and the play, and between various elements within the play itself. Conceptual understanding was thus aided by physical re-framing: by moving the text around, by trying it out in speech and movement, by transporting it to different periods of time etc.

In summary, then, from the original conception of *As You Like It* to contemporary versions of it, there are a series of framings and re-framings that will have, have taken and could take place. These are, as in many cases of framing, highly complex to account for. The main point to be made from this section, in relation to the book as a whole, is that re-framing (as a verb) does take place in the creation and interpretation of cultural works. It is a creative and critical act, often practical and pragmatic, but always involving a transformation on the part of the participants. This transformation is both actual and (ideally) emotional, cerebral and sometimes spiritual. It is closely allied to the act of learning.

As You Like It and Company: A Different Kind of Re-framing

Dusinberre (2006) tantalizingly cites Beckett's 1980 novella *Company* alongside *As You Like It*, without elaboration: "Samuel Beckett's subtle reinvention of *As You Like It* in *Company* embodies the … perception of authorial power invested in Rosalind both '*within* the play' and '*beyond* [its] confines'. Rosalind's epilogue highlights the 'artificiality' of the work of art" (p.142). The stepping outside the play by Rosalind at the end of *As You Like It*, when she addresses the audience about the play in which she has just been the main character, does indeed transgress the frame of the deeper fiction of the play's action and makes one keenly aware of the artifice. But the stepping out is itself an artifice. The consciousness of framing is high at this point, and the audience leaves the theatre with Rosalind's words *as an actor* in their ears, rather than as a part in the play. Beckett's *Company* does this too, in a different way, bordering novella with (dramatic) monologue. It has been given on stage as a monologue. Its voice is both embodied and disembodied.

If *Company* is a 'subtle re-invention' of *As You Like It*, in what other ways does it re-frame Shakespeare's play? First, what is the nature of this novella? *Company* consists of a voice coming to 'one' in the dark. The one is you, as a reader or listener; but it is also anyone, including the narrator. And yet we do not hear the voice directly, but rather reported as if it had happened, and continues to happen. 'You' are "on your back in the dark", perhaps in prison, perhaps in bed, perhaps on your death-bed, and in other supine situations, being the recipient of the voice. The narrated account seems to have no connection to *As You Like It*, and it is not clear that this was a conscious re-invention of Shakespeare's play on Beckett's part.

Company is a novella. In the 1996 edition, it runs to 89 pages, but each of these pages only carries about 125 words – about a quarter of what one would expect on a page in a printed novel or novella. The effect of having relatively few words on each page – and printed in a type size larger than normal – is to slow down the reading, make it more like the kind of reading you would give a poem, and thus attend with more concentration than usual in reading the prose. The prose is framed in the book in order to achieve this effect, like Solzhenitsyn's *Prose Poems* (1973). And yet the ghost of the novel sits behind the novella, creating the expectation of story, plot, character, setting and the world created by narrative.

Company is an ostensibly bleak piece, seemingly very far away from Shakespearian comedy. But let us run with the idea that it is a re-invention of *As You Like It*. What are the correspondences?

One is that the narrator in *Company*, from his perspective "in the dark" is taken back to childhood and to pastoral moments. These moments are not ideal, not idealized; they are sometimes moments of pain and recognition:

> A small boy you come out of Connolly's Stores holding your mother by the hand. You turn right and advance in silence southward along the highway. After some hundred paces you head inland and broach the long steep homeward ... Looking up at the blue sky and then at your mother's face you break the silence asking her if it is not in reality much more distant than it appears. The sky that is. The blue sky. Receiving no answer you mentally re-frame your question and some hundred paces later look up at her face again and ask her if it does not appear much less distant than in reality it is.
>
> (pp.12–13)

The mother shakes off the hand and makes a cutting retort "you have never forgotten". In *As You Like It*, in the first part of the play, set in the corrupt court of Duke Frederick, Rosalind suffers retorts from him (her uncle) and is banished from court, for no apparent reason other than that she is daughter to the exiled Duke Senior. She sets off on a journey with her cousin, Celia, into the countryside and forest, with the court fool as company.

Here is the second parallel: the bleakness of the (symbolic, life-changing, soul-discovering) journey in *As You Like It* is signified in the play via weariness and exhaustion, largely on the part of Celia and the fool Touchstone. On this journey, Celia and Touchstone provide company: a touchstone of realism, the burden of injustice and baggage and companionship. This is no journey by a single, romanticized and existential being, but a social journey: one tinged with comedy and despair (cf. Beckett's other works concerning journeys). The resonance of the less-than-perfect pastoral is marked in *Company* by:

> You are on your back at the foot of an aspen. In its trembling shade. She at right angles propped on her elbows head between her hands. Your eyes opened and closed have looked into hers looking into yours. In your dark you look in them again. Still. You feel on your face the fringe of her long black hair stirring in the still air. Within the tent of hair your faces are hidden from view. She murmurs, Listen to the leaves. Eyes in each other's eyes you listen to the leaves. In their trembling shade.
>
> (pp.66–7)

We know from the play that the Forest of Arden is no garden of Eden; it is inhabited by the melancholy Jaques as well as by the more benign and holistic Duke Senior and his attendants. The corrupt court is not contrasted to a perfect Eden, but to a working countryside of pastoral effort, as well as to a forest of complexity and transformation.

Third, the sense of 'company' as a band of actors. Already mentioned is the heightening of the artifice of *As You Like It* as marked by Rosalind's epilogue. But 'company' in *Company* is not just about friendship, or – slightly lesser – the presence of some other voice as you like in the dark; it is about common experience, a life outside the internal musings of an individual consciousness, however alone that consciousness and self is in the end. In *As You Like It* the notion of company manifests itself in the self seeking out its other (the gender-crossing in the play, both intrapersonal and interpersonal, is pervasive); in the camaraderie in the first among Duke Senior's men, in the world-weariness of Celia and Touchstone as they accompany Rosalind in their journey of exile; in the company of actors as a whole that perform the play; and in the fact that most us, when we read, usually read alone, but when we see a play, we usually see it with others.

Lastly (though there are probably other correspondences) the loss at the end of *Company* is one of confinement, imprisonment:

> Thus you now on your back in the dark once sat huddled there your body having shown you it could go out no more. Out no more to walk the little

winding back roads and interjacent pastures now alive with flocks and now deserted.

(pp.85–6)

The walkabout that Rosalind takes is a journey of self-seeking, completion, removal of injustice, reconciliation, with encounters with flocks and shepherds along the way. The space that she allows herself, forced initially by exile, is restorative. What the re-framing of *As You Like It*, as *Company*, does is to bring to the latter the complex mix of pastoral, comedy and romance of the former. The bleak interior landscape of *Company* is tinged with regret, with memories of pain but also with remembrances of absorption and loss of the self in the sound of leaves. What a reading of *As You Like It* can gain through the lens of *Company* is a sense of the darkness in the play, both within the corrupt court and the Forest of Arden; of the darkness carried with the exiled trio as they make their way through pastoral fields and forest; of the 'knowingness' of the main character, Rosalind, as she manipulates the other characters in the play as well as engineering her own redemption. An increased emphasis on darkness in the play would enhance its brightness, its summery comedy.

Comparison of these two works – a play and a novella – highlights the fact that Bakhtin's notion of dialogism and interglossia runs through literature as well as through speech. Shakespeare took stories from various sources and re-framed them as a play; Beckett (perhaps) takes a play and re-frames it as a novella. As readers and listeners, we have the freedom to bring frames to bear upon an experience of a new text or performance.

Traversing the Frame, Erasing the Frame

It is one thing to work within a practice and theory of framing, understanding the various physical and conceptual, subconscious and conscious ways in which acts are framed and re-framed. Multiple levels of framing can be accounted for in an elaborate taxonomy to explain a particular interpretation or creation. There can be, as there is in the present book, an accent on framing as opposed to frames. But what happens when frames are transgressed or traversed, and furthermore when they are erased?

In the conception of framing that informs the present book, the tangible nature of frames is not the most important feature. It is rather the *act* of framing. The tangible nature of some frames, however, provides an inevitable invitation to traverse the frame. People, phenomena, ideas cannot be confined within a frame. If there is an awareness of what is outside as well as inside the frame (either from the perspective of the outside or inside), then the desire to get to the other side will manifest itself. What is the psychological motivation behind the desire to traverse and transgress? Partly it is human nature to need to see what is on the other side; to break free from confinement; to transgress and in due course to erase the frame, in order to create new ones.

In terms of theatre, traversing the frame has a long history. As suggested in the first part of this chapter, first the frame must be set up in order to create difference between the actors and the audience. The frame suggests that what is on one side of the frame is fictive, and that the laws of the other side of the frame do not necessarily apply. Outside the frame is the 'real world', a world in which the audience is fashioned into a unity by the very fact of being positioned in this way. The frame allows a different kind of contemplation and attention, always suggesting that what is within is related to what is without, and that the audience's role is to make those connections. At the end of the spectrum defined by Brook as the empty space, the frame is hardly visible; at the other end, in a conventional Victorian theatre, it may be marked by the beginning of the raised stage, by barriers, by other devices.

In a 1978 production of *The Taming of the Shrew* by the Royal Shakespeare Company at Stratford, Jonathan Pryce played Sly. While the lights were on in the house, prior to the start of the play, a drunken man staggered from the stalls towards the stage holding a bottle of beer and a flash camera, shouting at the audience and knocking over several ushers on the way. Making his way on to the stage itself, he began to destroy the elaborate set while half-dressed actors, stage managers and other officials came from backstage to see what was happening. By this time, half the audience was on its feet in an effort to see every detail of the disruption; some members of the audience walked out in disgust. There was a struggle on stage, with the police called in to restore order, but not before the set had been completely destroyed and the character fallen in a collapsed heap, centre stage, with smoke and mayhem in his wake. This was the cue for the lights to dim in the house, for lights to come up on stage, for Sly (as he now turns out to be) to first be discovered by the hunt and then be taken away on a hospital trolley and for the beginning of the play proper, where he returns as Petruchio.

Theorists and practitioners who transgress frames do so because they are unhappy with the conventional framing, and/or they want to make a point about the two sides of the framing line. They may wish the conventional framing to remain intact, to comment on it and to make the audience aware of it. But is it possible not only to transgress or break the frame, but to erase it altogether? For the purpose of the performing arts, it would be possible to reach a state in which there was no frame and no framing: this would be a state in which it was impossible to determine what is art and what is not. In such a state, there is no art: simply a continuum of experience in which there is no projection of any other state. As soon as that continuum is reflected on and distinguished from other states, framing begins.

In the case of the Chinese playwright, Gao Xingjiang (see Conceison 2001), much of the work is performative without text. Conceison agrees with Zhao (2000) that his plays "cannot be understood or appreciated without at least visualizing (if not experiencing) them as performance" (p.750), and that "Gao employs a dramatic language for his actors/characters that deconstructs

conventional gestures of representation in provocative and refreshing ways"
(p.751).

Framing without Words

So far this chapter has considered theatre (and by implication, opera). Do the
same kinds of framing apply to non-verbal art forms like mime, dance and
music? The answer is yes. In fact the lack of words in these art forms makes
the point, as in the visual arts like painting or sculpture or other forms of art
installation, that the framing that occurs in creating and interpreting them is
independent of words. Even though paintings, mimes, dance and music are
accompanied by programme notes, rationales, verbal introductions and other
verbal marginalia, their framed activity does not depend on words. A sculpture
can stand in a park or on a street without mediation by words; a dance can
take place without words; a concert can be completely unmediated by words.
Words are often used as one form of framing around the core experience of
such artworks and events, but are not essential. When they are, they act as
steps up towards the central art experience itself, rather than as an integral part
of it. The actual act of framing, though based on the physicalities of a framed
painting or a theatre space, is conceptual.

So mime, dance and music operate within space and time, physically, visually
and/or aurally, and framed by institutional, conventional and generic expectations in the same way as artforms that include the verbal. A choreographic
score, or a musical score, is written in a language that is transformable into
performance. In themselves, these scores are highly framed within their own
languages.

Framing in Sport

There are significant distinctions between sport and the performing arts, but
much in common too. As far as framing is concerned, sport provides a highly
regulated, highly formalized location for performing. Take football (soccer)
and tennis, for example.

Every week, hundreds of thousands of football and tennis fans attend
matches. As in the performing arts, they go through the ritual of buying tickets,
traversing the boundaries of the pitch and its stadium (however non-existent,
modest or grand) and entering a fiction in which they not only form part of the
audience, but actually help to frame the action themselves. Unlike theatre or
other performing arts, the pitch or court frames the action – and although there
is some variation in the size of football pitches, most of them – and all tennis
courts – are of a standard size. Furthermore, the matches are played according
to very clearly defined rules, regulated at a high level by football or tennis associations at international and national level, and mediated by referees/umpires.
In terms of framing by time, football operates on the basis of two 45-minute

periods separated by 'half-time' – a break of 10–20 minutes. Tennis is framed temporally by the number of sets that are played: formally, these number three or five, with tie-breakers to curtail the sets if they look like extending beyond the standard length, except in the last set which can take as long as it takes for one player or pair of players to get two games ahead of their opponents.

An interesting issue arises in the framing of football and tennis. Some stadia have the crowd almost encroaching upon the pitch or court: a matter of a few feet or metres between the edge of the playing area and the audience. It is said that the closer the crowd is to the action, the more 'atmospheric' and sometimes 'intimidating' the feel is within the stadium. Football teams that have moved from such intimate stadia to bigger newer ones with plenty of space between the crowd and the action, often seem to do less well playing 'at home'. The proximity of the crowd, in the previous location, had been an asset to them.

What happens when the framing is transgressed or broken (it is never erased, except in the most informal and chaotic versions of the games)? Within the confines of the games themselves, there are rules, penalties, fines and all the paraphernalia of maintaining 'respect' for the game. Between the audience and the game, boundaries are set by walls, fences, barriers and policed by stewards, ushers and, sometimes, by the police themselves. These boundaries can, if possible, be crossed by jubilant fans 'invading' a pitch after a particularly significant game; or they can be transgressed by streakers, protesting fans, rioting fans. Very rarely, the trangression goes the other way with a member of the playing team leaping into the crowd, either aggressively (as Eric Cantona did for Manchester United at Crystal Palace in 1995) or in jubilation and camaraderie. An example of the latter is when tennis players ascend into the crowd to embrace their family and/or coach after a particularly significant win.

Some more General Questions

So far in this chapter we have considered issues of framing and frames concerned with the performing arts and with sport. A spectrum has been proposed running from informality and minimal framing at one end and formality and highly wrought and multi-levelled framing at the other. Let us now move up a level to performance and the arts in general and also begin to reflect on the relevance of framing in these fields to framing in the language arts.

The Spectrum

The spectrum can be extended. At the informal end, we can posit a state in which there is no framing. In such states, there is no distinction between the arts and 'reality', or no rules whatsoever to a game (because there is no conception of a game as being separate from 'reality'). It is hardly chaos at the farthest reaches of the spectrum, but a state of indivisibility, being without difference, complete unity between self and non-self, being and not-being: a state of immersion in the day-to-day, and at the same time complete absorption in being in which presence and absence are undifferentiated. If that sounds like a state of being that is charted by Buddhism and other paths as one to aspire to, then that is because its very nature, beyond the pale of framing itself, is a religious or quasi-religious state.

At the other end, ironically, is fully-fledged ritual: a ritual so formalized and conventional as to become 'meaningless' or arbitrary within the parameters of human consciousness. Such ritual points beyond the spectrum of human framing to other unimaginable states of grace or enlightenment. The ritual provides a mechanism via which the human spirit is transported beyond itself. Again, it is no surprise that theatre has embodied both ends of the spectrum: for example in the movement towards *sartori* (enlightenment) in the Noh theatre of Japan.

To step back into the formalized end of the spectrum, what Brook (1972) characterizes as the 'deadly theatre' is heavy on framing and light on significance; it has lost its *raison d'être*.

Sketching the outer limits of the spectrum of framing in this way helps to make clear that framing is a distinctly *human* act. It is employed to make meaning, and to provide a framework and frame via which meaning can be shared and negotiated.

Framing as the Sine Qua Non of the Arts and Sport

The function of framing in the arts and sport appears to be to give them identity by separating them from the stream of experience. In the case of sport, there is no identity unless there is a high degree of formalized framing to characterize the activity, except at the informal end of the spectrum where kicking a ball against a wall, or bouncing a tennis ball on a racquet, are activities that practise a skill or prefigure the fully-fledged sport itself.

In the case of the performing arts, the function of framing is closer to that in the visual arts. By drawing a line – however informal or informal – a distinction is being made between what is inside and outside the frame. What in 'inside' is space of particular concentration; an invitation (almost a requirement) to look, listen and experience more intensely; an expectation that what is inside the frame – by the very fact of its being framed – operates differently. As with all the arts, those differences are that: i) there will be a higher expectation of unity within the frame; ii) patterns of elegance and beauty will be emphasized or de-bunked; iii) the contents within the frame will be expected to 'say something' about what is outside the frame; and iv) freedoms of juxtaposition will apply. Outside the frame will be characterized (even though it may be highly regulated and patterned in its own way) as less differentiated; 'the general flow of experience'; a 'background' for what is being said inside the frame. If there is no framing, there is no art.

Implications for the Verbal Arts

Apart from the reference to verbal texts in the section above on text, script and performance and *passim* (as one mode via which meaning is communicated), what are the implications for the verbal arts (speech and writing) of the focus in the first two chapters on the visual and performing arts? In these fields, the act of framing is more evident, more a part of the presentation of the experience, than in the verbal arts. Part of the aim of the following chapters will be to show how framing bears upon the creation and interpretation of the verbal arts, but it has been important to demonstrate first that framing is a tangible, inevitable, creative act in the visual and performing arts. Without framing in these arts, there is no art; and without framing there is no human, communicable, negotiable meaning.

Frames in the verbal arts are often less tangible and certainly less visible. In print, they may not be marked as frames as such, but simply as white space around a text. In speech, they may occur as invisible *schemata, mores* or conventions. In both speech and writing, they manifest themselves as genres, both in the sense of social action and as text types (indeed they provide a means of making sense of the relationship between social action and text types).

All speech and writing exists in a time/space continuum that can be defined. Sometimes loosely identified as 'context', the spatial and temporal framing of a speech/listening act or writing/reading act is a multi-levelled and complex picture of historical, social, political and economic perspectives and influences.

Once again, it is important to note that the focus of the present book is on the act of framing, not on the frames themselves. Each 'frame' has a particular characteristic, and there are few situations that can be explained by the description of a single frame (just as a picture in a gallery or a performance of a play in the theatre is multi-framed). A taxonomic approach to frames has been attempted and has proved to be interesting in terms of categoric proliferation, but unworkable in terms of practice or dynamic applicable theory. That is why the lessons of framing in the visual and performing arts are significant for the verbal arts: they are transferable, easily understood and *active* in that they can be changed, are flexible, are arrayed on a spectrum of possibilities.

Chapter 4

Visual and Verbal Frames

This chapter looks at the problem not so much from a visual arts perspective as from a verbal arts viewpoint. So rather than consider with a group of artists how the verbal is included in or mediates their visual work, the chapter, in keeping with the argument of the book as a whole, considers various aspects of printed written material: how writing itself is a visual art; how writing relates to other graphic arts; how writing, in combination with more purely visual forms, shapes its messages; and what exciting contiguities are emerging between written language and the visual within an overall theory of multimodality.

The Nature of 'Visual Literacy': Problems and Possibilities for the Classroom

While educators in the USA have been using the term 'non-print text' to describe sources of information in the English classroom which are not traditional books and magazines, English teachers and art educators have been coming together in England to think about the role of the visual and of information technology (IT) in English. This section of the chapter considers two converging strands within the subject 'English', strands which were laid out in a paper from the UK's National Council for Educational Technology (the precursor of Becta, the British Educational Communications and Technology Agency), *The Future Curriculum with IT: Implementing English for the 21st Century* (Tweddle et al. 1994) and in Dave Allen's 'Teaching Visual Literacy – Some Reflections on the Term' which appeared in an issue of *The Journal of Art and Design Education* (Allen 1994). There is much common ground between art and design, IT and English, and future conceptions of the subject English are going to have to come to terms with such convergence. It may be that a consideration of the issues confronting art educators will shed some light on the teaching of language and literature within 'media literacy'.

One of the main frames within which the convergence takes place is provided by computer screens and/or television screens. Just as word processing, searching databases and computer literacy are commonplace in English, so too art educators look at monitors as well as at paintings. As Allen notes (1994, p.134):

> However much we might like to claim a more significant place for practices like painting and drawing or ceramics and printmaking, we cannot pretend that they are as common in people's daily lives as the visual artefacts of the mass media

like cinema and broadcast television. Critical awareness in the face of screens seems to be one of the goals of the educators in visual literacy. Another is a heightened awareness of the links between being critical and being creative. Like *critical literacy*, the emphasis on not being duped by the media is a strong one,[1] and the recognition is that drawing, painting and allied arts and crafts are not sufficient in themselves to educate children and young people for the world out there. Of course, computer screens are not the only place where there is a dynamic relationship between word and image: magazines, newspapers, children's books all combine the two semiotic systems.

'Visual Literacy'

From a visual arts point of view, *literacy* is an interesting term to choose to define education in things seen. Allen charts the emergence of the term, coming into common use in art education in the 1990s, principally as a result of its appearance in the various documents which led to the publication of the National Curriculum regulations and guidance for art and growing from a critical studies movement in the 1980s. He then quotes a definition of visual literacy from Eisner (1989):

> By literacy I mean the ability to represent or recover meaning in the variety of forms through which it is made public. In our culture, words, numbers, movements, images, and patterns of sound are forms through which meaning is represented. To read these forms requires an understanding of their rules, their contexts and their syntactical structures.
>
> (p.8)

In other words, this is literacy as metaphor: the suggestion behind the term 'visual literacy' is not literal – that would almost be a contradiction in terms – but metaphorical. That is to say, a broad understanding of 'literacy' as reading and writing, as constituting a semiotic *system*, is used to describe what *could be* a way of accounting for a 'visual grammar'.[2] The source of the metaphor is not only Hoggart in *The Uses of Literacy* (1957), the widely acknowledged stimulus for seeing language in its social and cultural context, but also the very different tradition captured by Chomsky in *Syntactic Structures* (1964). Once Chomsky had attempted – but failed – to identify universal structures in language that were not only applicable to language and the other semiological systems, but to the innate structure of the mind itself, the enterprise of accounting for symbolic systems developed into semiotics: the study of sign systems. The history of the term 'literacy' goes back further, at least to the late-nineteenth century, when it was claimed in 1883 that Massachusetts was the first state in the Union in literacy achievement in its native population. The definition given in the OED is based on a 'knowledge of letters' and on the broadly accepted conception of an ability to read and write.

The definitional emphasis on *rules* and *syntactical structures* in Eisner (1989), as well as on the *contexts* of art forms, suggests that art educators think that there is a firm foundation in language and literacy studies that might inform their own practices. Linguists are not so confident about the validity of sentence grammar or syntax, however. Structuralists have tried to secure a reasonable account of the internal structures of language, and given up in the face of the enormous contextual and contingent factors bearing upon language; similarly any attempts to 'teach the grammar' of English in schools as a way of becoming a practitioner in the use of language have failed in the long-term because: i) the grammar is too complex for any other than linguistics graduates to understand; ii) it just doesn't work because it isn't necessary to learn 'grammar' to become competent and skilful in your native language; and iii) the 'grammar' cited is a grammar of sentence construction (see Andrews et al. 2006a). It does not account for the other levels of language like the text level. *Rules* are hopelessly limited (and much of language is not rule-governed, though it might be norm-oriented), *syntaxes*[3] hard to define and *structures* as much in the eye of the beholder as inherent in the language.

So, when Allen (1994) acknowledges that "research in the field [of literacy] is problematizing the term even as we art teachers appropriate it" (p.141), his acknowledgement needs to be amplified. No doubt the visual arts world is riven by the same debates as is the world of verbal language. It is dangerous to build on a foundation that is itself shaky, even though one way to look critically at the practices and assumptions in one's own discipline is to compare them with a *seemingly* unified picture in another discipline.

There is more to be gained in theoretical clarity and in practice from being realistic about the state of each discipline, and looking for convergence and contiguity between them in a different way.

A Map of Verbal and Visual Kinds of Communication

Which media do we use to communicate? Table 4.1 suggests that perhaps the norm is a combination of the verbal and the visual, i.e. the second and third columns.

Table 4.1 A map of verbal and visual kinds of communication

Visual	Visual/Written	Visual/Spoken	Written	Spoken
Art galleries[4]	Comics	Most television	Most novels	Telephone
'Pure'	Most recipe	Most film	Most academic	conversations
landscape[5]	books	Face-to-face	articles	
	Catalogues	conversation	Most emails	
	Magazines			
	Newspapers			
	Multimedia			
	programs			
	Children's			
	books[6]			
	Non-fiction			
	works			
	Manuals			
	Most			
	advertisements			

It should be clear from even a crude listing of this kind[7] that most communication takes place simultaneously in more than one medium, and that certainly the popular forms of communication combine the visual with the verbal. Books and journals on the subject of the relationship of word to image – like *Word & Image*[8] – always well received in literary and artistic circles, do not give a real indication of the vast interrelationship between word and image that most of us take for granted.

Visual Critique

When looking at the design of cars on the market, or arranging furniture in a room, or relating what is seen in art galleries to the angles, shapes, lines and colours of the gallery itself and to the buildings and people outside the gallery, do those working in the field of letters and language think of their activities as acts of 'visual literacy'?

Words in their written form are part of the visual world. Whether in type standing alone, or in close proximity to more purely visual signs, words can be seen to stand in relation to other visual forms.

It is worth reflecting on the spectrum in which those relationships can be understood. At the 'visual' end of the spectrum, there are purely visual forms: paintings, for example. Then, taking a step towards the verbal, words can be used to overlay or be embedded in a picture (as in the work of Schwitters, Kitaj, Miró, Blake, Juan Gris, Picasso, Basquiat et al.). In this zone, words are usually iconic in function.

Somewhere in the middle of this spectrum, there is a delightful balance and/or tension between the verbal and the visual, as in maps (perhaps slightly

Figure 4.1 Saul Steinberg, cover for *The New Yorker*, 24 May 1999.

Drawing for the *New Yorker cover*, May 24, 1999, altered after submission to the magazine in the 1990s. Pencil, colored pencil, and collage on paper, 14×11 in (36.6×27.9cm). Collection of Ian Frazier and Jacqueline Carey ©The Paul Steinberg Foundation/Artists Rights Society (ARS), New York.

to the visual side) and in many books for children up to about the age of 7, in comics (for children and adults), in cartoons (political; work by Hogarth, Lichtenstein et al.), in the work of Magritte and Steinberg (where word and image often subvert each other – see Figure 4.1) and in advertisements.

Moving over further towards the verbal, there are long traditions of Arabic and Chinese and Japanese (for instance) art and calligraphy (see Figures 4.2 and 4.3), illuminated manuscripts predating the printing press (including musical manuscripts which incorporate yet another symbolic system – musical notation), early printed books (e.g. Donatus's Latin grammar, the 42-line Bible),

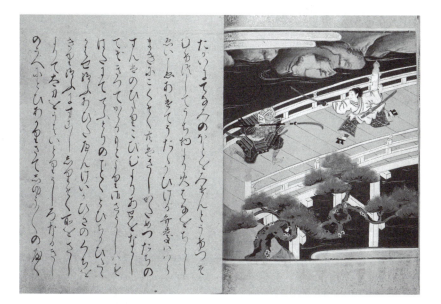

Figure 4.2 Quran, Surah XCIII, Egypt, fourteenth century.

Figure 4.3 Fight on bridge between the young hero Yoshitune and the warrior-monk Benkei.

illustrated drafts and notebooks (Lewis Carroll, Edward Lear, A. A. Milne, Pablo Picasso, Vincent Van Gogh – see Figure 4.4), illustrated books and manuals with illustrations; finally, at the verbal end of the spectrum, there are articles, novels, regulations etc. which have no visual presence other than the typographic.[9]

What is the significance for framing theory and practice of these examples, and more generally of the spectrum from the visual to the verbal? The combination of two modes within one frame sets up tensions and contiguities that

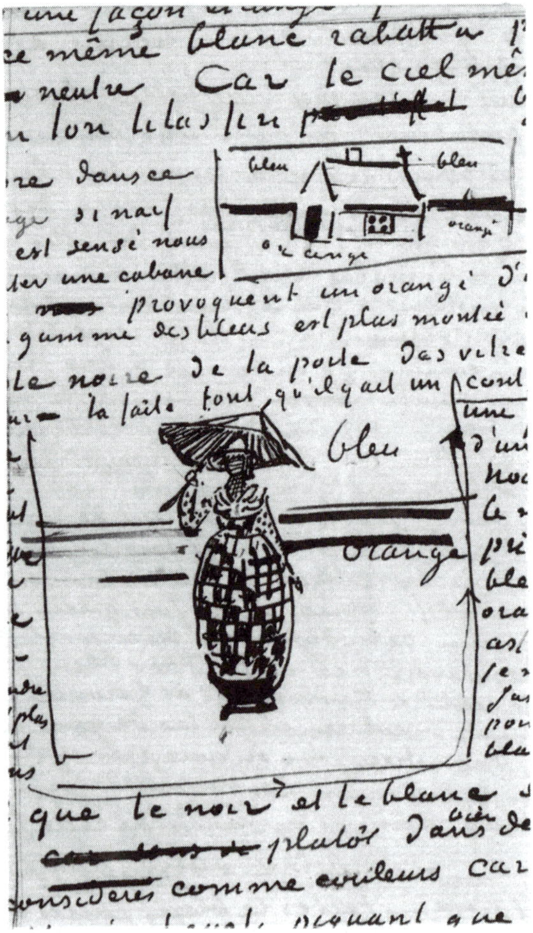

Figure 4.4 Van Gogh, autograph letter to Emile Bernard with a sketch of a woman with a parasol, Arles, *c.*7 June 1888.

are generative. They are generative in the sense that they are visually interesting and require attentiveness; the eye and mind are drawn to puzzling out the relationship between the two. They are also generative in that, consciously or unconsciously, the balance between the two modes is in question: does the visual dominate, or does the verbal? Where there is a delicate balance between the two, the question is even more tantalizing. In the case of the Steinberg (Figure 4.1), it is hard to tell whether the original conception was typographic or visual (or both). The framing of the block of stores in bold, three-dimensional lettering, with additional two-dimensional lettering on the front of the stores and on adjacent signs, is arresting. The word 'and' is implied between the 'HERE' and 'NOW', so the reader unwittingly offers conjunctive links between the building and the street. In the manuscript pages from the Quran and *Benkei Monogatari* (Figures 4.2 and 4.3) there is a difference between the Arabic script, which is used as the basis for the visual decoration (as in medieval illuminated manuscripts in English or Latin) and the Japanese script which sits alongside the illustration. In the latter case, the equal division of the page between the script and the image provides the sense of balance and ambiguity: it is hard to say which mode has dominance, so the balance between the two becomes part of the message that is conveyed.

Finally, in the extract from the autographed letter from Van Gogh (Figure 4.4), the clearly framed sketches are inserted into a written letter. But what is evident is that the framed sketches must have gone in first, or certainly before the written text was wrapped around them. Again, though the images seem on first appearance subsidiary to the text, they provide a counter-balance, a different way of communicating, setting up complementarity and counterpoint in relation to the written script.

It thus makes sense, within the notion of 'visual literacy', to see the verbal not as a metaphor for the visual, but as standing alongside the visual.[10] Contiguity is the crucial relationship: the attempt is to bring images and words together in a dynamic, provocative, generative way.

Both English teachers and art educators want their students to be critical. They want this because being critical is seen as both the function of education and as a sign of an educated person. It is considered to be the highest of the high-order intellectual skills. It reveals the structures and ideologies behind what is 'taken for granted', and protects us from indoctrination. It also enables us to compose appropriately (or inappropriately) according to our audience and context. The key text on critical literacy is probably Fairclough's *Language and Power* (1991).

To get the critical spirit into perspective, it is necessary to place it in relation to interpretation and reading – which is exactly what Scholes does in *Textual Power* (1985). Scholes sees reading as a largely unconscious activity that naturally fills in the gaps in texts "without confusion or delay". Interpretation depends "upon the failures of reading" (p.22) and requires the reader to work to fill in the gaps. It is largely consensual, whereas criticism requires a 'negative hermeneutic' (Ricoeur's phrase), a willingness to suspect:

> If wisdom, or some less grandiose notion such as heightened awareness, is to be the end of our endeavors, we shall have to see it not as something transmitted from the text to the student but as something developed in the student by questioning the text.
>
> (p.14)

That is, students must be fully aware of their own reading positions and practices – of the frameworks and frames they bring to the text. This kind of openness will enable them to be critical of the text in question, and to be able to argue with the text, seeing it not as a sacrosanct totem but as another voice in a dialogue. An excellent justification for teaching critical skills in the arts in the widest sense is to be found in Buchanan (1995).[11]

So, if art educators want a curriculum in which there is a shift from art as practice to art as heightened visual awareness, or a combination of practice with critical awareness as in some English composition practice, how are they best to go about it? Perhaps not by using a term like 'visual literacy' in which the term 'literacy' is fraught with baggage from the language of a complicated discipline called 'English'.[12] What literacy might mean to one person might mean something very different to another. On other grounds, the development of the study of linguistic structures (mostly at syntax level) into semiotics offers a better position from which to inform the teaching of the visual arts. The limitations of this approach, however, must be realized: literacy can be no more than a metaphor for the visual arts, otherwise frame will disappear within frame like a set of mirror reflections.

As interim summary, then, what might be more useful and productive, as well as reinforcing the position of the visual arts in the curriculum, is an alliance (already suggested by Allen) between English teachers and art educators to look at the relationship between the arts and language in general, and in particular at the way the two are brought together in many of the popular and not-so-popular forms of communication we use in society and education. More particularly still, the contiguity of images and texts, and how we read those contiguities, is going to be important.

The Role of IT

To borrow the theoretical terminology of MacLachlan and Reid (1994) the particular *frame* in which these contiguities are played out is increasingly that of the monitor, whether a TV monitor and/or one attached to a computer.[13]

In a paper from the National Council for Educational Technology (Tweddle et al. 1994), referred to earlier in the chapter, various propositions have been put forward, along with questions that have a bearing on the issues discussed in the present chapter.

The main propositions put forward are that:

- IT is providing an information-rich society for some
- the culture of IT is global (though unequally accessed)
- IT is generating a collaborative culture
- the polarities of home/school, teacher/learner and reading/writing are dissolving
- images, icons and sounds are used alongside and instead of words for constructing and conveying meaning.

One of the many consequences of such a set of propositions and of the changes already taking place is that the distinctions between English/media studies/ communication studies/visual studies are being redrawn. One of the important breakthroughs made by this conception of English is that reading and writing are reciprocal. This is not a new perception. Barthes, with his notion of the 'writerly' text, and reception-theory and reading response-theory, with their re-framing of reading as a creative act, have broken down barriers between reading and writing, suggesting that readers 'make' or compose the text as they read it, and that writers are all the time informed by their reading to different degrees. The analogy with 'speaking and listening' makes the reciprocity clear (though the nature of those reciprocities is different), and the irony remains in successive versions of the National Curriculum in English that although 'speaking and listening' are seen as reciprocal, they are afforded less than an equal share of curriculum time than the still separately conceived 'writing' and 'reading'. The true reciprocity of writing and reading is well described in, for example, Jones (1991).

How, then, does the computer screen facilitate the close connection between composition and critical literacy? The simple answer is by allowing the reader/ viewer to manipulate texts, change texts, interfere with the sacrosanct nature of the text: to change their shape, to change words within them, to split them up and re-formulate them, to write into existing literary works, to join voices with another text, to create split column texts. Thus the 'dialogue' – to borrow a metaphor from speech and listening, and to use the dominant metaphor in discourse studies post-Bakhtin – between writer and reader, between text and writer/reader, is made an active and interactive one.

The interactivity is not only between reader and text (reader, that is, who becomes writer). It is also between collaborating readers. Much of the evidence of the value of computers in the classroom to date has suggested that the conversation that goes on between students as they sit in front of a screen and manipulate/create text is probably the most valuable activity taking place. There is a renewed critical dialogue taking place, and it is about making things with words (and images) and/or interpreting words (and images). The dialogue is also evident in more distant types of collaboration between readers and writers that technology enables, e.g. in emails in response to questions and messages on the Net. The making and remaking of words and images on the computer screen seem to link with post-modernist ideas about intertextuality and re-presentation.

Implications for Art/English

Let us take these observations about what IT can do for English back into the discussion about the relationship between Art and English and the notion of visual literacy.

The nature of a discipline is to question its own practices. The very nature of life in a discipline is that it is constituted around arguments about its practice. This much is suggested in Sally Mitchell's account of the place of argument in sixth forms and higher education (Mitchell 1992 and 1994).

Arguing within one's discipline is often accompanied by references to still points outside the discipline; in the case of the present debate, the still point is 'English'. Similarly, debates which rage within English – like the relative weight of literature and language study, the nature of fiction, the value or not of teaching 'skills' – often look outside to practices like Art for illumination. Almost always, the outside practice is conceived rather simplisticly and conservatively by the practitioner/theorist from the perspective of his or her own practice. The striking thing about the articles by Allen and Buchanan is that despite some oversimplification of the case of English (as inevitably, in the other direction, with Art), they make insightful and potentially creative connections between the two subjects, not least that there is much to be gained by English and Art teachers looking at each other's practices and approaches to composition and 'reading'. As Allen suggests, "we need a more sophisticated sense of what people actually do with images – in their totality – and how that relates to pedagogical practices" (1995, pp.6–7).

Visual *Rhetoric?*

A better approach to visual literacy or the frame in which the visual and the verbal are converging, and in which the contiguities between them create a new dynamic, is *via* a contemporary conception of 'rhetoric' – as suggested at the end of Chapter 1. The 'contemporary' tag distinguishes rhetoric from its Aristotelian version and defines its area of interest as informed by cultural studies, linguistics and theories of dialogue. It is political, tying personal expressiveness to notions of audience and the media of communication; it is also a down-to-earth pragmatic way of thinking about how best to frame a message in a real situation. Rather than repeat what is set out elsewhere (Andrews 1992, 1993, 1995a), below is a reprise of the advantages of seeing the verbal (both spoken and written) and visual – and the tactile and dramatic/gestural – as coming under the umbrella of rhetoric.

- Rhetoric is socially and politically situated. It sees communication as taking place between a creator/speaker/'rhetor' and his/her/their audience in a particular situation. The situation partly determines the 'meaning', as do the creator and the audience. It is thus not prey to theories of 'reader-response' *or* 'author-centred ideology' *or* Marxist social analysis, because it embraces all three perspectives.
- A rhetorical perspective allows the production and analysis of different media alongside each other, as the level it operates at is one of communication, action and purpose. It brings reading and composition closer together in the way that speaking and listening were in classical rhetoric (the 'art of persuasion'). If art educators are concerned about a separation between the tactile/expressive domain on the one hand, and the critical domain on the other, a rhetorical perspective unites the two – and does so in a way which, although powerful theoretically, is also very pragmatic and practical.
- Crucially, for those concerned with education, rhetoric mirrors the natural learning situation in which education is an effect of community – a situation which, as pointed out earlier in the chapter – is the most common one in which children learn to read (in the fullest sense of that word): a situation in which the visual and verbal are rarely far apart.
- By perceiving schools and art galleries as rhetorical communities, we are freed to see them in a wider context of social communites in general: families, local community groups, nations, international communities, electronic communities, communities whose sensibilities are determined by television or radio. Such liberation from the confines of the classroom or gallery/museum widens the possibilities for learning, and also allows us to see the value of classrooms and galleries, framed as they are with particular functions and by particular ideologies.[14]
- Rhetoric foregrounds argument, allowing positioning in relation to existing works, and questioning of them to take place more readily than in conventional approaches.
- A rhetorical perspective provides a theoretical unity to the verbal and visual arts (arts of communication, arts of discourse) at a time when they need to defend and justify their presence in the curriculum.
- Rhetoric does not privilege one art form over another, nor one mode of expression over another. It both allows image and text to stand alongside each other and their relationship to be analysed; and it throws new light on, for instance, the relationship between fiction and documentary.[15]
- More practically, rhetoric might help in providing a language to describe the elements, relations and functions of a multimodal screen.

Two articles from *Rebirth of Rhetoric* (Andrews 1992), Patsy Stoneman's 'Reading across Media: The Case of *Wuthering Heights*' and Prudence Black and Stephen Muecke's 'The Power of a Dress: The Rhetoric of a Moment in

Fashion' drive home the importance of an umbrella-like perspective on visual and verbal communication. Stoneman traces the development of visual images derived from the novel, suggesting that the novel is transformed completely in the process. Black and Muecke analyse a photograph of Jean Shrimpton at the 1965 Melbourne Cup, using the notion from Barthes of the rhetoric of the image.

Given the exciting potential of analysis and production of word and image, perhaps a rhetorical perspective is the best one to take if we are not only to understand what is happening to us as we read from computer screens, but also to help us compose more effectively and to develop our own (and our students' and children's) use and awareness of the range of discourse communities in which verbal and visual languages are learnt.

Questions for Research

Most printed and electronic communication (at least in popular culture) is now verbal/visual, rather than purely verbal or purely visual. Indeed, purely verbal communication (*Oxford English Dictionary* etc.) is rare, and if we go further along the spectrum of the verbal/visual to the very end, we would be hard pressed to find verbal communication that is not associated with the visual in some way. Radio is perhaps a classic exception (though radio is an interesting case in that we always seem to be doing something else while listening to it; the senses, the body is engaged in some other tangentially related way). Printed verbal communication almost always has a visual dimension of some sort that helps the reader frame it. Similarly, at the other end of the spectrum, where do we find unmediated 'pure' visual communication? Certainly not in cities, which are verbal language-rich, but perhaps in uninscribed landscape, in images that are language-free and also unmediated by language.

Perhaps, if you follow the argument of Richard Lanham (1993) and his notion of 2,000 years of multimedia, it has always been the case that the verbal and visual work together. To quote Lanham, 'pure' printed written communication (to be more precise) operates via an 'aesthetic of denial'; as if, outside the frame of the black-and-white printed page, colour, texture and tone are desperate to get in.

But where, in this welter of the verbal/visual, are the really interesting areas for research? What is the exact nature of that relationship in these interesting areas? What is the evidence of how children bring together the verbal and visual, and what are the implications for language learning? And finally, what model of communication might best account for and generate new insights into the relationship between the verbal and visual in communication?

What's interesting about the screen in Figure 4.5? I'll take the second, third and fourth questions first, and by degrees come round to the first one. First, it has to be said that the verbal and visual don't simply coexist here; rather, they

Figure 4.5 Screenshot of bilingual email.
Courtesy of Yu Ge.

are contiguous. That is to say, they are equal in status and they create a complementary tension. You both 'read' them at the same time and you read them differently. You switch codes, most obviously when you click on one or the other to
foreground it on the screen. Is it possible to say which has pre-eminence? When
the text is being attended to (and here 'text' is used to mean the manifestation of
the verbal language), the images are secondary, contributary – they fulfil the function of illustrations. Similarly, when an image is foregrounded, the text becomes
caption-like. To explore the different nature of the messages being received, we
probably would have to go into cognition theory and brain science. This brief
analysis of what is happening – or potentially what might happen – in the making
of and response to this screen is of course partial. It is an academic approach which
can only operate by shutting out much of the vitality of the multimodal format.

The second question follows from this position: how do we – as adults – read
material like this? How do children use it? Are there differences? I would suggest from observing children in classrooms at primary and secondary level, and
also by reflecting on my own use and my children's use of multimedia for
homework, that the skills of scanning and skimming – so well described by
research into reading in the 1970s – are finely tuned in the twenty-first century.
Scanning is often followed by more concentrated reading of text by children
doing research; but scanning remains scanning as far as the visual goes. In some

ways, then, the practices of reading follow the technology … just as theories of reading that have developed since the 1970s are book-based, fiction-based, narrative-based.

Scanning, however, is a term to describe the way machines read text and images, as well as to describe the way people do it. As in colour supplements or junk mail, you are invited to scan. More interesting questions – for example, how young children process and respond to and learn about verbal language alongside the visual, and how the visual helps (or hinders) the learning of the verbal – are subjects for further research.

Third, what model of communication best suits a world in which email, multimedia, old-fashioned print, speech etc. are prevalent; in which the *managing* of communication for people at work is close to defining what work actually is; in which children and adults, education and the workplace are making sense of digital data in verbal and visual form, often simultaneously in the same message? That discipline in which such a model finds its home might be linguistics, but a linguistics much transformed. Single-channel linguistics (i.e. linguistics based only on a study of verbal language in speech or writing) must surely wither into obscurity as it increasingly ceases to represent the real contexts of language use. Multi-channel linguistics – almost a contradiction in terms – is a different animal. It won't be concerned so much with the internal dynamics of one channel or mode, but with the relationship between different channels or modes and their relationship with their functional contexts. In the history of linguistics over the last 50 years, that seems a logical enough step, but we've now come to a point – helped by linguistics' charting of the levels of language description and their relationships to each other – where we have to step beyond linguistics.

What does emerge, as was discussed in Chapter 1, is the idea that frames (brought into discourse analysis from sociology, and borrowed metaphorically from the art world) can be useful ways of making sense and also of creating communication, however many channels are used.

In opera for example, the heavy framing (opera as social institution, high cost of tickets, ornate theatres, lavish costumes, the largely huge frames of the singers, the bringing together of song, recitative, music and acting) allows for a multi-channelled, highly formal art work. In conversation across a kitchen table between two adults, framed by social conventions of marriage and/or partnership and/or friendship, a cup of tea, the table, the room, the house, communication is going to be of a different order. Different kinds of dialogue exist in the two situations; different channels are used (if there is a printed or handwritten letter between the two conversants, the social and communicative dynamic is changed yet again). In each case, the framing partly determines the nature of communication. At the same time, the frame can always be broken, transgressed for comical or revolutionary effect, or simply to enhance the awareness of the frame. In the emergent model of literacy learning that is set out in this book, considerable emphasis is put on framing both in the teaching of reading and writing. Children of any age can subvert, transgress, change the frame in order to inject some humour, energy and fun into the process. That element of fun, of gaining command of the act of framing, seems to be missing from curricular initiatives in the UK between 1996 and 2010 around literacy that are derived from Australian genre theory.

Frames are not the same as genres; that is why the preferred term here is 'framing'. Framing is an act, not a tangible thing. It is called into play in order to give historical credence and shape to an encounter, i.e. to give it 'meaning'. Even genres conceived as social action (Miller 1984) rather than text-type do not convey the fluidity and flexibility of framing. But framing of itself is not sufficient for a model, because frames come in different shapes, sizes and natures according to their contexts. Framing is, however, the agent of action and cohesion (and coherence) in a theory of communication underpinned by rhetoric.

Lastly – and if you go along with the notion that the visual/verbal interface in education is worth exploring from a framing perspective – what are the really interesting areas for research at the interface of the verbal and visual? Some of them are:

- how 'work' and 'education' use them to transact their business, and whether there are mismatches between the two principal uses. If there are mismatches, does it matter?
- the way the visual and verbal work with each other in the development of children's capacity to use language
- the way the visual arts world conceives of and uses the verbal
- the differences between high art (which tends to be relatively mono-modal, e.g. Fine Art practice, poetry, 'prose', fiction) and popular art, which tends to be multimodal
- the question of whether education prefers an 'aesthetics of denial' in order to induct its students/pupils into a single channel of communicative discourse, and into a particular semiotic system
- the very future of linguistics or semiotics in such a volatile and rapidly changing communicative landscape.

The shift away from semiotics and language-based theories of communication towards rhetorical theories has been marked since about 1990. Contingency, the move away from Modernist systematizing of communication and a need for a more grounded model of communication have contributed to this shift. It marks not so much a turn to the visual as a return to a *modus operandi* in which channels of communication – the visual, the aural, the physical – and modes of communication – speech, writing, other visual modes, dance – are considered alongside each other: an acceptance of the multimodal nature of most commu-nication, whether electronically driven or not. Mitchell indicates this shift in the prefatory notes to 'What is visual culture?' (1995, p.208; see also 2002), where he records how a faculty working group on visual culture at the University of Chicago in 1993 rejected an emphasis on semiotics and sign theory as a starting point "in favor of an introduction that would stress visual experience as its point of departure". The first point to emerge from such a paradigm shift is that it is partly brought about by the breaking down of the separation of humanistic disciplines into 'verbal' and 'visual' camps along with the distinction between high art and mass culture; this breaking down of walls has implications for both the verbal and visual.

It was with this new landscape in mind – glimpsed but hardly explored – that Viv Reiss of the Arts Council of England commissioned a research project from Middlesex University in London. The appointment of a research fellow, Karen Raney, to the project 'Framing Visual and Verbal Experience' in 1996 led to a year's investigation into the notion of visual literacy: a term much used in art education circles but with a weak sense of core definition that would provide a foundation for debate or a coherent pedagogical programme. Mitchell's aim (1995, p.210), "to provide students with a set of critical tools for the investigation of human visuality", comes close to what the project was about. Mitchell's own formulation of signs (iconology, visual literacy, taxonomies and histories of visual media), bodies (race, vision and the body; gender; the gaze and the glance) and worlds (institutions of the visible, visual media and global culture, architecture and the built environment, the ownership of the image) seemed inappropriately programmatic for our needs.

In relation to framing in the macro-sense of institutional programming and the design of courses for schools and universities, Mitchell's observation that it is the permeable boundaries between the various 'insides' or 'outsides' of disciplines that were most noticeable in the study of culture in the late twentieth century is a salient one:

> One can deplore these developments as a degradation of eternal standards, or as the predictable corruption of advanced capitalism; one can celebrate them as the hyper-fun of advanced postmodernism. Or one can do neither, and attempt to assess dialectically and historically the contemporary relations of artistic institutions to what lies outside them in what I have been calling 'visual culture'. This will not rescue us from the contradictions of what Panofsky calls an 'organic situation', but it might provide a way of making those contradictions the very subject matter of the field, rather than embarrassments to be finessed in the name of disciplinary coherence.
>
> (1995, p.217)

In summary, there are various types and levels of frame that have been discussed in this chapter, specifically in relation to the contiguity of word and image. First, a spectrum has been suggested with the 'purely' visual at one end and the 'purely' verbal at the other, though these polarities exist merely as dialectical ideals. Along the spectrum, combinations of word and image, yoked together through framing, are set in relation to each other. Sometimes that relationship is complementary, sometimes it is equal and sometimes there is a difference in status between the two modes. At other times, the two modes are in (usually) productive tension. But such relationships, and the communicative possibilities they offer, would not be possible without framing. Framing puts them together in a composition that invites inquiry: why are these two modes put together, and what is the relationship between them? The frame is therefore like a heuristic device.

Figure 4.6 Workers on scaffolding in Shenyang, China, 2009.
© Press Association. Used with permission.

Second, much of the chapter has been concerned to unpack the term 'visual literacy' moving it from a loosely metaphorical way of denoting competence in reading the visual towards a more precise sense in which the visual and verbal can be seen to have commonalities and significant differences. It is argued that the term 'visual literacy' is too vague (too fuzzy a frame) to be anything other than confusing in the debate about modes and signification.

Third, the affordances of the computer screen have been explored for what they suggest about the combination of image, word and sound. The computer screen is the principal interface of this medium, either writ large in wall-to-wall television screens, in large- to medium- to small-book size on desktops or laptops, and even smaller in handheld devices like mobile phones. These frames allow for multimodal and seemingly monomodal communication. While studies in multimodality seemed to coincide in the 1990s with the rise of the internet and increasing availability of mobile phones and other forms of computer in digitized communication, they need to be separated for analytical purposes.

Finally, to borrow Goffman's conception, frames operate within other frames. The hierarchy of frames is not absolute and fixed. In other words, perception and composition do not always take place driven by an overarching ideological framework that then transforms into a series of smaller frames to delimit and make sense of specific phenomena. Rather, the process is one in which different frames are applied in different circumstances, refracting with others, coming into the foreground and then receding into the background or into invisibility. Such relativity in framing makes for difference in interpretation, for debate and conjecture about the nature of frames that are in operation and the continued possibility of innovation. There is rarely a case where a single framing exercise provides all that is required for making or interpreting meaning. Larger frames give context and meaning to smaller frames, and the very act of composition and interpretation is one in which frames have to be played off against one another.

Like scaffolds (see Figure 4.6), these can be constructed and re-constructed in order to provide a way in which a building can be put up. And like scaffolds, they are temporary light structures that, in the end, are taken down and rendered invisible because they are a means to an end, not the end of communication itself.

Chapter 5

Frames of Reference

Framing in Relation to a Theory of Multimodality

What implications do theories of multimodality have for a framing approach to composition? What place does framing have within such theories? This chapter suggests that the two sit well with each other, with rhetoric as the overarching theory, multimodality as a palette of possibilities in shaping and communicating with others, and framing as the creative and critical act which can bring such communication into being/action. The chapter suggests that 1980s and 1990s approaches to genres, which often saw them as static text-types and/or recognizable patterns of social action, need to be updated to allow for rhetorical, multimodal and framing perspectives – and to provide a way in which the creative and critical can be included.

Introduction

In the 1990s it looked like 'visual literacy' provided a way of bringing together the verbal and visual. By analogy with other kinds of literacy, like 'emotional literacy', 'political literacy' and so on, the phrase suggested competence and capability in the discourses of the field of visual perception and application as well as "a rising area of concern" (Raney 1997, p.14). Indeed, 'visual literacy' seemed the most salient of the literacies, in that it was concerned with the common ground between two 'languages': that of words and that of images. But like many such hybrid terms, its apparent surface elegance and presence were underpinned by an iceberg of controversy and debate below the surface. This chapter starts with a further discussion of visual literacy, but then moves on to an exploration of framing from a perspective of multimodality.

Raney (1997) provides a comprehensive summary of the field. It looks back to Berger's *Ways of Seeing* (1972) as a turning point in conceiving the visual arts as part of visual culture; of urging us "to think of pictures as being 'more like words and less like holy relics'" (Raney 1997, p.7). The liberation of the visual arts – not from frames as such, but from a cloistered art history approach – was engineered by photography, which enabled copies of images to be put alongside words, other images and music into ever-varied hybrid compositions. One of Berger's memorable examples is the comparison of the Mona Lisa hanging in the Louvre with a poster of the painting in any student's room. He asks, 'What is the value of the original, in the broadest sense: as a cultural icon, in monetary terms, as a tourist attraction, as a work of craftsmanship etc.?' In a digital age in which the notion of 'originality' or 'the original version' has been questioned, Berger's questions remain pertinent. Essentially, what Berger was doing was asking us to look politically and critically, to be aware of the changing landscape of visual culture. In a sense, he was re-framing the way we looked at art.

The complexity of the task of defining and exploring visual literacy is partly to do with the fact that it is of interest to the fields of "perceptual psychology, artificial intelligence, visual education, literacy studies, art history, art criticism, visual theory, cultural and media studies, philosophy of the arts and aesthetics" (Raney 1997, p.13). This range makes the problem of definition a near impossible one to solve, but at the same time a tantalizing one. The approach used by Raney was one in which the uses of the term by practising artists and/or theorists and their attitudes towards the visual were explored and charted. There was no preconception of what it meant to be visually literate or illiterate.

It is impossible to do justice to the report on visual literacy in the present book. What it helps us to see with regard to framing and re-framing is how a particular nexus of problems and issues in the visual arts, and in visual culture more generally, have been framed at a particular time (say, in the second half of the twentieth century) for a particular purpose. That purpose appears to have been to explore the degree to which pictures are like words, and conversely, the degree to which they are not. Not explored by the visual literacy debates is the complementary issue of the degree to which words are like images. Such concerns play along a spectrum from the 'purely' verbal to the 'purely' visual, with visual literacy operating like a moving frame along that spectrum, bringing different relationships between the two codes into focus. There are paradoxes and conundrums in this relationship between the verbal and the visual, like the fact that the printed verbal code is always visual (via type, handwriting etc.) but that the visual is not always verbal. There is also a sense as particular framings come into focus that sometimes the visual is dominant, and sometimes the verbal. The most interesting relationships between the verbal and visual occur when there is a balance and/or tension between the two. In these cases, both the composition and interpretation of the message is likely to move backwards and forwards between the two modes.

Framing and Genre Theory

Well before the publication of *Framing and Interpretation* (MacLachlan and Reid 1994) Ian Reid and colleagues at Deakin University in Victoria were debating issues of genre and framing. In *Shifting Frames: English/Literature/ Writing* (Hart 1988), a distinction is made at the outset between frames and framing. Frames are seen as fixed cultural entities that set certain limits and are subject to critical investigation about the ways in which they are "devised and regulated" (p.1). But the key point as far as the present book is concerned is to do with framing as a verb: "to frame something is not simply a matter allowing the thing to declare itself, to present itself as it really is, but rather of permitting it to be constituted in one way rather than another" (ibid.). In other words, framing is positioned as an act that allows critical re-shaping to take place; that sees frames as highly provisional; and that marries theory and practice.

Framing and (especially) re-framing in this sense can be seen to be part of another movement in language studies, broadly known as critical literacy. Critical literacy asks, 'What frames are we bringing to bear in reading and interpreting the texts we have before us?', 'What are the political values and influences that are brought to bear in the shaping of that text?'and 'Can we change those frames?' Although there is interest in how writers and composers deploy critical literacy in the making of texts, there is an emphasis in critical literacy on *reading* and interpreting. This may be because there is a sense that composition is not always a fully conscious act (an element of it may depend on suspending full consciousness) but that reading is, or should be, highly critical and conscious. There is certainly less literature on writing and composing in the critical literacy field than on reading and interpretation. 'Criticality' is not the main focus of the present book, though an assumption is made throughout that being critical is part of the creative/critical approach to composition that permeates framing theory. Because the terms 'critical' and 'literacy' have been over-used in different and separate configurations ('critical thinking', 'critical literacy'; and 'emotional literacy', 'visual literacy', 'computer literacy' etc.) their meaning has been dissipated. And yet critical literacy – the movement which ensures that power and issues of equity/inequity are always considered in the interpretation if not the making of texts – remains a constant presence, a necessary condition for clarity, full political awareness and thus understanding of literary and non-literary texts.

Green (1988) in the same volume, discusses the emphasis on reading in literary studies, linking it to perceptions about the framing of English as a subject based on reading practices. Such issues of *curriculum* framing and English as a school (and university) subject will be the focus of Chapter 7. For the time being, the focus remains on framing in relation to genre theory and multimodality.

What Reid (1988) and Medway (1988) separately point to in this volume is the notion of "genre as a resource and not as a straitjacket" (p.93). It is in this sense that I see framing: not in terms of frames that act as straitjackets and that have to be taught and learnt like the Greek *progymnasmata*; but as a resource that helps writers and composers, readers and audiences to bring to bear on the creation and reception of a work that awareness of difference, of separateness, of the 'inside' and 'outside' of the text that will raise awareness of what is going on and make for a better communicative experience. Such an approach is not entirely coincident with critical literacy, as pointed out above; nor with 'genre as social action' (Miller 1984), though it is a great deal closer to this conception of genre than to the one that sees genre as text-type and which has given rise to the derivative practice of scaffolding frames within the English curriculum throughout the 1990s and 2000s. To distinguish the framing approach from 'genre as social action': framing is a creative and critical *process*, deeply practical both for composers in any modes or medium, but also for teachers and students in classrooms. It is *pedagogical*. Genre as social action makes us keenly aware of the differences between school genres and real world genres, but it is essentially a critical tool for understanding the intimate and complex relationships between texts and contexts. It is not a pedagogical approach, though it could be used as the basis for an exciting approach to teaching and learning that breaks down barriers between the school and the outside world in order to become more aware of the nature of those barriers as well as to explore the common ground between the real world and the world of schooling.

Framing and Multimodality

Framing is variously mentioned in Kress and van Leeuwen (1996/2006, 2001) and Kress (2003). In *Reading Images*, framing is listed as one of the key components of composition along with 'information value' and 'salience' (2006, pp.176–7). Interestingly, framing is mentioned along with the possibility of *absence* of framing devices, though it must be the case that absence of material framing is just another kind of framing (as in large abstract art works or photographs which bleed to the edge of a page). A better conception seems to be that of 'stronger' and 'weaker' frames (ibid., p.203) where the degree of framing presence is gauged. These frames can be realized by white space, by changes of colour and discontinuities as well as by lines. Kress and van Leeuwen also point towards deeper elements of framing in the visual and spatial fields in the style of drawing or painting (and by implication, sculpting etc.). These styles will take various degrees of delineation according to the focus of the (metaphorical or real) lens that is used.

Within multimodal works, framing takes place both within the composition and around it. There is a natural separation, say, between verbal text and imagery on a magazine page, though also instances where the verbal becomes iconic (as in logos) or graphic (as in graphic design elements). In general too, if we widen the aperture, the page as a whole has a visual presence even if it is composed entirely of words. In fact, words have a visual identity but images do not necessarily have a verbal one. The visual mode thus dominates the world of static (not time-based) multimodality. However the verbal, because it can take oral or written/printed form, is able to escape the confines of the material, visual page or screen and break free into speech via the medium of sound. Its materiality – its confinement to the material world – is less constrained than the visual.

As Kress suggests (2003, p.123), in a discussion on punctuation,[1] that "[f]raming marks off, but in doing so it establishes, at the same time, the elements which may be joined". The elements which may be joined as a result of framing is an interesting concept and one which needs to be pursued further. Once a frame is identified, it gives unity to the elements inside it, however disparate they are. There is an assumption on the part of the composer and the reader/audience that what is inside the frame is there deliberately, and that it 'coheres'. The principle of unity is a strong one and it is marked and reinforced by framing; indeed, we could say that there is no meaning without framing, no sense that things may be connected or brought into a relationship of connection. Such juxtaposition itself generates meaning, because a gap is created then bridged: difference is acknowledged then – if not always resolved – at least, the two or more parts are brought into proximity and contrast. Juxtaposition is a key principle in composition. The lines of connection may be made explicit by the composer/writer, or they may be implied, or the reader/audience may make their own lines of connection. 'Unity' thus emerges from an overall conception provided by the frame, and also by the interconnections within the frame. The notion of unity also validates the connections made (though these can be debated, as in literary critical discussions about the validity of internal connections in a text). Even in postmodern works in which the principle of unity is questioned or rejected, the very fact of a frame (however intangible or invisible) brings the principle of unity into operation.

Unity (and its opposite, diversity) are partly what framing is for. If we approach framing from a social semiotic perspective, we are likely to emphasize the way meaning is embodied, realized and exchanged in signs. Those signs can be relatively monomodal or multimodal, and the different affordances of the modes and media come into play according to the dynamic between the modes and media (the *inter*modal, the *inter*media). Social semiotics is always reaching beyond the magic of the sign itself to the meanings beyond it: social meanings that inform and are informed by the operation of signs. From a rhetorical perspective, unity does not matter much in the delivery and reception of the message, nor to the relationships between the speaker/writer/composer and the listener/reader/audience. It does matter when it comes to the aesthetics of the message itself, which subliminally sends out an indication of intention, coherence, meaningfulness and reasonableness. Unity thus matters deeply in the arts – visual, performing, time-based etc. – which is why classical literary theorists paid much attention to it. Without unity, there is no statement of truth, no patterning of experience which can lift an audience above the quotidian. The seeking and identification of pattern – and then its relaying to the audience through visual, verbal, aural, rhythmic and other means – are core to the generation of meaning and significance (just as they are to learning, research and teaching). With disunity within the frame, there is no meaning. Even if there is apparent disunity, as in the juxtaposition of a seemingly disparate and unconnected cluster of elements, the cultural programming to look for unity will operate. Rhetoric includes *the arts* of discourse in its contemporary definition because there is artistry in the act of framing and the juxtaposition of elements within the frame. Again, even if a frame is drawn around a seemingly random and coincidental configuration of phenomena, the artistic drive to seek and find unity will come into play. It is possible that there can be more order and unity outside a frame than inside it, but the principle remains the same: the act of framing marks off one degree of unity from another. It asks us to interrogate what is outside the frame in terms of what in inside it; and vice versa.

The power of framing is underestimated in terms of what it can do to make sense of a theory of English and literacy teaching, and also what it can offer practice in teaching situations and in learning. Framing can be seen as meta-theoretical in that it is behind all kinds of theory building and the Miltonic architectural weight of what can be brought to bear on the analysis of even the seemingly simplest sign. But it can also be intensely practical, in that the act of framing and re-framing is something that is available to all learners, of whatever age or ability. It is a way in which they can take control and bring meaning and sense to their worlds; and also control the mediation between the different communities (of learning) in which they operate. Such boundary crossing in real life happens all the time – every time we get out of bed, or cross the threshold of a house, or enter a workplace, or have an encounter with a friend or acquaintance on the street. Again, if framing is a central multimodal principle, it is the *act* of framing that is important rather than a mutliplicity of frames.

Framing in Time

Much of the discussion in the present book assumes framing, although an act rather than a tangible phenomenon, operates without regard to time. But the temporal dimension needs addressing for two reasons: first that all framed entities operate in time as well as space; and second, because time-based arts (film, theatre, music) have a particular nature in which framing is horizontally applied (moving from A to B) rather than vertically (how does one frame of action sit within another, and another in order to give meaning to signs?).

Kress and van Leeuwen (2001) note that:

> In time-based modes … 'framing' becomes 'phrasing' and is realized by the short pauses and discontinuities of various kinds (rhythmic, dynamic etc.) which separate the phrases of speech, of music and of actors' movements.
> (p.3)

That phrasing can be at macro-, mezzo- and micro-levels. At one of the micro-levels, the use of emphasis in speech can change meaning. In a simple sentence like "I can't believe you are here today" the emphasis, via subtle rhythmic shifts, changes the meaning: "*I* can't believe you are here today" is different from "I *can't* believe you are here today" and from "I can't believe *you* are here today". Without labouring the point, every word in that utterance could be emphasized and slightly change the meaning by emphasizing or foregrounding a particular word. With the addition of gesture (imagine what could accompany "I can't believe you are *here* today") the variations can be further defined.

At the mezzo-level in texts, the way a text is arranged – the classical *dispositio* – is part of the rhetorical dynamic apparatus. Classical rhetoricians proposed several different patterns for good arguments, ranging from two-part configurations to six and above. All are possible, but the most sense (and the most appropriate for contemporary composition) comes from Quintilian who suggests that parts of a composition can be used in any order appropriate to the purpose of the composition and the elegance of the art[form] itself. Whether we are looking at acts and scenes in a play, or movements in a piece of music, or edited sections of a film, the way the elements are structured and sequenced is crucial to the meaning and understanding. An example will illustrate this principle of mezzo-rhythmic structure. In teaching a course on dramatic approaches to the English classroom at New York University, I chose to focus on *As You Like It*. It is notoriously difficult as a teacher or director of the play to get a sense of the whole structure by reading it in the arbitrarily divided pages of a book, but a simple pedagogical device helps. As initially described on p.63, I cut up two editions of the play and pasted the pages of each scene on to a continuous strip of paper. Each scene, therefore, hung on the wall, clearly indicating how many scenes there were in the play as a whole but also what their respective length was. These scenes can be divided into acts (a classical reconstructive move by early editors of Shakespeare). What becomes clear, visually and at a glance, is that the scenes are of irregular length; some are very short indeed. There is no obvious balance between the scenes or acts. And yet there is a dynamism and momentum to the play that comes from the rhythmic shaping of the scenes in relation to each other – the 'phrasing' of the work as a whole. The shift from the corrupt court to the Forest of Arden is clearly delineated. The ritualistic killing of the deer in Act IV, Scene 2, is the shortest scene, yet it has symbolic resonance within the play as a whole. You can also see where you could cut the play, as a director, and what impact cuts and re-arrangements might have on the work.

At the macro-level, a whole text can be framed in time. To stay with the example of theatre, a production of any play at a particular place, at a particular time, is influenced by the *zeitgeist*, by the director of the play who interprets the play in the light of his or her interpretation of the *zeitgeist*, with his/her own ideologies and what he or she sees in the play; and also by the resources available (staging, actors, time for rehearsal and performance etc.). So *Waiting for Godot* can be performed in the Abbey Theatre, Dublin production, in a theatre in New York (as it was in the autumn of 2007) and be a very different version from the more jocular, music-hall production including Ian McKellen, Patrick Stewart and Simon Callow at the Haymarket Theatre in London in the spring of 2009. The fact that the former received rave reviews and the latter, with its star-studded cast, had mediocre to good reviews, is yet another take on framing by audiences and reviewers. Something about the conception and direction of the latter production was missing: a gravitas, a tragic dimension perhaps. To concertina the various levels of rhythmic identification discussed in this section, the macro-level of the director's conception informed the articulation of the movements and sub-sections of the play itself, which in turn had a combined influence on the actual delivery of the lines.

Phrasing in Poetry

If framing manifests itself as *phrasing* in music and poetry on the temporal (horizontal) dimension, what does that look and sound like, exactly? In poetry that operates within regular rhythms – metres – it is relatively easy to identify the rhythmic pattern. Take this opening quatrain from Shakespeare's 'Sonnet 57':

> Being your slave, what should I do but tend
> Upon the hours and times of your desire?
> I have no precious time at all to spend
> Nor services to do till you require.

It should be said, first, that the sonnet form of 14 lines provides a frame for the expression of a complex of thoughts and emotions (the structure of feeling). Such a frame can be specified in some detail. In Shakespeare's case, he is using a pattern of three quatrains – rhymed ABAB, CDCD, EFEF – with a rhyming couplet to finish. The frame is visual (you can identify it by looking at the pattern on the page) and mathematical (the rhyme scheme), but both the visual and mathematical shape give identity and form to the rhythmic movement of the poem. Within the frame of the whole, then, the poem operates via iambic pentameters:

$$x / x / x / x / x /$$

with the 'x' marking an offbeat and the '/' marking a beat. Most simply, that rhythmic pattern is sometimes characterized as diDUMdiDUMdiDUMdiDUM diDUM. But the metre in the case of the four lines above is adapted by Shakespeare so that the actual lines of the poem vary it. The iambic pattern is established – most clearly in line 2, with reinforcement in lines 3 and 4. In the first line, however, we would be hard pressed to identify it as iambic pentameter without the pattern that is established in the following lines. It is close to speech, and in fact starts with an emphasized beat, a reversal of the iambic foot: "*Being* your *slave* ..." with the rest of that first line falling into the iambic pattern: "what *should* I *do* but *tend*". The horizontal drive and momentum of the expression (hard to represent, even on a printed page) is the opening sentence which conveys the meaning in the compressed rhythmic form of two iambic pentameters: "Being your slave, what should I do but tend upon the hours and times of your desire?" In discussions at the outset of the Cambridge Schools Shakespeare series in Cambridge in the early 1990s, I suggested that we should print the plays without a capital letter at the beginning of each line in order to de-emphasize the clunkiness of starting each line as if it were a new unit of meaning; and in order to allow the sense of the script to emerge more strongly in readings by students – but this suggestion was not taken up. What happens in Shakespeare's verse is that there is a continual tension between the horizontal, everyday speech or prose drive of the language on the one hand; and the rhythmic patterning of the verse on the other. These tensions set up expectations which are either met or not, and which create nuances of meaning that characterize the subtlety of the poetry. For example, "*Being* your *slave*" follows the natural rhythm of speech, but sets up a counterpoint at the start of the poem in broad rhythmic terms. If we were to give a full account of the way this sonnet works in formal framing terms, we would first start with the genre of the sonnet as adapted by Shakespeare from the tradition of Petrarchan and other Elizabethan sonnets; then move to the particular pattern adopted by Shakespeare; account for the rhyming scheme; then shift into temporal mode, to capture the rhythmic identity of the verse; then come down to a more detailed level, analysing the particular nature of each quatrain and couplet, as begun above, balancing the meanings of the poem with the formal properties of the visual and mathematical patterning – the function of which is to generate an identity in sound. We can thus say that phrasing (the rhythmic identity of the line) is only one aspect of poetic form in which framing manifests itself.

If we look at a different example, we can see how phrasing can work without a regular metrical pattern underlying it. Claims have been made that Ezra Pound's work has the ghost of regular metres behind it, but my own analysis of Pound's *oeuvre* indicates that his attempt to "break the pentameter, that was the first heave" (Pound 1964, p.553) was successful, and that he wrote in rhythmic patterns that cannot be accounted for in regular metrical terms. Take the first three lines of 'Canto CX' (Pound 1970):

Thy quiet house
The crozier's curve runs in the wall,
The harl, feather-white, as a dolphin on sea-brink ...
(p.7)
('Crozier' = the curled tip of a young fern, the head of a bishop's staff; 'harl' = barb of a feather.)

Here is an example of *additive* rhythm, in which the first line establishes a phrase against which the second line defines itself. Following that, the third line, longer than the first two, creates a yet more expansive phrase. We could analyse the three lines grammatically to show a variation of a different sort, not unrelated to the rhythmic variation: the first line a noun phrase; the second a full sentence with noun phrase, verb and predicate; the third, a different kind of noun phrase with a qualifying simile but no verbal closure. In terms of punctuation, the rhythm is loosely marked: the comma at the end of the second line is hardly necessary in rhythmic terms, and marks more prominently the end of that particular phrase. Apart from that, punctuation is used to separate the qualifying adjective "feather-white" from its noun, placing the adjective after the noun to which it refers (an unusual order in English). The lack of a punctuation mark of any kind at the end of this opening three-line section reinforces the effect that Pound is trying to create: of free verse ("No verse is free for the man [sic] who wants to do a good job"), articulated in rhythmic subtlety via the notion of the line as the unit of rhythm, rather than the metrical foot. The wider framing structure for this extract from 'Canto CX' is that each of the free-form cantos ('songs') forms part of a larger collection, a vast attempt to measure the spirit of the age in fragments against the history of civilization.

The rhythmic identity of these three lines by Pound, then, is very different from the pattern informing Shakespeare's quatrain. Shakespeare's language uses the underlying metrical pattern to shape itself, and also to identify variations from the underlying pattern for semantic, rhythmic and sonorous purposes. Pound eschews a regular underlying pattern and builds up his rhythmic shape line by line, letting the meaning and the sound operate as a single phenomenon: we cannot separate a metre or a rhythm from the meaning of the words themselves.

Framing in Space and Time

What we are moving towards in this chapter is a position, a model, in which there are three dimensions: space, time and the psycho-social dimension. In the spatial dimension, acts of framing take visual form, like the white space that surrounds a poem on a page; the stage that is separated from the audience and which circumscribes the dramatic action; the museum that includes a gallery space that, in turn, contains a painting that is either framed against a white wall or provides its own frame. In the temporal dimension, framing manifests itself as phrasing and in rhythmic form. Those phrases have an identity in time: they are utterances in speech; musical phrases as part of a larger work that is itself structured in time; poetic feet, lines, stanzas, of various shapes and sizes.

These two dimensions of framing refer to each other. More commonly, framing in the spatial dimension, like the score of a musical work, indicates how that work might be performed in time. But temporal framings can provide the material for spatial framing, as when the hours of a day can be characterized in numerical terms and displayed on a clock.

In terms of the psycho-social and physical external and internal framing that goes on in the everyday operation of thought and action, both the spatial and temporal dimensions provide means of expression and informing patterns that help to bring meaning to experience. From the perspective of an individual, the framing of scenarios is one way in which these spatial and temporal possibilities can be realized. Imagine a person walking along a street. She is on a track from A to B, with a clear purpose in mind: to attend a meeting and put the case of her company on the table in order to win a contract. She has already framed the possible outcomes of the meeting and imagined three or four ways in which it might go – and what her response would be. But as she is walking along, she imagines another scenario (another framed possibility): that she needs to find some way of introducing the idea at the outset that will appeal to those sitting around the table, especially those that are likely to be most resistant. As that scenario is rehearsed and she feels comfortable with it within her repertoire, her mind wanders to other scenarios in her private life: a relationship; a need that will take her to a particular shop or gallery after the meeting; a problem she needs to resolve at home; another contract that is dependent on this one.

The process of framing and re-framing in everyday life is captured in fictional terms in Pavel's *Fictional Worlds* (1986), where framed worlds of different shapes and sizes, of different natures – and crucially, at different distances from our own worlds – are depicted in order to help an understanding of the function and position of fiction. But the everyday scenarios depicted in the example above are no less fictional, even though they are generated from real-world preoccupations. They are devices that are framed in their own complete way that are used as comparisons to the real world, as engines that shed light on it, and that provide possibilities for action. They are linked to the philosophy of modal logic. Pavel's work is discussed further in Chapter 10.

Framing Theory

Could a theory, or at least a model, be constructed that provides a guide to the possibilities of framing; that indicates how frames relate to each other, and how they inform and afford the possibilities of expression?

Such a theory, it must first be reiterated, could not be a comprehensive one which took account of every frame that is in play in the creation or interpretation of a cultural act. Such a project has been attempted, and it results in a plethora of interlocking frames which, in due course, overburden and defeat the process of analysis. If, however, the accent is on framing rather than frames, could that perspective be captured in a model?

The best option seems to be one that draws on polyptical framing, as far as spatial framing is concerned. I will go on to argue that rather than use such polyptical framing in a temporal dimension, thus creating a complicated four-dimensional model that will hardly be operational, the same polyptical grid could be used to map temporal framing. The basic idea is simple (see Figure 5.1).

First, some characteristics of the grid. The individual units that make up the grid are uniform in this diagram. They have been drawn as squares, but they

Figure 5.1 A basic polyptical grid.

need not be. They are simply drawn in this way to suggest that the vertical axis is no more important than the horizontal, and vice versa. But a grid can be imagined that is more like a tessellated pattern with various shapes, sizes and configurations of pattern.

The grid can be made up of any number of frames. The one above is four-by-four, again to suggest no particular preference for a horizontal or vertical pattern overall; but the number of units could be adapted to needs.

Layering

One way to address the problem of multiple frames and framing is via the notion of 'layering'.[2] Again, it is not so much the *layers* that are important to the discussion in the present book, but to the act of *layering* in the composition and interpretation of texts. By 'text', I mean any monomodal or multimodal semiotic entity that is framed as such. To address the problem concretely, let's go back to the Shakespeare sonnet discussed, in part, above.

> Being your slave, what should I do but tend
> upon the hours and times of your desire?
> I have no precious time at all to spend,
> nor services to do till you require.

Nor dare I chide the world-without-end hour
whilst I (my sovereign) watch the clock for you,
nor think the bitterness of absence sour
when you have bid your servant once adieu.

Nor dare I question with my jealous thought
where you may be, or your affairs suppose,
but like a sad slave stay and think of nought
save where you are how happy you make those.

So true a fool is love that in your will
(though you do anything) he thinks no ill.

This is a monomodal text, but as I have argued elsewhere in the book, the other modes press in around the edges of the text, asking to be let in (speech, the visual, sound). Typographically, there is a shift from the quotation in the previous section: in this one, the capital letters have been moved to lower case at the start of lines unless they indicate the beginning of a sentence. My deliberate intent here is to allow the sentence to assert itself within, and in relation to, the metrical shape and rhythm of the poem as a whole; rather than see the poem as a line-by-line creation.

What kinds of framing and layering are suggested by the text? There seem to be at least three formal layers and at least three interpretational ones. The formal ones are formal, linguistic and modal; the interpretational ones are historical, interpretational and dialogic. Rather than undertake a full literary critical analysis, the rest of this section will set out these layers or frames, and test them against the poem.

Formally, the most obvious feature to notice is that the text on the page takes the shape of a poem. Even from a distance of several yards, it is possible to see that these words take the form of a poem, as the lines do not go up to the right-hand edge of the page (as they do in prose). Closer examination reveals that the words on the page form a sub-category of poetry: the sonnet. As indicated in the previous section, this is a Shakespearean sonnet with its characteristic structure of three quatrains and a couplet, rhymed ABAB, CDCD, EFEF, GG. These are formal properties, identifiable visually, but indicating a *rhythmic* shape. The rhythm comes alive when the poem is read aloud, transposing it from print to sound.

Next, at even closer range, is the linguistic layering. In the particular linguistic mode of the English language – it might be different if the poem were translated into Spanish or Mandarin – there is the overall controlling metaphor of slavery to a master or mistress in the name of love. The metaphor allows two levels of layering to operate at the same time: the literal reference to slavery, and the metaphorical one to love. The interplay between the two layers is richly suggestive. This overall metaphor of slavery permeates the poem, so that 'time', 'services', 'your affairs' and other such aspects of slavery and service all emerge as 'natural' references from the overarching metaphor. They too operate on two levels at the same time.

The modal framing or layering can be identified in a number of respects. First, in the fact that this is a monomodal text. But the tightly framed mono-modality is a permeable fence that invites transgression from the other modes and their associated senses and dimensions. The imagination, generated by the words of the poem, invokes the visual and the aural, the spatial and temporal. In this case, the form of the poem (thus linking modal issues to ones of form, already discussed), invites other responses: the Shakespearean sonnet's final rhyming couplet reinforces the overall sense that these sonnets are not just lyric outpourings, but arguments. Who is addressing whom, and where does the reader/listener stand in relation to that statement? What are the lineaments of the argument? In this case, the speaker is addressing him/herself as well as his/her master/mistress (my very identification of the gender of the slave and 'boss' as either male or female is itself a reading that is provided by the frame I am bringing to the poem – there is no indication in the text itself of gender). So through modality the question of rhetorical positioning is raised: yet another 'layer'.

These three or four textual frames or layers are closely related to the inter-pretive ones, because interpretation must depend on recognition and analysis of the intra- and inter-textual features of the work under consideration. Layers of interpretation inevitably bring to bear other frameworks, which in turn feed back into the analysis of the textual features. There is thus a synergy between the writer-as-reader and the reader-as-writer.

Interpretatively, then, we can identify at least three frames or layers: that of the historical dimension; that of the dialogic aspect; and that of the reader. Again, all are inter-related.

Let us take the historical dimension first. All texts exist in time. They are created in a particular place and time, and their immediate historical context is brought to bear on their interpretation. We cannot escape the fact that this poem is by Shakespeare, and that we read it differently, as a result, than if it were by Marlowe or Jonson. Furthermore, particular words had particular nuances at the time, and the poetic diction of the time (e.g. 'nought', 'save') reveals both a meaning and reference to a limited diction that was the (poetic) language of the age. 'Slavery' is a particular poetic conceit, but was also preva-lent in attitudes promulgated by a highly hierarchical society. Another dimen-sion of the historical layering is that we now read the poem, in the twenty-first century, from our own vantage points and contexts; scholarly readings can be traced back through the centuries, through editions of the sonnets, and can inform our own contemporary reading.

Dialogically, we return to the formal question of the rhetoric of the piece. We position ourselves, as readers or listeners, in a number of ways in relation to the poem: as the master/mistress; through empathy with the slave him- or herself; as a bystander or witness to the conversation; as a detached critical reader.

We can operate all of these positions at the same time, thus making the reception and interpretation of the poem a complex one, with many perspectives. Furthermore, the poem as expressed on the page can be seen as part of a conversation or dialogue. Here, Bakhtinian theory helps us to see that such utterances do not exist in a vacuum, but are a response to a particular circumstance – even if that circumstance is a distillation of a number of events as well as of the history of the poetic form itself. In other words, the poem could stand as a speech in a dramatic form: we can imagine what went before it, and what might come after. And we can imagine tension in the exchange as well as consensuality.

Finally, the text as text has a life of its own beyond its composition by Shakespeare. It exists as print on a page, but can be realized in a number of media. It is like a score, but different. It is similar in the sense that the print on the page can act as the score for a reading; it is different in that the language of the poem is also the language of speech. In music, the score bears no modal resemblance to its performance in sound, other than through the translation that occurs from one mode to another. So the multimodal relationship between writing and speech is of a different order than that between a musical score and actual music.

Part II

The Case of Language

Chapter 6

Pre-school Writing and Drawing

Before Framing

This chapter is about the home/school dimensions of making marks on paper and on electronic screens. Research has often explored how children learn to paint and draw; similarly, there have been several studies on the development of writing in pre-school children. This chapter not only brings the two strands of research together, but adds another dimension: the use of multimedia packages by pre-school children to compose. The chapter draws, then, on existing research in the area – particularly over the last 25 years – and an empirical research project by the author in which all the graphic output of a four-year-old child over a six-month period has been collected and studied.

Various Debates about the Verbal and Visual in Early Mark-making

One of the most significant publications on pre-school verbal and visual literacy is Gunther Kress's *Before Writing* (1997). Kress writes from a social semiotic perspective: signs are seen as evidence of meaningful communication in a social context. This chapter aims to develop the ideas and challenges set out in that book in looking at a four-year-old's mark-making on the way to literacy from a rhetorical point of view.

It is not clear that all the cultural production of the child is communicative. This can only be true in a very broad sense, and theoretically rather than in practice. While not wanting to fall into the late Romantic fallacy that all cultural production is *expressive* and only expressive (i.e. it has little sense of audience or little *function* other than to express thought and feeling), it did not seem that all the productive work in the verbal and/or visual modes by the four-year-old discussed later in this chapter was communicative. Rather, her graphic and painterly production over the six-month period fell into three kinds: 'gifts', or works specially created for particular people and/or occasions; experiments with visual and verbal language; and consciously crafted stories or figurative paintings/drawings. It is the second of these categories that seems not to fit too readily into the frame of 'production-as-communication'. Works such as these may have 'meaning' of a sort, but their primary function seems to be to explore the medium – certainly the 'meaning' cannot be easily translated into words.

The emphasis could be altered slightly, suggesting that the child – located within the community of family and friends – explores various modes and media in free and expressive ways in order to i) find out more about those modes/media in relation to his/her own command of them, and ii) find out more about him/herself within that community. So whereas a social semiotician might see all sign-making as being informed by meaning, I would want to preserve a space for the arbitrary – the zone in which meaning in the conventional sense is suspended. The preservation of this space is especially important to the development of the syntagmatic or serial dimensions to language learning, as opposed to the paradigmatic or 'meaning-informing' dimensions. Syntagmatically, the child experiments with systems. If the progress towards command of the alphabetic writing system is partly a matter of getting to know that system through emergent writing, copying of letters, reading-and-writing, dialogic writing and other means, there must be scope for experimentation and exploration within that system. 'Meaning' is brought to it by the calling up of one or more levels of signification (either via a top-down or bottom-up – or both – approach) on the paradigmatic axis. The point is that, while most mark-making will be 'significant', some of it will necessarily and pleasurably be without translatable meaning. The key to learning is not only the exploration of the syntagmatic and paradigmatic in language *at every level*, but also the *integration* of the various levels and dimensions. Hence the complexity of learning to read and write, irreducible to a single-level approach like the ill-termed 'phonics'.

Let us try to tease out the particular magic of the transition from multimodal production to writing, without wanting to suggest we are talking about an abandonment of the visual as a child learns to write. The complexity of the transition is very well described in *Before Writing*. It is essentially a transition from a multimodal practice to a relatively unimodal one; from a visual/verbal ground to a system based on sounds (the alphabetic system) rather than on pictures (the pictographic, like Chinese characters); from a first-order to a second-order semiotic system, to adapt Vygotsky's description. Lanham's comments on prose are helpful here. He suggests that prose – the same goes for poetry – operates via an 'aesthetic of denial'. That is to say, the printed or hand-written marks on the page gradually come to carry the burden of meaning. The visual dimension – the imaginative read-off from the page – is supplied by the reader on the basis of the controlled and ascetic black-and-white symbols on the page. These are surrounded by a frame: very obviously, white space with poems, and less obviously so in prose. The frame is there to be transgressed. The writing invites transgression – indeed, it does not count for much unless the frame is reshaped by the reader and moved beyond.

If learning to write is a matter of keeping the visual at bay (outside the frame) and suggesting it, the gradual process of separating word from image until it can stand on its own is worthy of further study. It can only be a partial approach to say that because most popular printed communication combines word and image – with each crowding, complementing, acting in contiguity with the other – then we should preserve the multimodality of communication *pedagogically*. It also seems to be necessary for children to explore each of the semiotic systems in its own terms as well as bringing them together.

In terms of pedagogy, we can develop here one of the points made by Kress in his analysis of children's making in different modes – and in particular, the transition from mode to mode. Not only is it the case that humans need to make transitions from one mode of representation to another, from one kind of realism to another in both home and institutional (e.g. school) settings; it also seems to me to be the case that in these *transformations*, an act of learning takes place. It is notoriously difficult to pin down what constitutes learning (see Illeris 2007, 2008), but an account of the multiple transformations that take place as children and adults present and re-present material is closer to the mark than attempts at describing competences. A theory of learning based on transformations (see Haythornthwaite and Andrews forthcoming) is more dynamic, more about the creation of new learning and more likely to be able to bridge the gap between home and school than a model based on the description (and inevitable targeting) of competences which can describe only what a child or adult is able to do, not how he/she changes in the course of the doing.[1]

Another aspect of transition is described by Kress early in the book: this is where a child cuts around drawings, thereby lifting them off the page into the world of action; a drawn camel, for instance, becomes part of an immediate play-world when cut out and used like a toy. "Cutting out," Kress suggests, "acts as a kind of framing" (p.25). This observation helps us to develop further the notion of transformation as central to learning. If frames act as contextualizing devices – whether concrete or invisible – for acts of communication, then the changing of frames changes much more than a change of audience. Genre theorists and social semioticians would agree that the text as 'trace' rather than 'vehicle' better suits such an approach. Deriving from Peirce, the audience plays a constructive role in relation to the sender of the 'message' in the creation of meaning; the function of the encounter is to make some change, some transformation in social relations; what is left is the trace of that encounter, which itself enters the world as part of a semiotic web which, in turn, may influence subsequent communication. The act of framing, then, brings about the conditions for communication. Because the accent is on the act of framing rather than on a repertoire of frames, there is no taxonomy of text-types, genres or other such reified 'objects' of language to consider; instead a particular set of conditions which bring about particular kinds of language. These may be dissected and analysed after the event to determine what went on at the time. Like fossils or archaeological fragments, they give clues as to the real live communication that happened, and also enable us to predict patterns of communication that may happen.

More needs to be said about the relation of writing and the visual to the imagination. Most literally, the imagination is an image-creating faculty. Images on a page, however created, can be said to proceed from or give us a window to the imagination. At the same time, images are 'metaphors' for the real world; they 'stand for' things and clusters of feelings in the world. To say that "the formation of signs … is the same kind of activity as that which we call imagination; a sign is a metaphor; metaphor involved the new expression of individual interest, and is therefore always in a sense a facet of imagination" (Kress 2004) is to say something it would be hard to disagree with. The relationship between the signs that make up words and the imagination is not so simple. Words do not represent images. If we follow Vygotsky, words represent abstracted concepts, classes of objects. When they are combined in sequences, they can suggest a range of imaginative scenarios; indeed, these imagined worlds – 'possible worlds', 'fictional worlds' – are likely to be different for each individual, though mediated for the individual by the culture in which they are generated and 'read'. What is kept out of the frame by printed or handwritten language is precisely what the writer/creator/rhetor is wanting the reader to supply,[2] and what will become meaningful for the reader. This, perhaps, is one of the most striking aspects of written language.

The deeper shift which brings together the verbal and visual is cyclical: a look at Lanham's '2000 years of multimedia' – at illuminated manuscripts, children's books, surrealism, chapbooks – will only confirm that the verbal and visual have always coexisted in many different ways, with different emphases and with different degrees of power. If we are talking about large-scale cultural and semiotic shifts, it hardly seems the case that the verbal is being left behind in the 2000s, 10 or 15 years after 'the turn to the visual'. Rather, there is an increase in verbal communication, with some of it (email for example) increasing exponentially. Hence the centrality and power of rhetoric, with its perspective on real-world, social, communicative action in language, and its ability to embrace a range of modes. Rhetoric, unlike semiotics (but rather more like social semiotics), is not bound by the study of signs and their systems; its motivational drive is to support and understand communication in its social context, and its resource is to mediate between the particular situation and what it knows about language and other modes of communication. Rhetoric has the distance as well as the pragmatism to be open to different modes of communication as they best serve the requirements of a particular situation.

Not widely available, but a valuable contribution to the field is Bauers and Boyd (1989). In this study, the authors examined the writing and drawing – an approach in which the two are clearly distinguished – of two pre-school children over a period of 17 months. In the case of the first child (Jacqueline) it is assumed that she can draw but not write at the start of the 17-month period. The assumption is based on the notion that drawing must depict something, whereas 'writing' that consists of random marks cannot constitute writing as such. Writing is seen as a second-order symbolic (semiotic) system and emergent letter forms are identified, irrespective of the meaning they carry for the child or for the reader. The authors acknowledge the limitation of their study in this respect: they have based their analysis on the products only, not on the processes of composition; they do not know the intentions of the children in the composition of the writing and drawing. Nevertheless, the analysis of the shapes produced is comprehensive, and generates some interesting insights:

> Jacqueline is testing her hypotheses about letter shapes all the time, keeping those which she sees as 'correct' and discarding those which are not. Thus a whole range of 'invented' shapes which appeared in earlier work have disappeared and these particular shapes never reoccur.
>
> (p.12)

Another insight, not made explicit in the commentary, is that the command of writing letters (for example in writing one's name) takes a great deal of effort and self-discipline; drawing, on the other hand, is used freely. It seems that in the early stages, according to Bauers and Boyd, the alphabetic visual system is played with and explored for its own sake, not as a potential carrier of narrative or conceptual meaning. In Jacqueline's case, she is happy to put her name 'and some other words' – that is, random sequences of letters, clearly identifiable as 'words' (i.e. strings of 2 to 14 letters) but without meaning. The sense of a text is still some way off. As Bauers and Boyd suggest,

> what strikes us most forcibly about Jacqueline is that, while we as teachers usually tend to stress the importance of 'the message' in writing, she has been riveted by the formal aspects of writing.
>
> (p.33)

In a useful taxonomy showing how Jacqueline's understanding ('use' might have been a better term) of writing emerged, the authors identify categories from 'undifferentiated scribble' to 'words written as conventions':

1. undifferentiated scribble
2. writing is distinguished from drawing
3. cursive graffiti
4. printed graffiti
5. writing arranged horizontally across the paper
6. rehearsal of letter shapes/rejection of non-letter shapes
7. symbols recur
8. writing of own name has become stabilised
9. symbols grouped into strings
10. strings identified as 'words'
11. strings identified as names (of people)

12. word spacing
13. words are written according to conventions.

(p.34)

The authors complete their short study with a parallel look at another child's writing and drawing.

Wolf (1989) suggests that most studies to date of children's graphic development have been studies of single strands, for example the development of drawing ability. We can partly attribute this approach to at least a generation's influence by Piaget in urging us to think of cognitive rather than symbolic/semiotic development, i.e. the focus has been on the child rather than on his or her productions. She suggests that "[r]arely have there been observations or experiments that look either at all these abilities in the same children, or, more importantly, at the conversations or mutual influences among the abilities" (p.23). She makes the point that as children between the ages of two and six "make the leap from being exploratory animals to becoming symbol-using human beings … they begin to understand the demands and power of graphic representation" (p.25) and they do not think in terms of special classes of visual images, but gradually over these years "come to understand how a picture works, how it denotes objects, scenes, even imagined experience" (p.34). These are important points, but they are clouded by the assertion that *dialogue* or *conversation* between the different modes, and between the processes of making, looking and reflecting takes place. The act of conversation is used metaphorically and is not sufficiently defined to tell us more about the interrelationship between the different modes and media, or the symbiotic processes and acts of making.

Barrs' 1988 chapter, 'Drawing a Story: Transitions between Drawing and Writing' suggest that attempts to understand the beginning of writing had become preoccupied with the emergence of identifiable features of the written code, and cites Bissex's (1980) study of orthographic development as typical of this approach. Moving away from the idea that reading is decoding and writing in encoding, she thinks of learning to write as "'learning how to mean' on paper" (p.51). Drawing on Vygotsky, the essence of learning to write is the representation of meaning by symbolic signs. He suggests that "make believe play, drawing and writing can be viewed as different moments in an essentially unified process of development of written language" (p.52, quoting Vygotsky's 'The Prehistory of Written Language' (1978)). Another quotation in the Barrs chapter is from Luria, on the inability of four- and five-year-olds to conceive of the act of writing:

They grasped the outward form of writing and saw how adults accomplished it; they were even able to imitate adults; but they themselves were completely unable to learn the specific psychological attributes any act must have if it [is] to be used as a tool in the service of some end.

(p.53)

Barrs' suggestion that drawing and iconography support or 'make do' for writing until that system is brought under control is borne out by the following case study, as well as the thesis that text and pictures are more closely related in home stories than school stories. She posits a progression through the symbolic systems, from dramatic play through drawing to writing, with each new system carrying the trace of the previous one.

A Case Study

For six months between September 1996 and March 1997 I kept all the graphic, painting and collage (two- and three-dimensional) work generated by my four-year-old daughter, Grace. I should say at the outset that I was aware of the cliché-like nature of such collecting. The opportunity is too tempting: to see close at hand the early exploration of the visual and verbal, to know the contexts intimately in which the work is created, and in this case, to compare production at home with that at nursery and the first term of schooling proper. In Grace's case, there is the added interest of word-processed and multimedia compositions, created on a Macintosh computer with the help of her brother and sister and the software program *Kidpix*.

During that six-month period, I managed to collect 266 works from home and school combined. I do not think I caught every single piece of work, but probably over 90 per cent of those created. Of these, 55 (20.6 per cent) were principally writing, 120 (45.1 per cent) drawing, 45 (16.9 per cent) painting, 26 (9.7 per cent) collage, print and rubbings and 20 (7.5 per cent) word-processed or electronic multimedia creations.

In general, the output is principally in what we take to be the visual media: 206 of the 266 works are primarily or purely visual (77.4 per cent), whereas 60 are either handwritten or electronically written (22.6 per cent). To put it even more simply, over three-quarters of graphic production in the six-month period for this four-year-old was visual.

Of the entire production, 215 pieces were created at home, with 51 at school, making for a proportion of 80.2 per cent at home and 19.8 per cent at school – this is during a period in which Grace attended nursery for half-days between September and December 1996, and full days in a school reception class between January and March 1997, covering her age from 4 years 6 months to 5. In short, again, just over four-fifths of her graphic and 'fine art' production was from home.

A last set of statistics in this preliminary analysis: what proportion of the various media was created at home and at school? Of the 55 pieces of writing, 9 were produced at school and 46 at home, i.e. 84 per cent at home. Of the drawings created, 111 of the 120 were produced at home (92.5 per cent); of the paintings, 28 of the 45 at home (63 per cent); of mixed media works, prints and rubbings, 10 of the 26 at home (39 per cent); and all the 20 electronic texts were produced at home. It was a surprise to me that 84 per cent and 92.5 per cent of the writing and drawing respectively over this six-month period was created at home – especially the writing, the art form conventionally seen as being reserved for the beginning of schooling.

The material produced at home was almost entirely self-generated: it was composed at a small table in the kitchen or in a playroom; some of the paintings were composed on an easel that was unearthed from a cupboard under the stairs. The audience for the work was largely non-existent; that is to say, the work was generated by sheer expressive energy and the need to make marks, rather than for a particular audience. In five instances, the writing/drawing was a reply to a letter or fax from another 4- year-old; sometimes the work was produced as a 'gift' – "this is for you" (most obviously in Valentine, birthday and Easter cards, but sometimes a simple picture or piece of writing was offered as a gift); but mostly it was simply made – and if it wasn't enjoyed by sister, brother and/or parents, and displayed on the fridge or wall and occasionally mounted for display, Grace probably wouldn't have noticed if something made just disappeared. The energy was devoted principally to the process of making, and focused on the moment of creation and the next one rather than on the corpus of work created. There was huge graphic energy expended very freely during this period.

In contrast, the work produced at nursery school and in reception was 'commissioned', and labelled into categories like 'emergent writing', 'handwriting practice', 'seriation' and 'representation'. Both nursery and reception classes were in state schools: the first, a class of 35 (divided into three uneven groups, each with a teacher) attached to a primary school in St Albans, Hertfordshire; the second, a class of 27 in a primary school in Beverley, East Yorkshire. In both cases, work was selected and preserved in folders and large scrapbooks.

From the complete sample of 266 works, I have taken a sub-sample of 20 for analysis. The principles on which this selection took place were: i) to select a representative range of work created; and ii) to look for correspondence between the works in the emerging literacy or literacies of the child. The drive of the research is not primarily developmental, though some points can be derived from the data about development over the six-month period. Rather, the attempt is to take a broad canvas and try to understand the nature of graphic and 'fine art' production at home and at school over a pivotal period in a child's development.

My principal research question for the purposes of this study was 'What is the relation of emergent writing to other graphic and visual production in a four-year-old?' and subsidiary questions included the following:

- What are the functions of writing at home and nursery/school?
- How is writing consciously related to the visual at school?
- What can we learn about how children learn to write from this study?

Figure 6.1 Drawing of sister.

Analysis of the Sub-sample

I take the above subsidiary questions in chronological order, and will speculate later as to whether there is an emergent sequence towards initial command of the writing system. For now, the sequence cannot be taken to be significant. First let us consider two pieces from outside the sample proper that might be taken as points of reference: one produced at home on 10 November 1995, when Grace was aged 3 years 8 months (Figure 6.1); and the other in the first month of nursery school, January 1996 (age 3 years 10 months) (Figure 6.2).

The drawing (Figure 6.1), in felt-tip, is characteristic of those at this age: this is a portrait of Grace's sister Zoë, complete with pigtails and belly-button. The body is almost constituted entirely by the face, with the belly-button seeming to appear in disembodied form beneath the face/body. Pigtails, arms and legs protrude in bold lines away from the face/body. Some writers have suggested that the clear delineation of limbs from body is a precursor of the formation of letter shapes.

Soon after, the emergent writing at nursery school – 'Robins have black eyes'. The composition is the child's, with the teacher adding the 'translation' afterwards. In this case, it seems to me that, to follow the principles of emergent writing teaching, the teacher's version should have come below the child's. As it stands, the child appears to have attempted to 'copy' the teacher's writing – which would have little point. What is interesting about the writing is that

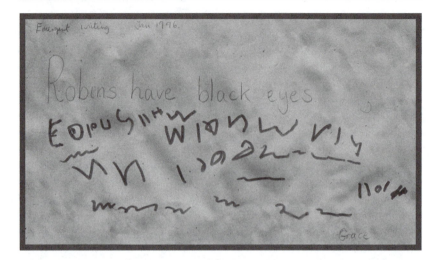

Figure 6.2 Robins have black eyes.

some identifiable letters shapes do appear: in the first string of letters, E, O, U, S and H. There also appears a W and a movement from formed letters to free-form squiggles.

The next four examples (Figures 6.3–6), from the first month of the sample proper – September 1996 (age 4 years 6 months) show different forms of visual representation, both of letter shapes and figurative drawing:

Figure 6.3 The letter M.

Figure 6.4 The letter G.

The illuminated letter M, painted freehand, has an animated vibrant energy about it, while the coloured-in G is a celebration of colour within a recognized shape. As with many children, the name proves talismanic throughout the six months of graphic and 'fine art' production, appearing on almost every piece of work as a signature, and sometimes written or painted for its own sake. The letters in 'Grace' thus provide a basis for moving outwards to the rest of the alphabet, and a touchstone for future development. They appear in the top right-hand corner of the lollipop painting (Figure 6.5) as well as in the teacher's handwriting, both here and in Figure 6.6. In terms of identity, their presence is strong.

Figures 6.5 and 6.6 are both nursery-produced works, experiments in form and colour.

The next piece (Figure 6.7) is a particularly interesting one in terms of writing. This is an unsolicited letter to a close friend. We moved from Beverley to St Albans for a 20- month period between Grace's third birthday and 4 years 9 months. The friend, Lyddie, lives in Beverley:

Figure 6.8 Story about USA summer.

Perhaps we can deduce from this kind of writing that Grace believes strings of letters 'stand for' (I use a deliberately loose term of connection) the story/ meaning she is wishing to convey. In two other very different examples (Figures 6.9 and 6.10) this belief is evident. The first example – two pages of arbitrary letters strings, with some shaping occurring through the starting of new lines, stands for a story composed orally by Grace and transcribed by her sister.

The transcribed story has the title 'Spring Holiday':

First page

A little girl was going to have a holiday and she went to the park in spring and it was a very lovely spring morning and she met an old woman and the old woman said "I wanna come to your house" and "What's your telephone number?" The little girl said her telephone number was 8874305T888. And she went down the slide and the old woman watched her. She said "Wheeeeeeee!" Then she went on the roundabout with the old woman. She shouted and shouted and shouted and shouted because she was sick. The old woman said "Quick! Quick! Let's go to the doctors!" The little girl had been injured by a cat. That's why she was sick. The little girl had to stay in hospital for 100 years, and she couldn't go to the park, and she couldn't go to the zoo, or her home. She was frightened, because the doctors were very, very, very rough and one lady doctor was very kind. She said "Shall I be gentle?" and the doctor gave her something to take home. It was very, very, very soft and it was a puppy dog, a real puppy dog!

```
ufkgjgjtihuthjithiueh
iugritiriitifufujeiruu382uru83yryryyry4tyr
y84tyr i777565 hyoyjuyy78 y6uiyju8
vthutybg bg9u0tgktgtu9u5tigk gcjfj9itr
jijtiojg jtirj tirj 7ugkojh tg
765678876lv6ihmymthmgmy6h6hj6yoret
mtrjgyuiyrthghuyigfdhigtuyfryuui6rihbhiu
gjihgjyuijkhghu7hnnkbjkgnjhjhfdmj hjtjn
g ngbngjkhmngfnhbjtn
jfnjvfnjgjrjhjkjihbtghjg gttrjhjuthjh
bjhtuyhjijojijitj
hkjhkjgrjijgjfhgfh5yhtht4bgbhghghthghuh
u jmgbklgjith7543532nhhnvghjbhbgnvb
jngjkn bg
vcnmkgjr4jugjthihg85jti4tj4ti5tit5oyk54it
ij8966586ym bhktyijriot 5tkktrjgt
yikrmkty b mg, llolrg lk43rioj5o4j rke
bvmk, kl gklhnkh hkmthntgk    kjhkt
mirgbfb fdhvnb nuun nkltjkrfhjrhu ijojogr
rujjknnugn blk5unb
grookmbkmbml,v,.k,gbghhtfgkfblfgkflgh
mot56ugf489t8745t421§ntrih3rerey4eehw
§§§§§§§§§ry8u9tu5tiuru5ui9uuu9
§§§§§§§3h8iyjjnth87iuy798iu8§i896uhyu
reg vnvjfdg mcn cv jnhgq§§ m, l §m
vfm e jn  m knn nk . nm mgtheu§ms
nfgbgjregjgrufej4t3gbjkerdhfvnc
isemdj§mznjcx §§§§§§§§§§§§§ blk
,nyblh,g,b mbmjkghkm b
```

Figure 6.9 Spring Holiday 1.

Second page

She was very very pleased because her mum and dad were visiting her and the little girl hugged them and kissed them. They picked her up and gave her a kiss and a hug. She could get out of bed and watch television. She watched her best video. It was called 'Go to the farm'. She finished the video and could go home! She kissed her new little sister and that's the end.

Three pieces of writing composed with a four-year-old friend reinforce the arbitrary energy of writing, in this case accompanied by much talk.

I then talked about the writing with Grace:

RA: What does the short one say?

GRACE: Please go to work at the right time. Please go to work.

RA: And what does the long one say?

GRACE: Please go to work at the right time and get some papers to bring home ... from the computer you're doing ... and then you'll be able to get a little surprise.

RA: Nice.

Figure 6.10 Spring Holiday 2.

GRACE: Please go to bed at the right time and before you go to bed look out of the window and see if the street is not flooded.

I then asked Grace to tell me the longer piece again, to see if the 'read off' from the writing was the same:

GRACE: Please um, um, um ... Please go to work at the right time. Before you go to work, get your handbag and mind you come back. On the computer you need to write that: 'my name is Richard'. And you need to write 'Andrews' ... and then you have to go to bed.
RA: Which piece of this writing says 'please'?
[Grace points to beginning of writing]

She then read the longer piece a third time:

GRACE: Please go to work at the right time and don't forget to print something down on the computer [inaudible 2 seconds]. Go to bed at the right time and before you go to bed look out of your window and see if the street isn't flooded.

It is not so much the connection between speech and writing that is of interest as the way narrative shapes the emergent writing. The sense of the whole is strong, and the sense that a whole story (Figures 6.8; and 6.9 and 6.10) can be represented by a complete piece of writing is there.

There is little formal correspondence, however, between the written letters and the meaning, except to say that the longer strings of letters do stand for longer utterances – so another connection of sorts has been made. In all the random writing, I have looked at the letter sequences carefully to determine whether there is a secret pre-convention code; there does not appear to be one. Apart from the minimal connection mentioned, this stringing together of letters is probably what Bauers and Boyd (1989) describe when they say that it seems that in the early stages, the *alphabetic visual* system is played with and explored for its own sake, not as a potential carrier of narrative or conceptual meaning. But take the next example, Figure 6.11.

This short piece of writing, composed in December, includes the word 'bacon' as well as other recognizable 'words'. Strings of letters are moving away from random sequences towards separate meaningful words.

One of the advantages of being able to observe the writing at close hand is that the contextual meaning behind the letters can be explored an advantage that Bauers and Boyd admit they do not have. Their work deals only with 'products' and their close and useful analysis of the emergence of command of the formal properties of the language is valuable in that respect. But writing takes place as part of a web of other activities – some close to writing,

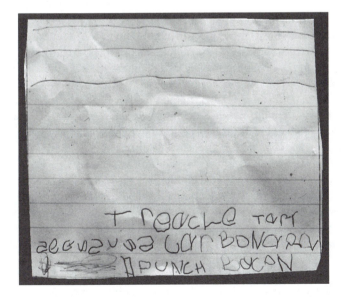

Figure 6.11 Story with the word 'bacon'.

like drawing, and other related activities, like painting and collage. Widening the context a little more, it also takes place within home and school/nursery situations, seeming to act as a conduit for expression that is sometimes personal and sometimes more social. Kinneavy's (1971) communication triangle is helpful here. At times, Grace's writing and drawing (and other related activities) operate in the top left-hand corner of the communication triangle, clearly within the zone of personal (but not necessarily I-centred) composition without cognisance of audience. More rarely, they operate with an audience in mind – either in the production of a letter or in the making of a 'gift'. So it cannot be said that the development of writing is purely an effect of community, any more than it can be said, post-Vygotsky, that speech is only an effect of community. I have come to revise my ideas about the notion that 'learning is an effect of community' too (Rogoff 1991), agreeing with Bauers and Boyd that, to a certain degree, command of the sign system of written language is about delight in taking control of the formal aspects of the system, just as much of Grace's abstract painting is an exploration and celebration of colour and form rather than having any figurative reference. In addition, there is the simple pleasure of wielding a pencil, fibre-tip, brush or mouse and making marks on paper or on screen. It also seems to me that too much has been made of writing as a 'second order symbolic system' based on *speech*. While this is an important insight into the nature of the written language in relation to other graphic and pictorial languages, it plays into the hands of those commentators on art who believe visual expression is primal and written expression somehow 'abstracted' and secondary. We can see from Grace's early marks (and from other work on this stage of development, e.g. Barrs 1988) that writing is conceived visually along with drawing; indeed, it is part of the same system. As it develops it retains its visual identity, only slowly coming to act as a second-order symbolic record for speech. In other words, framing begins to define itself as awareness of the different modes begins to grow. Although many of the works produced by Grace have their own social and institutional framing (she is 'framed' within a family, by the house she lives in, by the stark distinction between home and school), the formal textual framing emerges gradually in the pre-school years. My guess is that one of the reasons that teachers and children find learning to read difficult is that the children's own written (and drawn painted) works are not used as reading material; rather, the conventional emphasis is on 'readers' or books which act as primers for reading, and which are outside the child's immediate creative experience. If reading and writing are seen as reciprocal, and a child's writing used to prompt his or her reading (see Meek's study of weak adolescent readers, *On Being Literate*, Meek 1991), both writing and reading may advance more securely.

If the correspondence between the visual (as in drawing and painting) and the written were closer, as in the Chinese ideographic system, we would be in a better position to look for close correspondence between brushmarks on paper in a painting. But it is well documented that the ideographic system is a primary symbolic system (not emblematic, in which one symbol would be accorded one meaning) where constituent parts of an ideogram form a resource (not unlike morphemes) which can be combined to make further meanings. That is both its strength and limitation as a language: it is able to retain etymological presence in metaphor but, because it deals with ideographic elements rather than dislocated morphemes, it cannot signify more than a limited range of concepts without extending its vocabulary. Such a comparison drives home to us the fact that the letters of the alphabet are in themselves meaningless. Furthermore, we should not assume that the two systems are comparable in cultural terms.

But another helpful distinction suggested by a consideration of the Chinese written language is that, classically, children learn to write with a brush. In the English alphabetic writing system, pencil and felt-tip (and other fine writing and drawing tools) suggest that *writing* and *drawing* should be linked together, rather than, say, writing and collage or writing and painting. Children break these boundaries quite happily, but principally we are concerned with *graphic* production in the study of early writing. One of the interesting aspects of such early production is that drawing and writing are often included in the same work (see Figure 6.12).

So whereas writing-cum-drawing is one stage of learning the two systems, drawing alongside writing is an equally important stage. The drawing of Poppy and Grace not only uses the device of labelling, but includes the

Figure 6.12 Poppy and Grace.

Figure 6.13 Birds in the sky like letters.

motif-like bird symbol in the sky that takes the same shape as the letter U. Such correspondence between visual and verbal systems is also evident in the picture in Figure 6.13.

The birds appear again in this drawing, this time looking more like Vs. The clouds in the sky are depicted with the cursive lines that are the precursor of joined-up writing. In an interesting variation on the correspondence between letter and image, an October drawing of an angry pig caption inscribed by sister. Figure 6.14 uses a stylized visual language to convey the pig's feelings, working first within a square (again, the pig's face and body combined?) and then using a number of different devices – curly lines, lines moving directly outwards from the pig and even arrows – to express (almost literally) the anger. It is in these stylized drawings that the correspondence with the stylized visual language of the writing system is closest.

While we have been exploring the correspondences between the visual and verbal (written) systems in the autumn term, we should also note that there is much visual work beyond the verbal. Two very different examples are illustrated in Figures 6.15 and 6.16.

Even the seemingly abstract collage contains a polystyrene letter S, however, acting principally as a shape among other shapes and textures but nevertheless

Figure 6.14 Angry pig.

bringing an element of a different system into play with elements from other worlds: sponges, scrubbing pads, pasta, material, woodshavings, gauze and decorative grit. The sponge-print is a simple celebration in colour, shape and visual texture within the confines of a sheet of paper.

Figure 6.15 Collage.

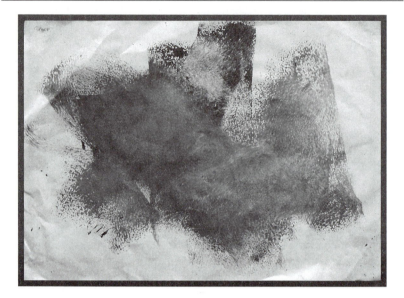

Figure 6.16 Sponge print.

A house move in December had two effects on Grace's writing and drawing: first, in the chaos and unsettling month of the move, there was little output;[3] second, once the move had been made, there was yet another reason for communicating with friends that were now 200 miles distant. Grace received a fax early in January from a friend in St Albans, Celia. This prompted a reply (Figure 6.17).

Perhaps there is little more to say about the relationship between the written and the visual here, other than the observable fact that drawing is becoming more dextrous, with details like the contents of sweet packets drawn in, pockets drawn and so on. This kind of detail is carried over into the drawing of a television (February 1997) with attendant channel and volume/brightness etc. controls, made when more television-watching had been banned; this drawing also marks the integration of the graphic arts with a three-dimensional paper work – the television stands up. As an act of defiance, the substitute television was watched, propped up on the arm of a sofa.

Drawings in these two months show evidence of seriation, the relationship between different elements, and narrative referencing as well as contiguous relationship (see Figures 6.18 and 6.19).

It is tempting to imagine analogies between these elements of visual language and advances in, say, storytelling and writing and other aspects of writing development. I have no evidence of such correspondence, so instead concentrate on the drawings and their relationship with writing. One work in particular, Figure 6.20, seems to be representative of this continued relationship.

Figure 6.17 Fax to Celia.

Figure 6.18 Seriation 1.

Figure 6.19 Seriation 2.

'Zoë with spiral and window' starts with writing at the top with the letters 'o', 'm' and 'c'. The name 'Zoë' (albeit with the 'z' reversed) follows the diaeresis clearly included. The spirals in the 'e' are reflected in the drawing below, which also includes a grid-like window with flowers and birds. Barrs' suggestion, set out above, that dramatic play may be the symbolic system that presages drawing and writing, provides a place for 'show' in the development of children's command of symbolic systems, though with all hierarchical or sequential models we tend to find in the individual acts of making a collapsing of categories.

The idea of a 'show' is carried over into the multimedia work on screen. During the six-month period in which work was collected, a number of shows were composed on a Macintosh computer using the software *Kidpix*. The facility in *Kidpix* that attracted Grace in particular was 'Slide Show' in which you are able to create and import words and images into a sequenced format, adding sound to make the show.

Apart from the pleasures of primitive animation, there is a strong narrative quality to these shows; they give huge pleasure to the child, even though they again have an arbitrariness about them that is often baffling to adults. Although in the early 1980s I posited a relationship between the development of narrative in the three-to-five-year-old age group and the concurrent development of word formation and syntax – and then subsequently scrubbed out that connection in copies of the article I wrote about storytelling in the East End of London (Andrews 1981) – I now think that the connections between word, utterance and the whole text, cemented by the need for sequence – which is, in part, provided by narrative – is probably stronger than I originally imagined. If learning

Figure 6.20 Zoë with spiral and window.

to read-and-write (I yoke them together deliberately) is a matter of not only exploring and eventually gaining command of the different levels at which language manifests itself, but also integrating and thereby bringing meaning to the different levels, then the narrative impulse may well play an important part in that complex process. In the examples discussed above, we can see that the forms which allow narrative development are storytelling and slide-show animation; neither of these is strictly based on the written language, but they act as frames for it.[4]

What, then, of the research question with which I have set out on an exploration of these various pieces: 'What is the relation of emergent writing to other graphic and visual production in a four-year-old?'? I think we can identify different ways in which the two are related. First, in the visual/proto-verbal language of early emergent writing, where marks on the page are endowed with meaning. Second, in the visual nature of the writing system itself as it separates itself from the visual core and establishes itself as a formal alphabetic system in its own right – not necessarily always carrying meaning. Third, in the renewed relationship between the visual and verbal, now as separate semiotic systems complementing each other in works which use them both: either using words to label drawings, or in speech bubbles, or contiguously without apparent reference, on the one hand; or using words themselves as vessels to carry visual loads, on the other. This movement of integration to separate development to reintegration marks a relationship that probably continues in such a way, particularly at home and in most communication in the everyday world; whereas schooling is characterized by a separating of the systems, a kind of aesthetic of denial that the other exists in order to enhance the knowledge of each of the systems, and to encourage the verbal and visual imaginations by suppressing them, or keeping them outside the frame of the composition.

Consideration of framing in relation to early visual and written production is therefore brought full circle. While creations by children are relatively free of framing devices, they are inevitably framed by the resources with which they are created: paper, writing and drawing materials, the electronic screen. Schools encourage a more framed approach to composition by concentrating on systems rather than employing a mix of different systems in order to fulfil a function – whether that function is purely expressive or embedded within a community, however small.

Re-framing Language Arts/English as a School Subject

Re-framing the English curriculum in schools is a pressing matter as current curricula appear to be increasingly anachronistic. When the selection of activities in schools and classrooms moves too far away from the social and communicative practices of everyday life, teachers and students begin to ask 'Why are we studying this?' and 'What is the significance of that?' Chapter 7 puts forward a new theory and model for English, suggesting that the very term 'English' itself is no longer appropriate for the activities that need to go on in the service of the arts of communication in the twenty-first century.

Introduction

In the light of the previous four chapters, a new model for English is posited which builds on a range of incomplete or partial models that have dominated thinking for the last 10–20 years. Essentially, the model is an inclusive one which embraces the various approaches from a basis in rhetoric and framing. It is shown that a range of good practice – not 'good practice' as a rather abstract entity in itself – can reveal an underlying coherence about English as a school subject. 'English' is only the name of the language which is used to teach a web of values, text types and approaches to the process of composition. This chapter establishes the foundation for a well-theorized model of English which will be able to hold its own in the curriculum and will form the basis for the teaching of communication at all levels in the twenty-first century. Distinction will be made between the approach taken in this book and the fixed 'frames' of the scaffolding movement in designing learning, which derives from Vygotskian as well as Australian genre school thinking.

Current conceptions of 'English' as a school subject are muddled and various, akin to what Bergonzi (1990) described in *Exploding English* as like the Spanish Empire in decline – with the rider that 'it could go on for a long time in this condition' (p.204). Bergonzi's subject was university-level English studies, but the same applies to school-level English. While the relationship between university-level English and school-level English is not the subject of the present book, the curriculum and studies in the subject at higher education continue to exert an influence on the subject at school level, with rather less of an influence in the other direction. The influence that is felt in school English is principally one of 'literariness': different conceptions of the canon filtered down to the secondary- or high-school-level curriculum. The other main influence in the twentieth century, at least, was one of method. I. A. Richards' aesthetic, 'practical criticism' approach, pioneered in Cambridge with undergraduate students in the 1920s and 1930s and enshrined in *Practical Criticism* (1929), became a staple method for sixth-form (16 to 18-year-old) advanced study of literary texts in the UK.

What is Missing from Twentieth-century Models of English?

In terms of school English, what has been missing from conceptions of the subject? To start the investigation, this section will concentrate on secondary- or high-school English (for 11 to 18-year-olds) and will inevitably take a broad sweep, focusing not so much on specific curricula and examination syllabuses, but on the elements of models of English that have been prevalent.

There are a number of books on the birth of English as a school and university subject/discipline. One of the most interesting is Dixon (1991), *A Schooling in 'English': Critical Episodes in the Struggle to Shape Literary and Cultural Studies*, which charts, first, the emergence of English from the university extension movement of the second half of the nineteenth century, along with a demo-cratic desire to establish critical reading of literature as a central activity for educational purposes. Its second focus is on the establishment of English (and related) literature at the centre of the university and school curriculum in the 1920s, partly manifested in Newbolt's report *The Teaching of English in England* (1921/2005) and partly in the development of a dynamic and tightly focused theory of reading promoted by I.A. Richards (1929) at Cambridge, resulting in what became the staple of English studies for 16–18 year-olds in England thereafter: practical criticism, with its intense focus on the text itself. The third episode on which the book concentrates is that of the period 1960–79, which is characterized as one in which an elite system is restructured on the principle of the emergent and more personal voice of the student.

The development of English in the post-Second World War period in England is currently the focus of a study undertaken at the Institute of Education, London (Hardcastle et al. 2008). The research project, running from 2009 to 2012, looks at the way English was conceived and taught in three London schools. Part of the thinking behind the project is that creative approaches to the English curriculum may have been given impetus in the mid-1960s, but that there was a good deal of creative and radical work going on in schools in the 20 years before that in the socially reconstructive mood of the time. Medway's chapter in *Bringing English to Order* (1990) captures the nature of English as a school subject in 1958: English was "the sum of its well-established parts: literature, composition, instruction and exercises in written language and (less universally) speech training" (p.5). The pedagogy was in transmissive mode, deriving from medieval *progymnasmata* or written exercises in a narrow (and, in this version, now discredited) conception of rhetoric. There was a strong belief in the civilizing and moral power of high literature, largely of English origin, to educate and protect students from the vagaries and temptations of popular culture. We expect the Leverhulme Project to reveal some more radical notions and practices of English in this period. From initial research, the picture is likely to show pockets of radical thinking in the subject, linking the reading of literature to social change and encouraging talk in classrooms; with the writing curriculum remaining relatively conservative.

The conventional practice at the time, and one that has pervaded twentieth-century thinking about English, is informed by an aesthetic take on language. This explains the emphasis on a canon of literature at the heart of the curriculum, with 'comprehension' geared to understanding and appreciation of literary texts. But the influence of a prevailing literary sensibility manifested itself also in the approach to non-literary texts. These were conceived not so much as texts for action in the world, as texts that showed linguistic features that were worthy of study. In looking at writing that was prized in the period, it is clear that the most highly valued work is literary in its style. It is as if there is a hierarchy of value in operation, with literariness marking the high style and prosaic language marking the lower styles. That distinction was reflected too in the English curricula used by the grammar schools (dealing with the academically 'top' 20 per cent of the school population) and the 'modern' or secondary-modern schools (dealing with the other 80 per cent) with their more functional, prosaic, supposedly vocational approach to English.

The élite English curriculum of the mid part of the century, then, was framed by sensibilities steeped in the (largely English) literary canon; but remained different from the less literary, more functional English curriculum.

What was new in the 1960s was a conception of English in secondary and high schools that gave more credence to the personal 'voice'. Such recognition manifests itself in the rise of talk in the classroom (see Barnes et al. 1969), in the coining of the term 'oracy' by Wilkinson (see MacLure et al. 1988), and the gradual emergence of 'voice' (i.e. unified personal imprint) in writing (see Graves 1982). While seeing the young person's self at the centre of experience, the notion of self was grounded in its social context. Those social contexts were reflected in the range of literature chosen for study, which drew on 1950s social realism rather than harking back nostalgically to a more pastoral English age. Photographs in textbooks of the 1960s reflect an often gritty social world, indicating the worlds from which urban students came. Establishing English as the subject of social change through the power of literature drew on the radical ideas of the 1950s, with the subject as the 'social conscience' of the curriculum. The increased emphasis on social contexts and their relation to the development of a single 'self' mirrored the rise in interest in Vygotsky, first published in the West in 1962 but available in unpublished translated papers before that. Vygotsky (1962/1986) appeared to give English in classrooms a purpose and identity as the agent for transforming not only cognitive learning through social engagement, but also social and political transformation through talk and writing, reading and listening in the classroom. Vygotsky's contribution to pedagogical theory is best distilled in Britton (1987).

'English' was thus seen to be about expression and social awareness, fuelled by the imagination. Part of the movement to autobiographical expression realized itself in the rising interest in narrative in the 1970s and 1980s. This predilection for narrative has had a considerable influence on both sides of the Atlantic, with oral storytelling emerging in schools in the early 1980s; narrative being asked to do the work of argument and exposition; and narrative being used as a primary means of expression not only at secondary-/high-school level, but in primary/elementary schools too. The connection between English and narration is a strong one, locating the subject in the nexus of everyday demotic speech and writing in which stories are exchanged; but also preserving the connection with narration in short stories, novels, plays and (some) poems.

Another strand to the development of English at primary and secondary levels was the focus on writing *process*. Psychosocial studies in composing by Bereiter and Scardamalia (1987), for example, provided scientific understanding of cognitive processes involved in writing that underpinned, in theory at least, drafting and editing practices in the teaching and learning of writing. An emphasis on process led to a revival of the term that had been prevalent in the 1950s – composition – and which duly reflected the nature of putting things together in writing. That term also served as a more accurate one than 'writing' when describing multimodal forms of composition from the 1990s onwards.

For a more detailed survey of English in England in the 1960s through to the present, see Andrews (2009b).

The emphasis on a literary core to the English curriculum persisted well into the 1990s, but began to fade as a conception of English based on reading and writing in a wide range of genres came to the fore. The conception derives from Australian genre theory, with notions of 'genre' itself deriving from the categorizations in film theory as well as Hallidayan linguistics. Before the surge of interest in genre-as-text-type (as opposed to genre-as-social-action), the different genres in written literary language must have seemed obvious: poems, short stories, novellas, novels, plays etc. – the staple of English classrooms and of English textbook collections. But widening the range of genres to include non-fictional text types like business letters, manuals, reports, notes etc. shed a different light on literary genres. No longer were they the exclusive preserve of a higher cultural approach to English education, but they began to be considered as different text types along with the non-fictional ones. One of the key texts that explores the distinction between fiction and non-fiction is Pavel (1986), who is discussed again in the final chapter.

None of the models of English described so far provided a comprehensive model of English in the school curriculum. As a school subject – indeed, as a university discipline – the field of English has been characterized by disunity rather than unity; by competing theories rather than converging ones; and by political tensions. In summary, the models on offer through the twentieth century have been based on a number of principles:

- a conception of English that is primarily literary. That literariness has often been a 'high' heritage tradition, linked often with notions of nationality ('Englishness', though ironically England is only a country that is part of a nation, the UK), high moral ground, the cultivation of the spirit and other grand claims made for the study of literature
- a conception of English as an agent for personal and social change or transformation. This model sees English as a space for expressiveness, for exploring the connection between 'self' and society, for developing a social conscience
- a site for the development of functional skills, largely through language. This distinctively unliterary conception reduces English to the teaching and (hopefully) learning, but not the appreciation or understanding, of basic language skills in speech and writing
- 'English' as a sub-section of cultural and media studies, in which study of literature and language in English is seen as just one sub-section of a wider theoretical category of 'communication'. This approach sits alongside conceptions of multimodality and because it de-emphasizes the centrality of the English language, is more international in scope.

All these approaches or principles only partially represent the activities of English, and none of them can provide a comprehensive unifying theory for the field. It is no surprise that English came under attack in England in the 1980s from right-wing parties that found it lacking in robustness, loose and ill-formed. Practice followed one or more of the above conceptions, but was under-theorized and could not, if pushed, justify its place in the curriculum. It is a relief, looking back to that period, that English as a subject held on to its pride of place at the core of the curriculum with mathematics (two 'languages' of communication, analysis and understanding), perhaps largely through a belief on the part of conservative reformers that it still justified its core position, held since the 1920s. But their motives must have been mixed.

Towards a New Theory and Model

There is thus a need for a new theory and model for English in schools. Theories are important because they provide a unifying overarching (or, if the metaphor is reversed, underpinning) set of concepts that enables all parts of the subject to stand in relation to each other. Such unity is important for justifying curriculum choices, for arguing the position of English within the curriculum, for resolving the conflicts between existing theories and models and, more generally, to justify policy and practice in the subject. Without such unity, there is no clear basis for disagreement, argument and resolution; a situation can occur in which those subscribing to one view of English can have almost nothing to say to those subscribing to another. So an overarching theory does not preclude argument. Indeed, it encourages productive argument within the same set of discourses, values and assumptions.

Models derive from and/or generate the need for theories. They usually take visual, diagrammatic, two-dimensional form. They are a schematic distillation of a complex set of ideas that may constitute a theory (which mostly takes verbal form); their virtue is that they are easily remembered. They can be applied more easily than theories, and can serve as an *aide-memoire* for discussions about practice (and, to a lesser extent, policy). Mitchell and Riddle (2000) have written about the nature and efficacy of models in a report on argumentation (see especially pp.26–8). Writing models are reviewed and discussed in Smith and Andrews (2009).

Reviewing the principles that have underpinned English throughout the twentieth century, it is hard to pin down the theories that have informed them. Theory for a wide and complex field such as English might be a projection from a set of social and intellectual practices rather than a solid body of theoretical thinking. On the other hand, there are cognitive-developmental theories that have had a significant influence on English practices, like those of Piaget and Vygotsky. Linguistic theories seem to have had less of an impact, but literary theory (e.g. whether to emphasize 'reader-response' or favour a text-based approach to reading literature) more so. Whereas cognitive-developmental theories have informed ideas of curriculum progression and even, in Vygotsky's case, of pedagogical practice, it is harder to declare that Marxist literary criticism or any form of postmodernist theory has had an equally powerful effect. The most prevalent form of literary response in the twentieth century – *practical criticism* – seemed, as was discussed above, especially suited to the study of literary texts for 16–18 year-olds in the phase before university study of English, partly because of its pragmatic, aesthetic and seemingly atheoretical nature. Finally, it is still the case that cultural theory has yet to make a significant impact on English, despite more than a generation's argument from film and media theorists that English must be seen as a sub-section of cultural practice. The stubborn presence of English in the school curriculum, and the continuing, rather sterile debate between 'language' and 'literature' have restricted a wider view.

A new theory for English, then, must start from the actual and *potential* practices that make up teaching and learning in the subject. It must also take into account values, assumptions and principles in the field that may have been taken for granted or overlooked in the formation of partial theories. It will also, inevitably, react against the perceived lack of unifying theory, outlined above, and work with or against particular theories that have had an influence to date.

What the new theory must embrace, then, is, first, the fact that English covers a wide and various set of practices. It covers the study of the English language and of literatures in the English language (some in translation). It is concerned not only with the study of these fields of enquiry, but also with the teaching and learning of elements of them, in particular learning to write and read in the language; learning to speak and listen; learning to vary register in different contexts and for different purposes. If we take the end of compulsory schooling at about 16 or 17, we would expect students of English to have a working competence in the use of the English language that would enable them to operate as citizens in society and to be capable in any workplace. We would also expect the capacity to read, view and, in general, appreciate the way verbal language operates in culture in various forms and in combinations with other modes.

Second, a twenty-first century theory of English must embrace the digital age and multimodality. These are separate entities even though they are often considered together. The digitization of reading and writing through computer use since about 1980 has had a much larger effect on the use of language in society than appears to be the case in the English curriculum. Within English classrooms in school and in homework, word-processing and more advanced compositional tools are being used to compose, with implications for the nature of composition. For example, a student undertaking the composition of a newspaper story might begin the work by designing a page, in columns, on a computer screen. He/she might then place an image on the page, write the story, then add a title (or carry out those three activities in a different order). Drafting and editing tools might be used to improve the piece; different type-faces might be experimented with, either at the presentation stage or earlier in the process. The point here is that the sequence in which the composition takes place in the digital age is not pre-determined; it may be the case that design issues take precedence over writing ones.

A simple example such as this one raises questions of multimodality. What is the relation between the image (probably a photograph downloaded from the net or supplied digitally by the student; or even scanned) and the verbal text? Is positioning of the image in relation to the verbal text significant? If so, how? What are the affordances of each mode for the composer and reader?

Not all multimodal issues are generated by the computer screen. Multi-modality has been part of the nature of communication for centuries and does not depend on digitization. What the digital age has brought to the fore is the ease with which multimodal composition can take place, and the ubiquity of it in contemporary communication. It is hard to think of English practices now without taking into account issues of multimodality, even in cases where an act of communication is seemingly monomodal (for example, the reading of a page of verbal text, where other modes of communication are present to one degree or another via the visual/spatial context in which the text is read).

Third, a new theory and model for English must bridge the divide between the fictional and the 'non-fictional'. This divide, as indicated earlier in the chapter, has reflected a divide in the structure of secondary schooling in England between the grammar school and private schools on the one hand, and the secondary modern schools on the other. The structural divide was bridged by comprehensive schools for the period from the 1940s to the end of the twentieth century, but has re-appeared under the guise of specialist schools, academies and other types of specialist institutions in the first part of the twenty-first century. Even within schools, the division is evident, through banding or setting of classes within a particular school year, into those 'at the top end' who study literature in itself; those in the middle who study literature as a means of accessing and understanding a wider range of language; and those 'at the lower end' who, as new qualifications come in at the start of the second decade of the century, will study a 'functional', largely literature-free syllabus towards examination at 16. The divide, then, between 'fiction' and 'non-fiction' has social as well as linguistic and cultural implications.

The divide itself, even in discourse terms, is an odd one. To cast one set of genres that includes poetry, novels, short stories and plays as 'fiction' (remembering that not all such works are fictional) is just about understandable. These are, more accurately, literary works which operate in a more highly framed space than so-called non-literary works. The space in which they operate is framed by expectations of unity, aesthetic considerations and attention to the language of the work as well as its content. But to define all other works as 'non-fictional' is not only a negative definition, like 'non-participant', 'non-believer' or 'nonentity' – defined, that is, in relation to fiction – but also inaccurate. Many non-fictional works have elements of fiction in them; many certainly have creative elements and imaginative ones too. By casting a broad set of genres into the non-fictional category, the individual genres are diminished. In curriculum and syllabus terms, too, to have fiction at the core and non-fiction at the margins indicates the status of the two kinds of text. Referring back to the discussion of Pavel's *Fictional Worlds* (1986), we need to understand more about the nature of fiction and how it works before we can characterize a large body of documentary, expositional and other work as 'non-fictional'. We also need a theory and model of English that gives status to documentary and other such works, and acknowledges the hybrid nature of many of them.

The last five elements that need to be taken into account are: i) the role of speaking and listening in English; ii) that of film, moving image, TV and other 'popular' cultural forms; iii) the political nature of the subject in the classroom and the school; iv) the very nature of the English language medium and the way it is perceived both nationally and worldwide; and v) the distinction between 'literacy' and 'literacies'.

Speaking and listening have come under the canopy term of 'oracy' (by analogy with 'literacy') since the 1960s. A key part of the curriculum and syllabuses for the middle and 'lower' abilities through the Certificate of Secondary Education (CSE) examination system in England in the 1970s and early 1980s (thus again reflecting an apartheid in educational provision), speaking became compulsory for *all* students at 14–16 with the advent of the unified General Certificate of Secondary Education from 1986. Such a division in the pre-1986 period marks an ambivalence towards speaking and listening: it was celebrated from the 1960s onwards as essential to learning, but adopted only for the 'lower' abilities as part of their assessment. Those of 'higher' ability were using speech as a means to an end in discussions and conversations about their literary studies, and optionally exploring it formally in debating societies. The unification of the examination system in 1986 provided an opportunity to bring the best of both worlds together for speaking and listening. The problem, however, turned out to be that speaking and listening (understandably, as ideally they are reciprocal and of equal weight) were yoked together and given a third of the English secondary curriculum; whereas writing and reading were given a third each, and not seen as reciprocal. Structurally, then, speaking and listening were subsidiary to writing and reading in the new 'national' (it covered only England and Wales) curriculum formed from 1988. Furthermore, listening has always been second to speaking and is not taught to the same degree as speaking, writing or reading. The move to whole-class teaching in the national literacy strategy from 1996 onwards in England further relegated the role of a wide variety of spoken genres in the curriculum.

A fifth lacuna in the conception of English has been the continuing resistance to moving-image media like film and television. The resistance has taken the form of marginalizing these media by seeing them as a separate field of study; by seeing the 'film of the book' as a tokenistic way of including 'media' and more popular cultural forms in the English curriculum (rather than a study of film in itself); by the inoculation of young minds through high literature of the wilder excesses and pervasive presence of media culture; and, it has to be said, by the reluctance of some theorists and practitioners in media studies to be subsumed by a subject they see as anachronistic and culturally narrow. Again, the tendency to build a hierarchy of cultural appreciation, with popular culture providing the base of a pyramid of which 'high' culture is the peak, has reinforced the divide. The efforts of the British Film Institute (BFI) in the UK to bring film and television studies into the mainstream of English as a school subject have been admirable; it remains to be seen whether the curriculum space protected and offered by English can accommodate media studies, and thus move forward as a unified area of interest in schooling. The next major review of the secondary curriculum is scheduled for 2015, a date noted by the Qualifications and Curriculum Authority – but that date is far enough in the future to be changed. At the time of writing (2009), there were minor changes to the secondary curriculum in 2007 concerning personalization of study paths, and there is a major review of the primary curriculum underway. Neither of these incorporated a consideration of the place of media studies within literacy or English. A new theory and model of English, it is argued, must include a consideration of popular forms of culture and of a wider range of media than that of books.

A further factor to bear in mind in designing a new theory and model is the political nature of English in the curriculum and in the classroom. We have seen that English in the 1940s and 1950s, in some radical departments in London schools, was beginning to associate itself with the desire for social change in the wake of the Second World War. The particular focus of literary texts that were chosen for study and the liberation of talk for working-class children were geared towards nothing less than a gradual revolution in the discourses of the classroom. This opening up of students' personal lives to discussion; the consideration of self and immediate social context; the parallels with experimentation in comprehensive schooling (to bridge the divide between the élite grammar schools and the secondary modern schools); the gradual recognition of an increasingly diverse school community as a result of increased immigration during the 1950s – all these factors conspired to make English the site of social discussion and inquiry. The emphasis on English as a place where such matters could be considered continued into the 1960s and 1970s with ground-breaking anthologies of poetry like *Voices* (Summerfield 1968; see also Summerfield 1965, 1970, 1979) which not only celebrated the voices of young people themselves, but put them alongside the voices of established poets, poets from the wider world, vernacular writers and documentation from social and political history. In particular, the black-and-white photographs that illustrated these anthologies opened up the sensibilities of young people to a grittier, more realistic world than the dreamy and/or heroic associations of poetry and literary prose that had characterized school anthologies in the pre-war years.

The parochialism of 'English' literature – the work of Masefield, Kipling, Lawrence and others – was evident in the literary curriculum up to the middle of the twentieth century, and has persisted at the core of the English curriculum since then. Andrews (1993) points out the multiple ironies of a National Curriculum in England that re-established a canon based on sea-shanties, patriotism, English landscape and insularity for the 1990s. The deep association between literature and the national identity and consciousness in the conservative mind is reflected in such a curriculum which, along with a mis-placed belief in the teaching of formal grammar to improve children's writing (Andrews et al. 2006a), forged a nostalgic and ineffective set of beliefs and practices on the part of policy-makers for a generation of students. That parochialism is also evident in the assumption that 'English' as a language is totally associated with England as a country: with its history, culture and identity. The assumption misses the fact that English in the twentieth century became a world language, and that its variations are global as well as regional. The agency that speakers of English feel in India, the USA, Canada, Australia and New Zealand and parts of Africa is more than a post-colonial state of the language; it is true ownership of the language, developing it in distinctive ways so that, in the twenty-first century, we can no longer consider a unified world English, but need to widen our understanding to appreciate and explore world Englishes. Even political devolution within the UK (the creation of the Scottish Parliament and the Welsh Assembly to govern in-country affairs) has yet to have a significant impact on English awareness of the strengths and limitations of English consciousness: its diversity, tolerance, openness to new ideas and to people from across the world on the one hand; and its insensitivity, close-mindedness and resistance to diversity on the other. It is thus essential in literary and linguistic terms that a new theory and model for English as a school subject should recognize the place of English as a world language among other versions of world Englishes; and the wider canon of literature that makes up not only the diversity and richness of literature written by a multi-ethnic English population, but also the range of literature written in, and translated into, the English language, worldwide. It will be clear from such a world-picture that 'English' can no longer be the title of the subject for the rest for the twenty-first century: it is too bound up with the country, the people, 'national' identity and colonial history.

Finally, in this review of the issues that must be taken into account in the formulation of a new theory and model for English and literacy studies, the plurality of Englishes signals another plurality: the distinction between 'literacy' and 'literacies'. The key paper in this regard is Cazden et al. (1996), 'A Pedagogy of Multiliteracies: Designing Social Futures' composed by the New London Group, and reprinted in a revised form in Cope and Kalantzis (2000). In essence, the tenor of this paper was that 'literacy' as a unified concept was inadequate to account for its diverse applications in a range of contexts. These were not just applications of a single notion of literacy in different contexts, but different versions of literacy, with their own rationales, discourses and practices. The distinction between 'literacy' and literacies' can be captured in the following definition, used as a basis for research reviews on the relationship between new technologies and literacies in the early 2000s:

> literacy can be defined narrowly, as the ability to understand and create written language. But first, the scope can be expanded so that written language becomes written language and graphical or pictorial representation. Second, the skill can be treated as social, rather than psychological; in this view literacy is the ability to operate a series of social or cultural representations. Since sets of expectations and norms differ depending on the situation, the social view of literacy entails a number of different 'literacies'.
>
> (Andrews 2004, p.2)

Street (1985) makes a further distinction between *autonomous* and *ideological* notions of literacy. Autonomous literacy refers primarily to a unified notion of literacy as a set of cognitive skills and abilities and their generic use. Ideological literacy refers to the social conceptions and uses of literacy. These broadly sociolinguistic, critical, social semiotic and anthropological views of literacy (embracing the plurality of literacies) need to be borne in mind as a new theory and model is designed.

In summary, a number of different tensions within English as a school curriculum subject; and within literacy as a set of social practices that are learnt within and without schooling, need to be considered and resolved in a new theory and model of English and literacy. Not least is the problem of how to integrate, if that is seen as desirable, the different perspectives of English and literacy. It is too simplistic to suggest that 'English' is the term for secondary- or high-school communication studies, and that 'literacy' or 'language arts' for the primary and elementary years. The terms carry ideologies with them. These need to be discussed and resolved in order for the field to move forward. It is to the challenge of forging a new theory and model that the chapter, and the book, now turns.

Framing: A Theory and Model for English and Literacy

The foregoing chapters have provided the background and rationale for a new conception in, and a new approach to English and literacy studies. The foregoing sections of the present chapter have set the parameters of the challenge. The approach is set at the level of framing because that level of generalization/abstraction – a mezzanine level – looks up towards theory and down towards practice and policy. The informing (and informed) theory is contemporary rhetoric. The social and political practices of policy formation, on the one hand, and pedagogies in the classroom as well as learning situations in and outside school, on the other, is the territory to be mapped on the ground. I will develop, by the end of this chapter, a model of framing in the language arts, as that is the central focus of this book. But first we must return to rhetoric and the overarching body of theory for the model.

Rhetoric

Contemporary rhetoric is the natural body of theory for a re-framing of approaches to English and literacy, and the beginnings of a justification for its position as an overarching theory for framing were set out in Chapter 1. It is not associated with one language, so instantly opens up all aspects of communication in a multilingual or plurilingual world. It can apply in Spanish, Mandarin, English and all other languages, or to any combination of these.

To address some of the problems with the English field set out above, in the present chapter: first, rhetoric is an alternative body of theory to cognitive developmental theory (which applies to all forms of subject- and discipline-based cognition, not just to language), so we can now leave the generation of Piaget and Vygotsky behind, grateful for the insights they have provided into conceptual development and pedagogy. They do not provide a coherent nor applicable set of ideas for the design and implementation of language and other modal work, though they shed a good deal of light on these matters. Neither do linguistics nor literary theory provide a comprehensive foundational body of theory, partly because they cover different sides of a coin: language on the one hand, and the use of language in highly framed aesthetic forms on the other. We cannot look for such a relevant body of theory in anthropology, sociology, political philosophy or philosophy itself: each of these is concerned with different epistemologies. The only possibility for a unifying body of theory is *contemporary* rhetoric, which provides a long history ('English' looks like a recent and short-lived phase over a 'geological' time-frame). But we cannot depend on classical formulations of rhetoric which were designed – as all subsequent versions were over the last 2000+ years – for a particular function in a particular period and location.

Contemporary rhetoric, with its definition of the *arts* of discourse, retains the aesthetic dimension that is so important to framing in general, and to highly framed works in particular. Currently, it is able to embrace notions of multimodality and the flexibile and varied forms of communication media in the digital age, because it is not tied to verbal language (a term used to denote the use of words in speech or writing) but embraces all verbal languages and all other forms of linguistic, mathematical, spatial and visual code.

Rhetoric, too, is interested in the distinctions between fiction and non-fiction, but would cast the latter category in a more positive, independent light. As Eagleton pointed out (1983), rhetoric is a political literary criticism, interested in issues of power, containment, framing and positioning of the literary text in relation to other texts and to the discourses of public as well as private life. Non-literary texts such as political tracts, newspaper articles, personal letters and even manuals for products of a capitalist, production- and consumption-based society, are *documentary* texts in their own right. They have a direct communicative function in the world, whereas literary texts have a somewhat different function: to hold a mirror up to nature; to create a possible world that can be used to reflect upon the 'real world'; to structure and reify feeling; to abstract, to varying degrees, from the world in order to see it better. From a rhetorical point of view, the difference between literary and non-literary texts is not a matter of imagination (in literary fictional works) or non-imagination (documentary texts), as imagination operates in both. It is a matter of the framing of compositional ends and interpretation – and we know that fiction can be read as literal and applicable in the real-world, just as non-fiction can be read as fanciful, projective, inapplicable, bizarre. Rhetoric repairs the fissure between literary and non-literary but de-emphasizing the literary, defining the previously negative 'non-literary' or 'non-fictional' as having identity in its own right, and approaching all forms of discourse with the apparatus of framing to understand the power relations inside and outside the frame, the constituent parts and elements that are contained inside the frame, and the various influences and contexts that bear upon the frame from the outside.

Speaking and listening are given their proper place from a rhetorical perspective. Rhetoric does not privilege the written form of verbal language or its particular manifestation in handwriting or print. Because its history was (as far as we can tell) grounded in the production of speech (specifically, public speeches in the crucible of democracy in pre-Athenian and Athenian societies), it can consider speech alongside writing and other modes with equanimity. The return to orality, or the 'turn to the visual' are matters of re-balancing for rhetoric, not significant turning points in the history of communication ... which has always adapted itself to whatever new technologies have been created. That is why a new theory of English and literacy – the terms are already beginning to fade in their usefulness as the argument of the book progresses – must embrace image, moving image, physical movement (as in dance) and other forms of spatial representation.

How can rhetoric re-establish itself as a theory for global understanding of the communication arts? The first heave is to disassociate itself from any particular language, most obviously English in the case of the present book and in the English-speaking, writing and reading world. Introductions to rhetorical theory, which at their simplest involve the communicative and political relationships between the speaker(s) or rhetor(s), subject matter and audience (see Kinneavy 1971) need to be written or re-written to take into account the multimodal and digital age, as well as the range (or not) of media and other resources that are available to composers and audiences.

Finally, in this sketch of how rhetoric can provide the informing theory for the field (the theory must be developed further in a different book), the distinction between 'English' (by which is implied 'Englishes') and literacy (by which is implied 'literacies') becomes redundant. These are vestigial terms that define, on the one hand, a cultural historical phase/nexus in world communication history that gave rise to English Language and English Literature; and, on the other, a description of social practices and expectations grounded in reading and writing print, but having been recently expanded to take in a wider repertoire of modes, media and contexts. It would, however, be naive to think that one set of difficult terminology could be replaced by no terminology, or that 'rhetoric' provides a suitable replacement term for the field and for curricular purposes. This question of what we call aspects of the field is left for the final chapter, which pans out beyond rhetoric.

Framing

Framing, as a model, sits readily within a theory of contemporary rhetoric. It does so because it suggests agency (the act of *framing* rather than the existence of *frames*), thus linking to the action of the rhetor/composer/speaker/writer and his or her motivation to communicate. It also provides a *structural* vocabulary (based on a cohering metaphor: that of the 'frame') to describe the dynamics and forms of communication. Third, it is always aware of the political choices that are made in communication: one form is chosen over another; a particular hybrid is created; it is aware of its audience etc. Having a body of theory to underpin notions of framing is helpful because acts of communication can be justified, rationally. The further advantage of an underlying (again, or 'overarching') body of theory is that progress with communication can be gauged.

Before going on to chart the lineaments of framing in more detail, it is necessary to discuss first what is meant by 'progress with communication can be gauged'. It does not mean that it is possible to measure precisely the generation or impact of particular acts of communication. Rather, it means that composition can be designed in full awareness of the options that are possible, and of the histories of the particular forms that are used to communicate (or the histories of elements of form that are forged into a new hybrid). From the point of view of the receiver/audience, the interpretation of acts of communication can be gauged against expectations of the use of particular forms in particular situations, and in the light of general patterns of response to these forms (and how new acts of communication stand in relation to the general patterns of expectation). 'Progress' in such a field as communication means a move towards clarity, full expression, fitness-for-purpose and positive communication between all parties involved. It is not a case of large-scale progress across generations and periods of history (though breakdowns in communication through poor framing are signs of a diffusion of rhetorical clarity, leading perhaps to war and other forms of non-verbal aggression) so much as the renewal of day-to-day communication between people. The micro- and macro-levels are related, but it is easier to gauge and see progress at the micro-levels. Getting on with the everyday business of the world is a result of clear communication, consensual agreement after differences are resolved through argumentation and discussion.

Framing appears to be a structural phenomenon, even when the emphasis is on the acts of framing rather than on the frames themselves. It lends itself to graphic descriptions like Kinneavy's triangles (see 1971) or to rectangular frames (see Chapters 1 and 2 of the present book). Once these basic frames are drawn, vectors and other lines of connection work within the frames, across the borders of frames and outside the frames to depict relations between textual and contextual factors structurally. It is essential that these structures are seen as *light* structures that are dispensable as soon as the main acts of communication are achieved. They are not to be associated with the heavy nature of steel scaffolding (the metaphor has been used by Cazden 2001, Wray 2004 and others to provide post-Vygotskian frameworks for writing and other acts of communication), but are to be seen as more like the bamboo scaffolding that is used in Asia to construct tall buildings. Such scaffolding is portable and human-scale, transportable, and easily and quickly erected and taken down. It emphasizes the building itself, which is seen emerging through the scaffolding (rather than being hidden and enshrouded by it). In other words, light framing of this kind is a means to an end, not an end in itself.

What are the key elements of a model of framing? As in rhetorical considerations, the act of framing begins with answers to the questions who? what? how? why? (and perhaps when?). To explicate these considerations more fully (see Andrews 2009c, Chapter 2, for a much fuller explication with regard to the specific matter of argumentation): 'who' concerns who is speaking, writing or composing as well as (crucially for framing and rhetoric) who is being addressed. 'What' is the substance of the communication; 'why' is the justification and rationale for the act of communication and the choice of particular forms; and 'how' is the technical dimension. Once these four considerations are worked out, attention can turn to the relations between them. This is where visual/graphic representation will help develop the argument further and with more (albeit, simplified) clarity.

Whereas Kinneavy (1971) operated with a triangle, the three points of which denoted the speaker/writer/composer, the audience and the 'substance' of the message, the model of framing in the present book starts with a rectangular frame in order to give it four points of reference:

These four points incorporate the three of Kinneavy's triangle (who?, to whom? and what?) but add a fourth: how? The addition of a technical category makes clear the fact that the proposed model is a pedagogic one: it is not just concerned with descriptions of discourses, but also with the *art* of how those discourses are brought into being and improved. The rectangular shape is immaterial. What is important is that it constitutes a light and easily memorable frame. Composing that finds its centre of gravity in the top left-hand corner will be driven by the composer, and may emphasize his or her presence in the work. For example, autobiographical or lyric writing would find itself primarily in this quadrant of the rectangle. Works that are audience-focused – like

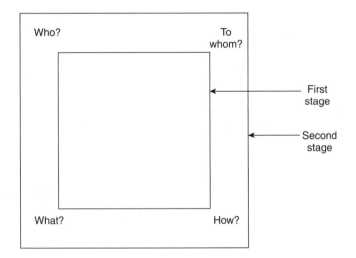

Figure 7.1 First stages in a model of framing.

speeches to elicit action or a change in ideological position, arguments (on the whole) and series of questions that are genuinely exploratory (as in counselling sessions) – would tend to find themselves in this corner of the rectangle.

These tendencies for particular types of composition to find themselves in particular quadrants of the frame are interesting in terms of genre theory, but should not divert us from the point of the framing, which is to gauge the best (most functional, most elegant, most appropriate) approach to the rhetorical demands of the situation. They also tend to divert us towards concrete entities like text-types, rather than to the act of composition itself. One of the advantages of a framing approach such as this is that it provides a neat theoretical/ practical way of representing the text in relation to its context(s). Put crudely (the subtleties of the case will be explored in subsequent chapters), the text is inside and the context(s) are outside the frame. Such a division allows for a clear distinction between text and context(s). The emphasis on contexts will be discussed in full later in the chapter.

A further advantage of the framing approach is that it naturally allows hybrid combinations of existing genres and text-types according to the needs of the situation. Furthermore, there is no specification in framing and rhetoric as to the modes and media of communication, hence allowing multimodal (e.g. speech, visual communication, writing etc.) and multimedia (e.g. film, computer screens, TV, radio, mobile phones etc.) composition, transmission and reception.

We can depict the relation of text to context in the addition to the emerging model shown below (Figure 7.2).

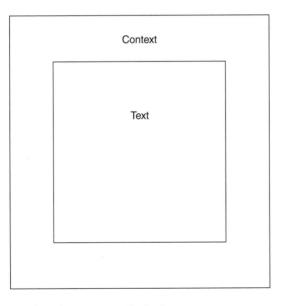

Figure 7.2 Text inside and context outside the frame.

What about the 'why?' of communication? This meta-consideration is often the starting point for communication: '*I* need to convey *x* to *y* for a particular *reason* or *purpose*'. The logic follows: 'therefore I need to use particular selections from the repertoire of communicative possibility'. The motivation(s) for communication are complex, but here is a simple example where communication was not particularly successful and needed to be re-thought. My wife and I were coming up to our thirtieth wedding anniversary, and happened to be holidaying in the place where we were married. I suggested I'd like to take her out to dinner on the actual evening of the anniversary, so might need to book a restaurant in good time. She had already had other ideas: that we might take a walk, climb a mountain, take a swim – in any case, something more improvised, less formal. The way I communicated this (the first time any utterance has occurred between us on the matter) may have come over as too much of a *fait accompli*, and certainly was mooted as an idea without prior discussion, so my half-formed plan went against her half-formed plan. It led to a small breakdown in communication, a minor 'stand-off'. There were contextual reasons why the stand-off might have occurred, but rhetorically – and in the frame chosen for the communication (late on a Sunday night before a complex working week) – it did not work. If we had (as we did soon after) discussed the possibilities, worked out a compromise and got on with the business of day-to-day living and communication, the rhetorical (framed) moment would have been simpler, more constructive, more positive. Contextual factors are complex: some immediate and evident, like too much planning in one day, planning too far in advance and too precisely, personal differences in attitudes towards planning; others subconscious and hard to define: tensions about family/personal commitments in the place we were to holiday; other matters bearing upon the visit as a whole; financial considerations etc. In the end, of course (why did not we see this at the time?) it was possible to plan *and* improvise, to eat *and* walk/swim.

The 'why?' of communication is not often considered, and yet it has direct bearings on the success of communication. If there is a tension between what is inside the frame (the textual elements and cohesion of those elements) with what is outside the frame (the context(s)) there will a problem. In most cases the why does not have to be made explicit, but when there is such a problem it needs to come to the forefront of attention so that the rhetorical problem can be solved through a re-framing alignment.

Text and context relate in other ways. In the following development of the model, each 'quadrant' of the central frame links to issues which are part of the context. We can also distinguish between matters of immediate local context on the one hand, and those of a wider set of contexts on the other.

The wider contexts that inform personal, local and immediate contexts and the text itself are social, political and temporal contexts. These wider contexts are akin to Toulmin's (1958/2003) concept of backing – perhaps the most difficult of the elements of his theory of argument. For Toulmin, 'backing' meant

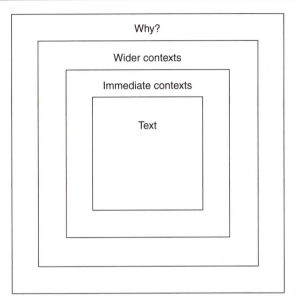

Figure 7.3 The distinction between immediate and wider contexts.

the sets of values, assumptions, *mores* and other aspects of positioning that underpinned the 'warrants' for the connections between propositions and evidence in different fields. In terms of the framing, these aspects of the wider contexts in which communication takes place are similar, though not applicable in the same way to disciplines and fields of enquiry. Whereas Toulmin's theory takes argument and argumentation as its focus (and so the elements of the model work towards testing the soundness of arguments in particular fields) the aperture of the present book is wider, concerning itself with a pedagogical approach to composition and reception in the particular field of English and literacy development. What constitutes an *argument* in this particular field is only part of the picture. However, the wider contexts bear upon the immediate context and the text itself in a number of ways; through the history of the genres that are used; through the history of the people that are engaged in the exchange; through the socio-economic and political contexts of the time; perhaps also through geographical issues of space. Issues of time (the 'when?' of the originally conceived list of questions that were important to rhetoric and framing) can be raised within the consideration of wider contexts: both in terms of how history shapes discourse, and in the judgement of timing in the exchange of particular communications.

In wider contexts, the question of 'why?' can be raised again, as its answers help to determine the broad approach to the matter of communication. As suggested above, such questions of rationale often include unconscious or subconscious issues of a psychological nature as well as social, economic and political issues of a more evident and tangible nature. There is no preference, in a model of rhetoric and framing, for a psychological over a sociological/social practice approach to discourse, or vice-versa. These are seen as dimensions of the wider intellectual context bearing upon the immediate contexts and textual choices that composers and audiences are informed by. The focus of rhetorical and framing studies is squarely on the arts of discourse. But such a focus raises one last question for this particular chapter: what happens to process theories of composition in a rhetorical/framing approach?

The answer is that the processes of composition and reception will be determined by where one starts on the model. For a designer of multimodal communication, the attention is focused on the inner textual box, informed by considerations of the contextual frames; he/she will go through processes that include how one mode operates with another, what their respective positioning is, whether one is foregrounded over the other etc. For a gestalt composer (in whatever modes and media) the ultimate starting point (though he/she might not actually begin the process of composing there) will be a holistic considera-tion of the expression of self in relation to the world and the demands of com-munication within it. For an immediate contextualized conversation between two people, the starting point will be negotiations at the level of the immediate context, informed not only by the wider contexts in which the conversation is to take place, but also by the available textual resources. 'Process', therefore, is a matter for the whole model, not just for one aspect of it. The distinction between 'process' and 'product' can be maintained within a theory of rhetoric and a framing model in that the former is concerned with the 'how?' corner of the initial textual frame; but as with all other elements of the model, the impli-cations run throughout the whole model and are interconnected with all the other elements. Process is thus inseparable from the framing and creation of a product, while at the same time being a constituent part of the model as a whole and distinguishable as such.

Chapter 8

Zooming In
Framing in Practice

What do the preceding chapters imply for the practice of English in elementary, middle- and high-school classrooms, and for the future of English studies at further and higher education levels? The framing of assignments, the place of writing in the classroom, the way texts are composed and the way they are 'read' will all be addressed. As well as setting out what might be done, this chapter will cite and demonstrate examples of what has been done. It will provide a colourful and generative set of ideas for use in the classroom, with an invitation to build on these in original ways.

Introduction

Framing and re-framing happens all the time in English lessons. Consider the following lesson. In a school in almost any country, a teacher enters the classroom, or the students enter a classroom where the teacher is waiting. The teacher has a short story – let's say Doris Lessing's 'Through the Tunnel' – to read to the students. Following the reading, there is discussions in pairs and then in small groups about the story. The students are then asked to write in silence for 10 minutes about an occasion in their own life in which they pushed the boundaries and/or were in danger. They complete the piece of writing for homework.

There are many ways in which the simple lesson described here can be made more complex. What is described above could take about an hour of lesson time, and yet the short story is so rich it could form the basis for a week's or even six weeks' lessons: on danger, on taking risks, on the experience of holidays, on adolescence, on the short story form, on Lessing, on the relationship between narrative and film etc. In other words, in curriculum planning terms, the possibilities are many, if not endless.

But in terms of the framing and re-framing in the one hour lesson itself, the picture is equally rich. First, consider the context of the lesson. The lesson is taking place in a classroom in a school. The school has a social context in a particular geographical area, and its clientele will determine the nature and conditions for learning (the linguistic profile of the students, their predilection for fiction, the experiences they bring to a particular piece of fiction).

For example, some students may have experience of swimming on beaches in the Mediterranean or other parts of the world; some may not. The school may be located in a far northern or southern part of the world where the temperatures never reach the level that allows the languid summery swimming described in the story. The school may also have an ethos that will have a bearing on the reading of this particular short story: it may, for example, see fiction as central to the experience (a right, and a rite of passage) for all its students; it may, on the other hand, allow only the most linguistically proficient students the chance to hear and read fiction of this kind. Despite the accessibility of the prose style in 'Through the Tunnel', some schools may see the story as too 'high' and too 'difficult', culturally, for some of their students. Furthermore, it may be a school which forbids the exploration of fiction of this kind, with its physical, visceral nature.

Within the frame of the school is the frame of the classroom. The lesson described is likely to be in a secondary or high school. The particular classroom might be an English classroom lined with books, posters, artefacts and other objects that provide a climate for learning of a particular kind. Or it might be a 'soul-less' room, or one that is anathemic to the reading of short stories. The desks might be arrayed in serried ranks, or in clusters; the numbers of students may range from a handful to over a hundred.

Into the frame of the particular classroom in a particular school come the teacher and students, each with their own backgrounds, sensibilities and expectations. The lesson is also framed in time: this could be an early morning lesson, or one in the later afternoon when the students are tired. But the fact that the teacher has chosen this story to read with his/her pupils is significant. He/she thinks that the story will mean something to the students; provide them with an experience that is valuable personally and educationally; might provide them with a means via which to produce work for assessment. The choice is heavily framed, deliberate, conscious.

So much for the contexts in which the experience sits. What about the story itself? There is a strong element of framing within the text. A boy is on holiday with his mother. He appears a little bored, distant from her. He finds himself watching some local boys diving off a rock into a pool and then disappearing for a while, emerging from the water breathless and triumphant some distance away. He works out that there must be a tunnel through the rock. Summoning up courage, and after an attempt or two, he succeeds (not without difficulty) in swimming through the tunnel. He returns to his mother, a changed person. She is concerned about him, but recognizes he has undergone some kind of *rite de passage*. The core experience described in the story is thus framed by the ambivalent yet cosier relationship with the mother. There is a host of nuances in the text that make it a rich multi-levelled read.

The fictional work itself is highly framed, as we have seen in discussions of Pavel in the previous chapter. The story is an engine for transformation. If you were reading it on holiday, or in your own home, the transformation would be personal, emotional, mental. But in the classroom, the transformations are more programmed, more explicit. The experience of listening to or reading the story is *re-framed*, in the example I have given above, first as discussions in pairs ('Talk with each other about experiences like holding your breath, or in which you felt some kind of challenge or were in some danger'), then in small groups ('Re-tell the story to each other in sections'). Most obviously, the story is re-framed as a new story or autobiographical work in which the students are asked to write their own version of such an experience. If the lessons were to expand to a series of lessons, the experience of the story could be re-framed in many different ways: as a short film, as a new short story, as a playscript, as a flashback from the point of view of an old man reflecting on the key experiences of his youth etc.

The example above is a simple one, but it reveals a great deal of framing and re-framing in even the most conventional of English lessons. The re-framing that is a result of the lesson design is more than a device to bring about learning; the act of re-framing by the students *is* an act of learning. Learning, in such a context, is a re-formulation of what is given; it is not so much the discovery of new (public) knowledge by private selves, but more the re-configuration of knowledge via i) making it one's own and ii) re-shaping it accordingly. These terms of re-configuration, re-formulation and re-shaping are all aspects of what the present book calls 're-framing'.

It could be argued that all subjects across the school curriculum ask the students to re-frame, and do so for much of the time, both at primary- and secondary-school levels. However, there is a particular focus to the re-framing in literacy and English lessons. The framing in these lessons is highly conscious of the form in which meaning is expressed. This is not just linguistic form, but includes expression and the making of meaning in all modes and via a number of media. In the example above, students are asked to take a story (in words) and re-cast it as an autobiographical piece in words. If they were asked to re-work the short story as a radio play, to present a newspaper feature (with photographs) on the events of the story or to film it, they would be switching modally – what Kress (2003) and Kress and van Leeuwen (2001) call 'transduction', i.e. from one mode to another. We must also remember that transductions of this kind are usually from hybrid forms into other hybrid forms – it is more rarely the case that modes are 'mono', especially if we take implication into account.

Let us push further the question of what is going on when a student transforms a text from one state to another. The re-framing is conscious, deliberate and a 'making new' of material that has existed in a different format. Usually, the student is asked to cast the material into a format, a genre that is already well-established in the school repertoire: an autobiographical account, another story, a poem, a radio play, a newspaper article. Thus the students learn the new forms while at the same time having some ownership of the process of transformation (the learning process) itself. The process is intensely practical or practice-oriented, and at the same time – if it is well carried out – enjoyable, satisfying, educational.

What has been described above is a very simple English lesson: one, indeed, that could have been taught in the 1960s as well as in the present decade. What framing theory provides is a rationale and a practical framework within which the transformations and activities of English can be unified and made sense of. Once that theory is in place, English can be defended more readily within the curriculum and the possibilities of new lesson design can be explored, safe within an overall model of the subject. To repeat the basic principle: framing and re-framing happen much of the time in literacy and English lessons. They are fundamental to English because re-framing, in particular, is what English teachers actually *do* with text in a largely untheorized way. They do not always bring the framing and re-framing to the attention of their students, but my argument in this book is that they should, not least because framing offers an intensely practical solution to the business of composition and interpretation in classrooms. The fact that framing is theorizable only strengthens its value for English and literacy curricula, and for teachers who need a rationale for their planning and teaching.

Queneau

The example used above to introduce the business of framing and re-framing in English is a conventional one. Many English teachers will have designed lessons like this, and will recognize the literary-based permutations that are involved.

The book now turns to a more creative and unusual example that is made possible by a theoretical lens of framing and re-framing in the teaching of literacy and English. In 1947, Editions Gallimard in Paris published Raymond Queneau's *Exercises de style*: it was translated into English as *Exercises in Style* for publication in 1979. The book presents a simple story about a man travelling on a commuter bus in Paris and needing a button sewn on the lapel of his over-coat. It is a disarmingly simple, if not inconsequential story. The *raison d'être* of the book, however, is that the story is told 99 times, always in a different style. The styles range from notation, precision and animism to alexandrines, official letters and mathematical. Rather than reproduce examples from the book here, I will generate a new story and re-frame it in different ways. There is no ur-story, or template, so let us start with the idea framed in notation style (and for the purposes of demonstration, each entry is shorter than in the Queneau volume):

> A street in a busy city. A woman is fixing a puncture on her bike. Passers-by stop and offer advice. Not all the advice is helpful. A man in a fluorescent cycling jacket stops his bike and offers some practical help. Together they attempt to fix the puncture but fail. The woman abandons the project. She hails a taxi, puts her bike inside it, and gets inside too. The man is left on the kerbside. He looks round and realizes his bike has disappeared. He thinks it has been stolen.

This is not much of a story. But it provides the kernel of a narrative that can be adapted and re-framed in many different ways. First, for example, as an official letter:

> Dear Sir or Madam
>
> I wish to report an incident that took place on the corner of Herbrand St and Guilford Street on the morning of 14 September 2012 at about 10.45 a.m. While stopping to assist a woman with a bike repair, I left my bicycle propped against a railing. When I looked for my bike after the woman had gone, it had disappeared. There were no witnesses, but I am sure it was stolen.

Second, in a negative pessimistic register:

> No point in having a bike, really. They get nicked all the time in London. You're riding along and a puncture is waiting for you. It happens. Nothing anyone says is any help. Even men who come along thinking they know it all can't fix them. Anyway, fixing punctures never works and is futile. The best thing to do is abandon the effort. You can't get a taxi when you need one, either. But here comes one – a miracle. Oh, I saw the man who tried to help me get his bike nicked. Typical.

Third, metaphorically:

> The street pulsates like a heart. In some obscure part of the blood system, a blockage: a splinter is removed but the body deflates. Various opinions are sought, then a doctor arrives. He tends to the wound, but it is hopeless. The patient and her life support are put in a taxi which, like an ambulance, sets off at pace. The doctor is left, his own life support dangerously missing.

And so on. Further styles that Queneau uses are opera English, 'Poor lay Zanglay' (the English translation has 'For ze Frrensh'), Spoonerisms, abusive, tactile, alexandrines and reported speech. It can be seen that the variation in style (an umbrella-term) includes exercises in genres, styles, registers, attitudes, arbitrary patterns (e.g. permutations by groups of 2, 3 and 4 letters), dialects, accents and rhetorical figures. I cannot resist one further variation, in (mock) free verse:

> The street.
> Its hard pavements and glass shards.
> She is punctured, the bike that was once
> one with her
> inert, separate;
> it burdens her.

No movement from passers-by.
A solitary Samaritan is no use;
the world whizzes by
including a taxi
whose interior beckons her.

The Samaritan is lost.
His bike de-materializes.
He stands,
a new victim
of the hard pavements and glass shards
of the street.

What kinds of re-framing are taking place, and what do they mean for English and literacy practices in schools? What are the pedagogical advantages of such an approach?

Each time the text is re-framed, a different kind of composition and a different way of reading is implied. Even in the barest and (seemingly) simplest of accounts, as in the notation offered above, there is a framing taking place and an expectation established. From 'experience', and/or from an observed scene, an initial framing takes place that separates the elements of the experience from the surrounding detail, from the continuous flow of existence in the world. Such a selection is a narrative schema that sees the event as constituted by a beginning, middle and end; by a visual framing (like a short film); and by the limits of the aperture that is used to select the constituent details. It is *re-tellable*, or rather tellable for the first time, as a story. Narrative is one of the key ways in which experience can be organized, packaged and framed. The narrative *selects* elements of continuous experience that together form a unity, and which suggest something significant and salient about experience that is seen to be reportable. How is 'significance' determined? By what is different, by what stands out in a life, by what is 'remarkable'.

Once that initial framing takes place, it is realized in the language of a mode: visual, verbal, aural, sculptural, mathematical and combinations of these, and in a particular medium (print, film, photograph etc.). Its first realization may be in note form, or it may move directly into an achieved form or genre (in the sense of genre as text-type rather than as social action). But it is always re-framable.

Pedagogically, the exercise inspired by Queneau is valuable for a number of reasons. First, the individual texts are short (it helps if they are no more than 100 words) and so are not as daunting to the student as a longer piece. The actual counting of words, at a later point in the composition, actually concentrates the mind on the particular words, and editing can take place to improve the composition. Second, the exercise of re-framing in a different style, mode or other category is an exercise in transformation. Referring back to what was suggested earlier as a core action in learning, *transformation* was key to the conception, because it involved the changing of a number of elements, reflecting a change in the framing of the work and a re-conception (mentally, cognitively). Furthermore, because the transformation resulted in another new work, a new framing is established – complete with notions of unity within the frame. Third, the exercise is fun. I have used it with primary/elementary school-children as well as with postgraduate students. The discipline of re-casting an existing text in your own words, in a number of different styles, can be liberating for a class: pairs, for example, can each be given two versions to create, and make up a third one of their own choice. Drafts and finished examples can be shared by reading them aloud or semi-performing them. Finished works can be collected and published. For example, primary/elementary students can be given tasks like 'Tell it from a dog's point of view', 'Tell it so it breaks all the [socio-conventional] rules', 'Tell it backwards'. Postgraduate students can be asked to summarize the plot of a play or a historical tract or any 'sub-body of knowledge' as the blurb of a novel, the brief for the design of new product, a satire or a cross-examination. Finally, it lends itself to drafting and editing. All the time, there is close attention to language, and there is no reason why multimodal resources cannot be used to create hybrid texts, photographs, short films, photo essays, soundworks or radio plays.

Re-framing in Curricular Design in Literacy and English Lessons

If we move up a level from lesson design to the design of, say, a six-week unit of work for a literacy or English class, we can see again how framing and re-framing operates. Such units can take the form of thematic, literary, linguistic, filmic, multimodal, functional or other categorization. Having used a Lessing short story and a book by Queneau so far as examples, let us move to a different principle of curricular design in literacy/English: autobiography. The advantage of such an approach is that it can be interpreted at different stages in young people's development, and indeed returned to recursively throughout education. Building on what was suggested about the framing of 'continuous experience' in the last section, autobiographies tell the story or stories of a person's own life – however, they can also be *projected* and imagined autobiographies as though you are in the shoes of someone else.

Autobiography assumes the operation of selective memory to incidents, state of feeling and being, relationships and self-awareness and self-understanding in a person's life. The operation of memory itself is a framing act which again uses narrative or particular sounds, phrases, images to capture or suggest a nexus of experience. Significance is a complex matter of identifying the salient, not only as a matter of difference but as a way of preserving the most important elements in a remembered life. These might be subconscious, but an autobiography will raise them to the level of consciousness to be displayed, clarified and (if necessary) resolved.

So, a skeletal design for a six-week unit of work could work as follows:

- use of the 'memory chain' device to elicit memories that are important
- sustained writing from salient points on the memory chain, linking parts of the chain together if they seem connected
- an emphasis on a language autobiography, or a visual one, or both
- working towards a finished product, e.g. a published autobiographical account, a short film, a radio presentation
- reading others' autobiographies or extracts from them
- composing an annotated bibliography of autobiographies.

In general, how is this six-week unit of work conceived/framed? It weaves the personal/autobiographical strand into published accounts by others. It uses a writing heuristic (teaching device) that draws out the main motivational elements for writing and gives pupils and students a start in their writing, a motivational wellspring from which to draw. It offers a range of modes and media for expression. It suggests publication, or at least a sharing of texts with others in the class to suggest a trusted audience, but also to provide a community of enquiry for what is likely to be a largely individualistic exercise. The framing of the unit thus encapsulates much that is distinctive in English: the combination and exploration of the private and public relationship; composing; reading and responding; and exploration of ways of composing.

Specifically, the 'memory chain' is a well tried and tested heuristic in eliciting writing. I first experienced it with the New York City Writing Project in the 1970s. It involves using sensory cues around the room or outside the window of the classroom to trigger a memory. That memory is written down in notated form. It is used as a trigger to another memory which is also notated, and joined to the first one by an arrow. This rapid process of association goes on for two or three minutes, with the brakes on automatic memory taken off as much as possible to allow the process of association to bring up the subconscious. Care must be taken to ensure that if a student is finding it difficult to undertake this exercise – either because he/she is 'blocked' and cannot release the brakes, or, conversely, by releasing the brakes has brought up memories that are difficult and/or upsetting – a technical or pastoral solution is found, which involves an escape from the exercise or a sensitive guiding through it. Once the chain is complete, students can be asked to share their experience, re-telling the chain and reflecting on the processes of memory that created it, in pairs and then as a whole group. It is always good if the teacher participates as an equal in this exercise.

Once the first phase of the memory chain exercise is complete, students are then asked to focus on a particular part of the chain that seems important to them, and to see if any other parts of the chain, through a process of association, could be linked to it. They are then asked to write – quickly, without concern for spelling or punctuation, for 15–20 minutes. I find that every group I have worked with on this exercise writes freely, in silence and usually at length – even groups that are talkative for most of the time. Following that intense period, there is a more relaxed one of sharing work with a partner again, with listening to a reading of the work to date and asking questions like: 'What made you focus on this particular memory?', 'How could you develop the piece further?', 'Are you happy with what you've written so far?', 'Is it in the form you think best suits the content?' etc. In other words, these are eliciting questions that do not make a judgement on the piece (e.g. 'That's great' or 'That's totally incomprehensible') but draw out the writer further, connecting him/her to his/her intentions and motivation to write. The writers are then invited to share some of their work with the group as a whole (again, it's good if the teacher puts him- or herself on the line) before being asked to work further on the piece, either in editorial mode or to continue in the same first draft vein. This approach to beginning writing can provide enough ideas to fill a six-week period, and set the autobiographical journey off to a powerful start. As a framing device, it is a classic of framing and re-framing because it starts with very little except stored up memory. It investigates the processes of memory, the processes of writing; and at the same time asks the student to frame and re-frame the work. Furthermore, it oscillates between individual work, pair work, small group work and whole-class work; between speech and writing; and it sets the foundation for multimodal work, if desired (the use of photographs could be a generative part of the whole work). It has the added advantage of tilling the ground, preparing it for the reception of autobiographical works by others that will be read during the course of the six-week unit.

Autobiographical composition of this kind need not manifest itself only in writing, though writing – like drawing with a pencil in the visual mode – is a fundamental ground on which other modes can be built. Nor does the memory chain need to take verbal form. It could equally be a chain of photographs, a mind-map, a short film resurrected from the past, an object or series of objects that are significant – or even a map. One of the most commonly used current forms for autobiographical expression, and as a basis for other kinds of composition, is the blog.

The emphasis has so far been on the productive side: the creation of a written, spoken or other form of composition. But a six-week unit could also incorporate annotated bibliographies of relevant reading – both other auto-biographies but also biographies. The latter do not tend to delve into the inner lineaments of experience, but they could. What both autobiographies and biographies tend to do is focus on key moments and their significance. Each time a work or an extract from a work is read, there is comparison in the mind of the reader/listener with his/her own work. The frames that are discovered and used in the composing of one's own work are aligned with, compared with, sometimes reconciled and sometimes not with the frames that others have used. Learning through the adoption of others' frames, and from resistance to those frames, is a fruitful exercise.

Finally, in terms of curriculum design, such a six-week unit of work could turn into something much longer. I have deliberately kept the design at a general level, and individual teachers will want to adapt it to their own circumstances, but suggestions for inclusion in such a unit include:

- Gorky, *My Childhood*
- *The Diary of Anne Frank*
- *The Great Gatsby*
- *Catcher in the Rye*
- Michael Rosen's *Sad Book*.

Another approach to autobiography is via 'language autobiography'. A unit of work or a briefer engagement with the topic can be framed by asking 'What is the history of your own language development?' and with cues like 'What languages, dialects and accents do you speak?', 'What were the key points or turning points in your linguistic development?' A number of issues arise: that of migration is one, with many individuals and their families choosing to migrate, or being forced to migrate and then take up different languages. Another is the range of languages offered in the schooling system, and whether that offer is made at age 7, 11 or later. Linked to the matter of migration is the relationship between language, dialects, accents and politics.

Language autobiographies can be framed as oral exchanges that take up a lesson or two; or they can be extended to include oral, written, visual (e.g. photographic) and other modes and take up six weeks or longer as a major project. The framing of the personal and individual idiolect within learning communities like families, education systems, countries of nationhood and residence is a compelling activity. As well as the individual gains that can accrue, such a project tends to create deeper understanding and stronger ties between members of a group or class (see Li 2005 for an example of a language autobiography, critically examined).

Re-framing the English and Literacy Curriculum as a Whole

'English' and 'literacy' have been used in the book so far as though they are synonymous. However, 'English' is a curriculum subject whereas 'literacy' is a social practice. Earlier in the book, the narrow and wider definitions of literacy were presented, with 'the ability to read and write' as the narrow dictionary-like definition on the one hand, and the following on the other:

> firstly, the scope can be expanded so that written language becomes written language and graphical or pictorial representation. Secondly, the skill can be treated as social, rather than psychological; in this view literacy is the ability to operate a series of social or cultural representations.

Since sets of expectations and norms differ depending on the situation, the social view of literacy entails a number of different 'literacies'.

(Andrews 2004, p.2)

To extend the understanding of literacy yet further, Barton and Hamilton's definition (1998) in the opening to their book *Local Literacies* is helpful:

Literacy is primarily something people do; it is an activity, located in the space between thought and text. Literacy does not just reside in people's heads as a set of skills to be learned, and it does not just reside on paper, captured as texts to be analyzed. Like all human activity, literacy is essentially social, and is located in the interaction between people.

(p.3)

Putting aside the debate about whether 'literacy' or 'literacies' is the best term to use (the existence of both suggests a dynamic relationship between a single generic entity – an idea of literacy – and the actual diverse social practices of language use – by using 'literacy' in this book I imply both) it is helpful to have 'literacy' as a counterpoint to 'English'. Why? The social practices of literacy help teachers and students in English classrooms to remember that their focus on language, literature and communication on other modes and media is intimately connected to communication outside school: in families, on the street, on the Net and elsewhere. 'English' in schools and classrooms is a part of that complex social practice, with its own history and variations, its power relations, its hegemonies and problems (pedagogical, political). English as a school subject is fraught with political baggage. It is a curriculum term used to identify a set of assumptions, ideologies and practices in schools across the world: as the space where the English language is taught to those for whom it is a foreign, second or additional language. But it is also a world language where agency for it use is owned by people across the world, not just by those in England or the USA or the 'West' (see Brutt-Griffler 2002).

At the macro-level, then, what kinds of framing take place? How can they be understood and, if necessary, changed? In England, to take one example, there is a distinction between the National *Curriculum* which enshrines the entitlement and the statutory framework of targets for performance in subjects; and the National *Strategies*, which set out how to get from A to B.

In understanding the nature of the National Curriculum in English, it is important to understand, first, that before the Education Act of 1988, there was no national curriculum. The National Curriculum emerged in the late Thatcher period from a number of sources and drivers: among them, the need to identify and measure progression in students' performance; the need to unify curriculum practice across the country so that student and family mobility was not compromised; a desire by government to establish and raise standards in literacy in competition with other countries and nations worldwide, principally for economic reasons. Other reasons for the creation of a National Curriculum were 'to establish an entitlement' for all students, irrespective of background; and to promote public understanding: "a common basis for discussion of educational issues among lay and professional groups, including pupils, parents, teachers, governors and employers" (DfEE/QCA 1999a, p.13).

A heartening statement on the values, aims and purposes of the National Curriculum includes, at the end, a key statement with regard to the present book and the state of English curricula at the end of a period of target-driven assessment-driven curricula worldwide: "the curriculum itself cannot remain static" (ibid.). The statement goes on:

> [The curriculum] must be responsive to changes in society and the economy, and changes in the nature of schooling itself. Teachers, individually and collectively, have to reappraise their teaching in response to the changing needs of their pupils and the impact of economic, social and cultural change. Education only flourishes if it successfully adapts to the demands and needs of the time.
>
> (ibid.)

The challenge of re-framing the English curriculum in response to this statement, particularly in the light of changes in the economy, in society and in schooling itself in the last two decades, is considerable. A first step is to identify the problems with the original conception of a national curriculum; and then to come on later to a consideration of the national strategies, though less time will be spent on these as the principal focus is on curriculum design and the existing framework in English and literacy.

Problems included the designation of the curriculum as 'national'; the nature of the assessment system that was imposed upon the curriculum; the internal nature of the curriculum balance within English itself; and the lack of a unifying theory or ideology to underpin the curriculum.

The National Curriculum, as conceived in the late 1980s, was never *national*. If we take the nation to be the United Kingdom, the National Curriculum only applied to the countries of England and Wales (Scotland and Northern Ireland have their own education systems). Soon after the establishment of the National Curriculum, the assessment system was designed, moving through ten levels from age 5 to 16, with progress expected in a linear, stepped manner at roughly the same stages as the maturational progress of students. (The ten levels were reduced to eight when the last two years of compulsory schooling, 14–16, were designated as the domain of the General Certificate of Secondary Education – GCSEs – rather than the top two levels of National Curriculum performance.) The linear stepped nature of the assessment system was not sensitive to learning or developmental progress and in itself has become part of the heavy machinery of high-stakes testing at 7, 11, 14 as well as in public examinations at 16 (those at 14 in English and other key subjects have recently been abandoned by the UK Government as a result of the system collapsing in on itself through inefficiencies in marking). Within the English curriculum itself, as conceived in the late 1980s, there is identification of programmes of study in Speaking and Listening, Reading and Writing. The first two are not given as much curricular space as the second two; and although the first two 'skills' are reciprocal, the second two are not seen as mutually developing alongside each other, and so there is a compartmentalization of the English curriculum. It should also be noted that within this conception of what constitutes 'English', there are gaps. Information and communication technologies, digitization, film and new media are peripheral to the conception, even though they are central to many young people's lives in terms of communication. Lastly, and connected to the previous point, there is no underlying theory or ideology to provide unity for the subject, either at primary (elementary) or secondary (middle- and high-school) level. The two strongest influences on the English curriculum have been the literary tradition and text-based genre theory. These two approaches have not been combined well, and do not constitute a theory that will inform practice and policy. This is part of the reason that the subject English floats without a rudder in the seas of curriculum theory. For more detailed critiques of the framing of English in the National Curriculum, see Andrews 1993, 2000, 2008a and 2009b; and Andrews and Gibson 1993.

In positive mode, what is the way forward for English and literacy in the curriculum, assuming that schooling and classrooms will remain as they are, with minor variations, over the next 10–20 years? How can the field be re-framed? English has a privileged position in the curriculum. It appears to have a seat at the table of the key subjects, along with mathematics and, to a lesser extent, science. Its position is a result of the centrality of communication, not only to the rest of the curriculum, but to the world outside and beyond school. That centrality now has to be earned, rather than granted as a privilege. I will use a framing approach *per se* to address the questions. Let us start from first principles at the beginning of the second decade of the twenty-first century.

As he/she enters the larger framework of the school system at 4, 5 or 6, the child brings with him/her (I will use 'she' and 'her' in the following section for style's sake, realizing that I am conflating and thus eliding gender differences that might be at play) a communicative competence that is made up of a number of influences. The particular linguistic profile may be plurilingual. The child may have been exposed to a rich, interactive, communicative world of speaking and listening in the home, or not; she may be highly literate (in the narrow sense) already having gained differentiated knowledge of writing as a system in one or more languages; she will almost certainly have watched television and/or film and been aware, even subliminally, of the multimodal nature of communication in play, in communicative acts, and in the two-dimensional but multimodal world of screens on computers and TVs. She may have been read to, thus imbibing story and other kinds of narrative aurally; she may also have been exposed to and learnt from the relationship between images (illustrations) and words in children's stories, but more surprisingly, she may also be aware that sometimes images carry the main burden of communication and are supported by words. She will have experienced first-hand the effects of the economy and of social patterning on her family; she will also have inter-acted with her environment, whether that is a rural, suburban or urban one. She may, if her family moves around, be aware of differences, of inequalities, of shared communicative principles. She will, above all, be either aware or una-ware, to different degrees, of her emerging *place* in the dynamics of different groups. The experience of school, and of a particular classroom – and crucially, for the purposes of the present book – the experience of English and literacy within that highly framed context, will all be part of her emerging literacy. An important principle at the beginning of this exploration of framing and re-framing is to acknowledge that the child enters the school with intellectual, emotional, social, spiritual and communicative capital. There may be difficul-ties that she has encountered along the way in her pre-school life that affect her ability to communicate, directly and/or indirectly, but these should not be construed as a deficit; they are, rather, areas to build on. It follows that part of the school's responsibility as the child enters is to find out what the communi-cative profile of the child actually is. Given that communicative competence is multimodal and developed in relation to a number of different media, as well as to the spatial, personal and political environments in which the child has grown up, it will inevitably be the case that she will have strengths in some areas more than in others. Such emphases and preferences will always be the case throughout the child's education and life, but part of the responsibility of schooling and education will be to make sure that she has a working under-standing, knowledge and use of a range of modes and media, and that she knows how to combine these to best effect.

It will be evident, even from consideration of the first moments in the transi-tion from relatively loosely framed worlds to more highly framed ones in school, that the education system, its schools, classrooms and curricula and the way these are interpreted and mediated by the teacher, operate via conventions that are different from any that she may have experienced before (except, in some cases, in highly formalized religious contexts or in tight family networks). First, the classroom (let us take this particular level of framing within the school as a working frame for the moment) is a place of *simulation* and symbolization. There are other places where symbolization is a major form of communication, but the classroom specializes in simulated communication. That means that instantly language and other forms of communication operate on at least two levels: that of the classroom and that of the (tangible or intangible) worlds to which it refers. Speech, for example, goes on inside and outside the classroom; but even within the school, the corridors and playgrounds and the edge-of-school environs are less regulated, less heightened, less intensely conscious of communication than the classroom itself. The classroom is a highly framed space sociologically. Its rules and conventions for talking, writing, drawing, making and action are tighter, clearer. There are sanctions for not following these conventions. This much is true whether the classroom is in a free school or in a highly formal school or somewhere in between: the classroom space is framed to allow, and encourage, talk and other forms of communication that are intended to develop the child, and ultimately for that development to be measured against state or national standards, and against the performance of other children in that classroom.

A Model for English and Literacy

To propose a model for English and literacy in the classroom is to constrain the conception, but the value of a model is that it distils the key elements of suggested practice and also mediates between theory and practice. It is an *aide-mémoire*, a template that can be used to make sense of the whole nature of communication in the classroom and school – and which can also serve as something to challenge. The particular model offered for bringing together the various dimensions of English and literacy education is three-dimensional and rather like a Rubik's cube in its colouration and dimensionality. Each mini-cube within the block as a whole can be re-configured with the other mini-cubes to form a particular text. But it is not a puzzle, and there is no final solution to the three-dimensional jigsaw.

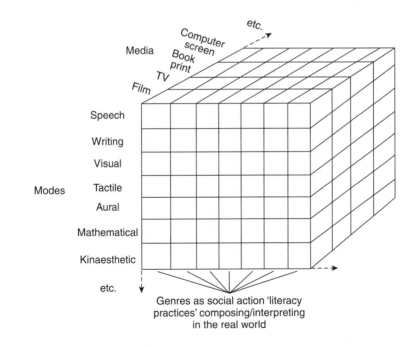

Figure 8.1 A model for English and literacy education.

Whereas the emergent model in the previous chapter took the text as its central point, the present model envisages the text as one cube within the whole picture. In effect, then, this is an English curriculum model rather than a textual one.

One axis or dimension of the model represents the range of modes that are possible for the representation of meaning within a social semiotic framework. These might include speech, writing (in various scripts), the visual, tactile, aural, kinaesthetic and other modes, like the mathematical (the 'language' of algebra). They can be 'read' (the metaphor is from writing) and/or inscribed (again, the pervasive metaphor is from writing); but simply arraying the range of modes is helpful in setting out the possibilities for communication. Multimodality would imply a combination of two or more of these modes in any act of communication. The number of modes is limited only by history and precedent on the one hand and the possibilities of human invention on the other.

Another axis/dimension is that of genres as social action: not the genre-as-text-type that has influenced curricular thinking in English for the last 20 years or so, but genre conceived more like the notion of literary practices: 'literacy [as] essentially social, and [as] located in the interaction between people'. Such an axis gives the model for English an embeddedness in the world: not only are 'real world' genres embraced within this conception, but fictional works find their place as engines for reflection, imagined projections that create parallel worlds along the real world. Such location in the interaction between people is consistent with reader response theory and, differently, with dialogic theory as expressed in the work of Bakhtin ... and the more recent notions of dialogic teaching. The number of such genres is endless, and can only be circumscribed by the plethora of human invention, activity and inter-action; but typical genres would be those that have reached some form of convention through their own evolution and use, e.g. the novel, the short story, the business letter, the report, the parable, the TV advertisement, the YouTube clip, and so on. Just as with the range of possible modes, the number of possible genres is endless (much greater than with any of the other dimensions). These genres are going to be of different shapes and sizes and, in themselves, multi-framed. A 'conference' or 'convention' for example, is a genre that can take place over a week in a city (or with multimedia help in a number of locations), in various buildings and online, with a variety of speech genres bound by different time periods – some addressed by a single person to an audience of thousands, others (at the other end of the spectrum) one-to-one conversations in bars and cafés on the edges of the convention itself. A good deal of writing might be going on, or filming, or blogs, telephone calls, or skyping. A much smaller genre would be the one-to-one conversation in a bar or café, with protocols of politeness around the buying of the coffee, the seating arrangements, the exchange of emails or phone numbers, the pledge to meet again, the beginning and end of such a schema.

One of the advantages of a dimension devoted to genre as social action is that the so-called home/school divide is seen not so much as a divide as simply two different communities in which learning takes place (cf. Rogoff 1991: "learning is an effect of community") alongside other communities. Genres do not migrate across these communities: they are differently constituted within them. The conception of genre as social action also provides a much more precise category than that of 'context' which seems to separate the textual from the contextual, and often does not specify the exact nature of that context.

Another dimension is that of media, to be distinguished from that of modes. Media are the hardware delivery mechanisms for multimodal communication. The medium could be the printed book, film, TV or the computer interface. A third or fourth generation mobile phone is a good example of a medium which itself combines a range of possible modes of communication. The inclusion of a media dimension in a model for English and literacy development obviates the need for a split between 'English' (principally linguistic, literary) and 'Media Studies' (principally TV and film) that has bedevilled the field since at least the 1970s. Always peripheral to the central curricular core of English, media education has made much more of a pitch for the centre ground in the last decade or more through the British Film Institute (specifically BFI Education) (Dickson et al. 1996, BFI 1999, 2008). Such inclusion of the various media that carry such modal and multimodal messages makes it ever clearer that 'English' is no longer appropriate as the umbrella term for the intellectual discipline and school curriculum subject. Moving image must be included in a conception of the field of communication studies that plays so central a part in the education of young people.

Four questions come to mind regarding the nature of the proposed curriculum model. First, how does it, or could it account for development? Second, what is the nature of metaphor that has been chosen for this particular model – that of the three-dimensional cube? Third, can the cube be extended to include new modes, genres and media? Fourth, are three dimensions enough to account for the complexity of the field? These questions, and the answers to them, are not unrelated.

The question of individual development within the period of schooling is complicated by maturational (naturally occurring) development in relation to *learnt* development and teaching. Without exploring the complex relationship between learning, development and teaching (see Haythornthwaite and Andrews, forthcoming; and Andrews and Smith, forthcoming) it is inevitable that learning trajectories and paths will be individualistic. Such a model as proposed above cannot, either metaphorically or conceptually, deal with development. Part of the problem is that learning development is often conceived organically, and represented by organic metaphors (growth) rather than by a cubic metaphor with its implications of structure, choice etc. Rather, what the cubic model can suggest is the total range of communicative competence that could be achieved in the course of an education. Such a three-dimensional model is an advance on previous models in that it does embrace a third dimension, and can be realized in material terms (we could build such a model). This kind of model is memorable and conceivable: it thus has the advantages of practicality, which is a key function of a model alongside its distillation of theory or theories. But a further advantage is a non-material one: the cube itself only depicts the possible relationship between the three dimensions: modes, media and genres. We have to conceive of the cube as extending potentially, in all three directions, and thus being able to embrace a wide range of categories in each dimension. There is no complete account of the 'world of discourse'(Moffett 1968/1987); only a model that allows for the description and placing (and thus analysis – see Gee 1999) of past, present and future discourses.

The last question is the most difficult: are three dimensions enough, and is there a need for a fourth and perhaps fifth dimension to complete the model? The personal individualistic learning trajectory has been discussed and cannot be accounted for in this particular model. The historical dimension (How do genres, modes and media come about and how do they evolve? How do the relationships between them evolve over time? What influences bear upon their evolution?) is imaginable and researchable/describable. It can be conceived as a fourth dimension, present in potential form within each mini-cube in the model as a whole. Bound up with the historical question are issues of economic, social and political influence upon the shape of English and literacy studies/education.

The way that these crucial dimensions – the personal and the historical – *can* be embraced within the conception that has been forwarded above is to situate the model within a theory of contemporary rhetoric. It is towards this overarching theory for communication studies that the book now moves, eschewing the terms 'English' and 'literacy' for a more all-embracing term to account for communicative acts and education in the multimodal and digital age: new rhetoric.

Part III

Re-framing the Picture

Chapter 9

Breaking the Frame
New Horizons for English

The foregoing chapters on the curriculum, on practice and on the place of framing in English are considered here in a chapter which draws out the implications for language use and study in education. Several issues will be considered: how to make space for creativity within practice that is shaped by framing; how a re-unification of practices in English will have implications for other parts of the curriculum; what the training implications are; how electronic English is making us come to terms with new conceptions of the subject and its teaching; and how English relates to rhetoric.

Introduction

We have seen in previous chapters that visual, conventional and institutional frames can be transgressed. That border-crossing or frame-breaking is partly what makes us aware of the frame itself. But the transgression of the edges of the frame means something significant, too, in theoretical terms. It suggests that the framing that has been taken for granted or used to define a space is no longer adequate to the task; something needs to be 'said' that takes us beyond the frame.

To start the exploration of frame-breaking, let us use a simple example from the visual and other arts. The Dartmoor Arts Summer School 2009 issued a small fold-out advertising brochure that used framing, multiple panels but also the taking of motifs and features across panels.

This is a typical piece of grid, multi-panelled, photographic framing with accompanying verbal text (or vice versa). At the macro-level, the verbal text on the page is framed by two visual elements: the abstracted 'textural' quotations from other photographs, used like a visual logo or motif on the left; and the six-panelled collage on the right. There appears to be some cross-over between panels in that the top two photographs in the six-panelled collection are made up of a single landscape photograph.

On the next page of the brochure (Figure 9.2), however, the framing principle is taken a little further. In this case the sequence of elements is reversed, and while the verbal text and the abstract textural motif are retained, the six-panelled element includes more subtle cross-over between the panels.

Figure 9.1 The Dartmoor Summer School 2009.
Dartmoor Arts Project.

The Dartmoor Arts Summer School 2009 is an intensive week-long programme of events and courses run by artists and aimed at anyone who has an appetite to engage with the arts and the creative process.

The Summer School brings together established and young artists, metropolitan and rural, providing a forum for experimentation and critical debate.

Figure 9.2 The Dartmoor Summer School 2009.
Dartmoor Arts Project.

Not only is there more cross-over, there is also textural/tonal variation, suggesting a much less figurative, less concrete impression of what is on offer at the summer school. Whereas the first set of images suggested a range of different arts and crafts that were available, the second set suggests that there is the possibility of inter-disciplinary work. The boundaries between the various images are transgressed, suggesting transgression is possible between the activities on offer.

Breaking Frames in English and Literacy: Preliminaries

Let us use this concrete example from advertising of an arts-based summer school to build a multi-panelled grid for English and literacy, so that we can see what the possibilities are for cross-over between the various elements. The grid that follows (Figure 9.3 in the present chapter depicts the possible elements of an English and literacy curriculum for the twenty-first century. But first, some principles need to be set out.

In a paper for England's Department for Children, Schools and Families (Andrews 2008b) I set out some elements regarding the 'productive' skills in English and literacy: speaking and composition. (In this sense, 'productive' means the act of making something; it is fully recognized that listening, reading or viewing can also be productive in the sense of making gains in understanding.)

Expression is important because it engages the self or personae and releases what may be felt and/or thought. It affords channels of communication and creates contact with others.

Articulation aims to make such communication clear. In speech terms, articulation is associated perhaps most readily with surface features like clear enunciation of utterances; more importantly, the notion of articulation ('joining') is about logical or a-logical connections between ideas, thoughts, feelings and language, in speech and/or writing. Andrews et al. (2006b), in a systematic review of research on the teaching of argumentative writing at KS2 and 3, draw attention to the need for cognitive as well as linguistic work in improving writing in this mode.[1]

With *framing* and *shaping* the emphasis needs to move from a focus on the end-products – the frames (pedagogic 'scaffolds', genres, text types, forms) and shapes that language uses and that need to be learnt – to the act of framing and shaping that is at the heart of composition (literally, 'putting things together'). Such a move will entail thinking more deeply about the early stages of composition: how ideas are formed; how they are framed; how inspirational ideas are supported by a climate for learning and development; how choices are made, early on, about the medium or media in which it is best to convey the message; how drafting and editing can be improved by critical dialogue and reflection at the deeper levels of composition (structure, voice, position, tone); how momentum and interest can be sustained; how speaking, reading and listening can contribute to the composing process in writing; how issues of design, balance and elegance ('when is a piece finished?') can be taught and learnt; and how a community of learners (speakers/writers/makers) can support such committed and high quality composing.

Ideas for writing come from speech (e.g. a story *told* can then be *written*); in response to other writing and other media; commissioned for particular purposes; and 'out of the air'. Providing a rich supporting context where a range of writing can be inspired and nurtured will require an appreciation of the written word. To develop such a climate, teachers and pupils will want to read and generate writing that gives pleasure (e.g. because it is funny, moving, well-crafted) and that makes a difference to personal lives and in the world. The early stages of the writing process – mulling an idea, developing the seed of an idea, trying various 'voices' or styles, gathering evidence via research, allowing a gestation period for the rhythm of a piece to identify itself – are important to share and discuss so that the writing process is made more evident (and thus open to discussion and development). Writing the first draft is usually a solitary act, requiring a high degree of concentration; but it is helpful to make the process public at significant stages, so that pre-writing, editing and proof-reading can play their part.

From a pedagogical point of view, techniques for improving writing will include practice in writing by the very teachers who are teaching it. In other words, English teachers will need to be *accomplished writers* in themselves, not only of literary and fictional genres but in informational and argumentative genres too. They will not only be able to produce final products in this range of genres ("Here's one I made earlier ..."), but also to reflect on and model the processes of writing in the classroom. It is probably true to say that most English teachers are already accomplished readers as degrees in English and related disciplines are principally an education in advanced reading skills in literature. Writing receives less attention.

Like all good teaching, *engagement* of the pupils at whatever age will be crucial. It is probably true to say that lesson planning has moved away from initial and sustained engagement (which is much more than stimulus) towards learning outcomes, compliance with the curriculum, and comprehensiveness. Some of the excitement may have been lost from routine teaching, so a new balance needs to be struck between meeting targets and outcomes on the one hand, and generating impetus and significant communication on the other. Too much emphasis on atomistic targets out of context tends to devalue the learning experience itself; we are more likely to attain targets if we concentrate on the substance and quality of what we need and want to do.

Following from engagement will be a much greater willingness to go into *depth* in whatever kinds of writing are being taught. This will require commitment, time and imaginative energy. It involves critical engagement on the part of the teacher with the emergent written texts of pupils *before* and *during* the compositional process as well as after it. It also requires the engagement of the pupils as thinkers, establishing in them a purpose and giving them a sense of their independent choices and voices as writers. Greater consideration to different types of planning and composition will be required, e.g. argumentative writing requires hierarchical and sequenced planning (Andrews et al. 2006b), as well as a sense of what mode(s) of communication (speaking, writing, reading, listening) is/are best for what purpose.

Dialogic teaching (Alexander 2006) will be an important element in improving the quality of interaction and thought on the part of pupils in the classroom. Dialogic approaches to teaching can support both speaking and writing, though it is not always the case that productive and purposeful talk translates directly into writing of such quality. As suggested earlier, we need to look not only at the transition from talk to writing (and vice-versa), but also at dialogic forms of writing in themselves, thus adding to the repertoire of largely monologic written forms that dominate the school curriculum and assessment regimes.

Finally, *audiences* and *purposes* need to be diversified so that communication has meaning (and is thus motivating) rather than a performance in empty or purely academic 'school genres' (Sheeran and Barnes 1991) served up for assessment. The writing across the curriculum of the mid-1970s understood this principle in its promotion of writing that made a difference in the world; such insight was continued in TVEI initiatives in the 1980s, getting English beyond the classroom.

Being *productive* in modes of language like writing and speaking can prepare the ground for advances and breakthroughs in the receptive skills – reading and listening. If the biggest gap in attainment is still that between pupils on free school meals and the rest, then one way to close that gap is to give *all* pupils the motivation, access and tools by which to express themselves, to articulate better, and to frame and shape via language within their lives and in society. Such an emphasis on engagement, production, and quality will benefit all students, and contribute to a general improvement of literacy skills in the school population at GCSE and beyond.

It has been noted above that a focused emphasis on improving writing can have direct effects on the generative relationship between speaking and writing. Recognition that we learn to develop the range and depth of our writing through its reciprocal relationship with reading, and *vice-versa*, will further strengthen the bond between the language skills. At the same time, understanding the strengths of the spoken and written verbal codes within a wider multimodal context is important in terms of contemporary communicative practices inside and outside school.

Such increased emphasis on sustained productive skills will not only benefit young people's communicative abilities; it will also make them more employable and better equipped to play their part as citizens in an inclusive society.

In addition to these productive compositional elements, we must add multimodal composition; and, as indicated above, the differently productive elements of reading, listening and viewing. Building on the models depicted in the previous chapter, which were concerned with the actual planning and design of particular works within the English/literacy classroom, and on the principles set out above, below is a curriculum model for breaking the frame of English/literacy as it currently stands.

Breaking Frames in English and Literacy: The Key Elements

Up to now, in England at least, the English/literacy curriculum has been based on the four language skills of speaking and listening, reading and writing. Even in such a simple formulation, the balance has not been right. In a literacy-driven conception of English, reading and writing are given separate prominence (thus, ironically, reducing the scope for exploiting the reciprocity between them) and speaking and listening, while seen as reciprocal, have a subsidiary place in curricular time and emphasis. While Australia and New Zealand were developing curricula that included 'viewing' as a key element, in order to embrace the visual and media arts, England continued to marginalize these key communicative elements.

Information and communication technologies have made significant differences to the way we communicate since the conception of this English National Curriculum in the late 1980s. Revisions of the curriculum in the period from 1990 to the present have not been radical, and so the curriculum has fallen behind actual social practices of communication.

The model above assumes an overarching theory of contemporary rhetoric, discussed elsewhere in the book and subjected to critique in the final chapter. Rhetoric's 'agent', framing, is the structural force behind the design of the curricular model, allowing the definition and focus but also, as I will go on to argue, the crossing of boundaries between the various elements. The model is a simple one in order to increase its applicability.

Basically, the curriculum model is concerned with communication in the current age. Its twin pillars are composition, on the one hand, and interpretation, on the other. Composition includes consideration of which media are being used to communicate: digital media, like television, computer screens and mobile phone interfaces as well as more established media like the

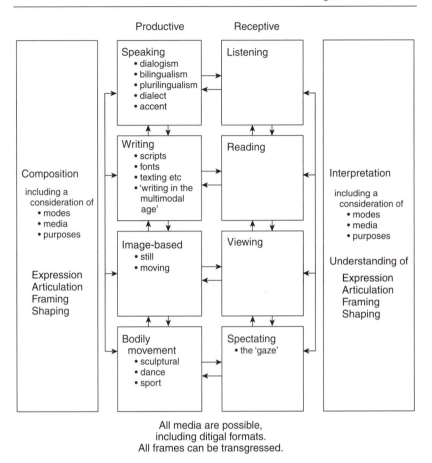

Figure 9.3 A communication arts model.

printed book, magazine and newspapers. In order to give speaking sufficient prominence in such a model, it is seen as a productive capability, like writing or image creation and manipulation. From a media point of view, speaking can be direct and face-to-face (more direct than the other modes), or via different media which literally *mediate* between the speaker and listener. Constituent elements of composition that apply to speaking, writing and other modes of composition like the visual (still- and moving-image) include expression, articulation, framing and shaping, as detailed in the previous section. A crucial element alongside these is editing, often seen as not such a creative act, but clearly the crucial creative act in the composition of a film, and much more central to the creation of writing than is generally considered. Creativity, in this model, applies to all kinds of making and not just to the fictional genres in writing.

Interpretation has a reciprocal relationship with composition. The same principles apply, except that the activity is concerned with receiving, decoding, comprehending and understanding the messages sent out in whichever media, modes and genres they take shape. Whereas psychologists tend to focus on decoding and on comprehension, the activity of interpretation requires an active bringing to bear of past enculturation, dialogic positioning in relation to the speaker/writer/composer (the 'rhetor') and stance (all aspects of framing) that are directly related to the constituent elements of composition. So receptivity to expression, articulation, framing, shaping and editing are all parts of the act of interpretation. So too are considerations of the media via which the message is relayed. A singer may be absorbed in the creation of a song (with editorial and mixing help) in a studio, but his/her composition may be received over the radio, via earphones from an MP3 player, via a CD on a sound system or as background as the receiver walks past a music store or sits in a restaurant.

If composition and interpretation are the twin pillars of the model, they are reciprocally co-evolving with digitization and attendant technological changes. In other words, it is no longer possible to conceive of a curriculum for English/literacy that is merely print-based. Between 1920 and 1990, it was evident that an English-based core subject in the curriculum was essentially book – or at least print-based. It was primarily about reading, secondarily about writing, with speaking and listening relegated to third place. Such a conception can no longer obtain. Relationships between digital new technologies and literacy themselves require a new perspective: one of reciprocal co-evolution rather than a case of new technologies coming along and having an 'effect' or impact' on an existing phenomenon, literacy (see Andrews and Haythornthwaite 2007). The new conception sees digitization as pervading communication in the twenty-first century. Indeed, even print media are now engineered digitally. What digitization means to communication, and specifically to the business of English/literacy teaching and learning – i.e. composition and interpretation – is that a myriad of media, modes, genres and forms are available to people as they communicate with each other. This myriad is the territory of English and literacy studies. Information and communication technologies (ICT) and their 'impact' on the field of English/literacy can no longer be seen as a peripheral/marginal factor. It is embedded in every type of communication other than the face-to-face oral exchange.

What is proposed for the space between the twin pillars is not *radically* different from previous curriculum conceptions about speaking and writing, though the surrounding spaces and the building itself *is* different. Hence the title of the present book. The conception of the curriculum area as a whole has been re-framed. Older frameworks have been dismantled and re-shaped.

Inside the subject are speaking, listening, writing and reading, differently configured from their positions in the curriculum to date. In addition, image-based production and image-based reception; plus physical movement in productive and receptive terms are added as elements of equal status within the 'building'.

The productive skills (if we can conceive of skills as more than mere technical competence, but rather as the development of fully-fledged capability in those areas) are thus arrayed equally as speaking, writing, image-based composition and bodily movement as communication. Let us look at these in more detail and also at the connections between them.

Speaking remains fundamental to communication and to the English/literacy curriculum. It is the mode of communication that is the most fluid, most natural (in the sense that it is a first order symbolic system) and most ubiquitous. It is also the case that, in the twenty-first century, it is likely to continue to maintain its position at the forefront of communication because of its seemingly untrained facility: most people in the world, including children, can speak at least one language (and can also use bodily movement to communicate) even if they cannot write or manipulate images. The telephone, and more latterly, Skype, have made global communication via speech a more accessible and cheaper means of communication. Speech recognition technologies, while they have not progressed as fast as might have been expected, might well replace the keyboard as the primary means by which written communication is realized. The other 'naturally occurring' aspect of speaking that needs to be taken into account in a re-thinking of English and literacy in the twenty-first century is the fact and the notion of plurilingualism. We know the majority of the world population is bilingual; many are multilingual. So any new conception of English needs to bear in mind that English as a world language (see Brutt-Griffler 2002) or, to see the phenomenon differently, world Englishes operate(s) in a context alongside other languages. Plurilingualism is a recognition that each of us has a plurilinguistic profile consisting of languages (it is good to include dialects and accents in this conception, so that the principle applies to 'monolingual' speakers too): some languages (dialects/accents) will be well developed; others may stand alongside that 'first' language in equal measure or be secondary to it; yet other languages may be known to different degrees of expertise and fluency. Some may be known better in writing; some receptively rather than productively. But essentially, it is likely to be in speaking that the range of languages is most evident. No English/literacy curriculum can continue to exist without defining itself in relation to other languages, to the students that it serves and the rich potential of exchange, comparison and cross-fertilization between English and other languages. Finally, with regard to speaking, the dialogic principle (cf. Bakhtin 1981, Alexander 2006) is most evident in spoken exchange. From this point it can be developed as a fundamental principle in rhetoric, and as a pedagogic principle (see Andrews 1995b and 2009c for an exploration of both in relation to argumentation and thinking).

Speaking relates closely to writing. To quote again from the DCSF report, *Getting Going* (Andrews 2008b):

> The relationship between speaking and writing is complex, and must be seen within the broader picture of how the language skills relate to

each other. Essentially, the relationship between speaking and writing is *generative* in that both are productive skills, and they can complement each other by directly giving rise to expression in the other. The means of communication in each case are, however, different.

The relationship between writing and reading (like that between speaking and listening), on the other hand, is *reciprocal*: in these relationships, the means of communication (e.g. print or speech) are the same, but the difference is between productive and receptive actions within the mode.

The National Curriculum in English and teaching within the National Strategies, where teacher-talk continues to dominate pupil-talk (despite efforts to the contrary),[2] have until recently (see DfES 2007) given precedence to writing and reading over speaking and listening. The latter two skills have been seen as more reciprocal than the first two, resulting in more curriculum time being given to writing and reading separately (with not enough time devoted to their reciprocity) and proportionately less to speaking and listening (which are almost always seen as 'going together') (Ofsted 2005). Often, speaking has been seen as a means to support writing and reading, rather than as an object of instruction in its own right (Cameron 2002, Myhill and Fisher 2005).

How can speaking continue to support writing, while at the same time establishing its own stronger presence in English and across the curriculum? The key is in seeing the generative relationship between speaking and writing as two-way.

First, speaking can be an important *rehearsal* for writing. Ideas can be discussed in pairs, small groups, whole-class discussion and larger forums, then distilled, translated and developed in writing. Such writing can be dialogic as well as monologic. Dialogic writing includes planning for Socratic dialogue (question-and-answer format), colloquia, playscripts and other dual- and multi-voiced text-types. Monologic writing includes the more conventional forms such as essay, story, letter and report, where translation from the multiple voices of speech to the single authorial voice of the writer can be more difficult.

Second, writing can be a *rehearsal* for speech. Individual and/or joint composition in writing can prefigure delivery in speech, as in the making of a speech, the production of an oral narrative, the composition of a persuasive case or the scripting of a (radio) play or advertisement. Speech as a product in these cases is more than mere performance: it is part of a dialogue that invites response in spoken, written and other formats. It is in such transformation between different means of communication and different genres within those means that the day-to-day practice of English in classrooms takes place.

Lesson planning and curriculum design, then, need to cater for speaking to come both before, during and after writing. Such bridging between speaking and writing will require imagination and consideration of the strengths of each skill in classroom, school and wider contexts.

The problem of insufficient *space* for sustained speaking and writing is compounded by assessment practices.

It is the case that speaking and writing are used to provide evidence of the quality of listening and reading, i.e. they are used to assess listening and reading as well as assessing themselves. The dearth of *extended* speaking and writing across the curriculum and in assessment across the curriculum may well have contributed to the relatively poor production skills of learners as they move through schooling.[3] Pupils are not being given enough opportunities and enough support or incentive to *discourse* at length. As Britton pointed out as long ago as the 1960s (Britton 1967, p.xiii–xiv) "a rough measure of [the teacher's] success in promoting the right kind of talk might well be the length of the span that can go on without word from him [sic]".

What is clear is that speaking and writing are central to learning in formal education because they afford the learner the ability to reflect, think, compose and re-arrange as well as respond spontaneously (particularly in the case of speech). Furthermore, as Meek (1983) proves, such emphasis on the productive language skills can be the key to improvements and even breakthroughs for weaker learners not only in speaking and writing themselves, but also in reading and listening as a result of increased motivation, commitment and investment in making meaning in language; and increased awareness and exploitation of the reciprocity between writing/reading, speaking/listening.

Less pedagogically, and more in terms of its function as a communication system and developmentally, speaking operates as a first order symbolic system. Learning to write comes after learning to speak, on the whole, though there have been moves to establish writing as not just a second order symbolic system (based on speech) but as a first order symbolic system in its own right. Let us consider, for a moment, what the idea of writing as a first order symbolic system means and implies. It suggests that, irrespective of speech or alongside it, writing developed as a means of communication that was self-sufficient. Marks on a cave wall or on the ground, alphabetic and calligraphic systems of written communication (though the alphabetic system is related to sound) could have meaningful communicative function without recourse to translation into, or derivation from speech. Even if we were deaf, we could use writing (in collaboration with image-making and bodily movement) to communicate the full range of meaning that could be conveyed in speech.

However, it is the transition from speech to writing and from writing to speech that makes for a rich productive connection in the developing curriculum model. Such a connection was largely absent from previous conceptions of the place of speaking and writing in the English/literacy curriculum, where the different elements were kept separate. They are different modes of communication, each with their own grammars, social functions and affordances; but they are also closely related, even in languages with non-alphabetic writing systems, and need to be explored and valued alongside each other.

Writing, then, is now seen no longer as the central productive skill in the English/literacy curriculum, but as taking its place alongside speech, image-making and bodily movement in a 'universe of discourse' (Moffett 1968) or, more appropriately for our present purposes, in an overarching rhetorical model of communication that values all the different modes equally. Writing includes everything from texting (a compressed diction based on a fuller sense of the grammar of the language) through minimal notes to letters, reports, essays, stories and other narratives – and ultimately to large-scale productions like theses and dissertations, novels and (auto)biographies. The key questions for writing, which had previously held prime position in the productive skills in English/literacy, are 'What function does writing have in the multimodal/digital age?' and 'What are its particular affordances and strengths?'

We have rehearsed the connections with speaking, particularly from a pedagogical perspective. From a multimodal perspective, writing has re-discovered a specialist function within communication. Whereas it was seen as the principal means of formal communication, with standardized versions enabling a (relatively) common diction, now writing is seen for what it can and cannot do. It is particularly good for: permanent or semi-permanent records of transactions; for enshrining long works (novels, reports, dissertations etc.) in print; formal exchanges (e.g. between solicitors); and as another form of expression ('How can I know what I mean until I see what I say [in writing]?') when spoken, visual or physical communication is not appropriate or desirable. Libraries are devoted principally to its preservation, though they are now grappling with digital storage of sound and image, if not of physicality. Indeed, libraries often have a policy of making a printed copy of anything they store digitally so that they have back-up in case the technologies that support the digitization (CD-ROMs, online storage at present) disappear. In that sense, the book and handmade paper manuscripts – complete with their illustrations – have survived and been an excellent form of deposit and archive.

Writing rarely appears in the multimodal and/or digital age without another mode alongside it, which is also the case with the other modes. Even the printed book of poems or novel has a visual and physical dimension. It manifests itself, after collective production, in a particular size on particular paper (a cheap paperback will have a different feel from a privately printed book of poems on hand-made paper) and with particular binding and covers, which may or may not contain a visual image. The text on the page, stripped down to its verbal code and allowing the words to do the work of communication, has a visual character too: the typeface and size, the fact that a poem does not run up to the right-hand edge of the page (thus suggesting concentration on the rhythm of the line, cued by its visual definition); the white space around the text.

Such genres as the poem can be identified at some distance simply by looking at the shape of the text on the page. But the more common experience is to find writing alongside images, as in newspapers and magazines and virtually all forms of popular literature. Sometimes the writing is foregrounded, as is generally the case in newspapers; sometimes it exists in tension with or complementary to images, as in magazines; and sometimes the visual takes precedence, as in *manga* and other cartoon formats. A look at a range of websites will also indicate which give written language prominence, and which do not. Their very structuration is indicative of a visual framing, within which written text or visual modes can predominate.

Visual composition includes conventional artwork; framing, taking and editing photographs; moving image work; and other two-dimensional visual design activities. It also includes three-dimensional work such as sculpture; interior and exterior architectural design; art installations; and even encroaching into the three-dimensional world of fashion design. When three dimensions are involved, or when a two-dimensional work has textural properties, the fourth element of physicality is introduced (to be discussed next in this section). An immediate objection to including visual communication in a conception of English/literacy is that the world of visual composition is already well served by Art as a school subject, and by the myriad of sub-sections of Art and Design that are available at further and higher education levels. My response is that the proposals in the present book are not challenges to the territory of Art, but that they provide theoretical justification for looking at visual communication alongside verbal (spoken and written) and physical communication. The theoretical perspective *allows* practical contiguities to be exploited and understood; and suggests, too, that in the curricular framework of schools, colleges and universities, the visual, physical and verbal arts could collaborate more on particular projects – not only on the production of plays in dramatic art, but on a more day-to-day basis in the creation of objects, the learning of skills and the development of capabilities. Framing and re-framing – the subject of this book – are more readily evident in the visual arts and continue to give shape to the forms of communication that take place in that world; they also continue to provide a metaphor for communication verbally and physically, socially and politically. And just as with writing, as mentioned in the previous paragraph, sometimes the visual is foregrounded, and sometimes it is not. It is most obviously foregrounded in catalogues of artworks, in paintings and in reproductions of artworks; but there is a productive ambiguity (a tension and/or complementarity) about genres in which the visual and verbal have equal status (advertisements, shopping catalogues, textbooks). The visual remains backgrounded as illustrations in books (unless they are foregrounded, as in some children's picture books); as addenda to verbal texts; and, in general, in newspapers.

The crucial creative act in visual work, in addition to framing and composition, is editing. This aspect of making is most obvious in film production, but the principle and the activity are evident too in the cropping of still images, in the manipulation of images, in the layering and re-layering of painting. Editing might almost be said to be an aspect of framing, but it is best seen as a more detailed re-working of elements within a frame, as well as the adjustment of the frame itself if necessary to the conception of the whole. Editing, because it generally involves cutting, re-arranging, re-working of some kind, has been seen within the romantic conception of creativity as a *secondary* activity, following the first surge of creative energy that makes the work 'out of nothing' or from the deepest self (in Yeats' terms, "out of a mouthful of air"). But editing is more centrally concerned with creation than the romantic perspective suggests. It is closely allied to selection of the elements for composition. Bakhtin in literary and dialogic theory, and Eliot and Pound in twentieth-century poetics, would all acknowledge that selecting and responding to existing cultural artefacts and utterances is an integral part of the act of creation; that a 'voice' is responding to other voices; and that composition is more a matter of the making of a mosaic than the outpourings from a clear fountain or spring.

Discussion of editing as a key creative act raises the question of *creativity* in the curricular conception that is being presented here: a conception that brings together speaking, writing, visual composition and physicality under the banner of contemporary rhetoric and, more practically, framing and composition. There have been two key points in the history of English/literacy education over the last 50 years, at least in England. One was the surge of interest in creative writing in the 1960s and 1970s, at both primary and secondary levels (and more latterly in university departments) that resulted in increased emphasis on expression; and on the 'creative' genres of poetry, prose and (to a lesser extent) dramatic writing. The second was the report *All Our Futures* (DfEE/QCA 2000) which recommended a broader infusion of creativity across the curriculum: creativity was seen to inhere in the sciences and other subjects as well as in the arts. Although that report failed to impact on the curriculum in the way it was intended (the assessment-driven target-driven ethos and practice, plus the narrowing emphasis on literacy and numeracy during the first decade of the twenty-first century continued to militate against it), it did spawn a Creative Partnerships movement, funded by the Arts Council, which has continued to breathe oxygen into the creative life of teachers and learners. Looking back, neither of these surges of interest and bursts of attention on creativity has embedded itself into the English/literacy curriculum to the extent that the curriculum can be said to be creative. Indeed the recent initiative from the Qualifications and Curriculum Authority to introduce 'functional English' at final examination level in schools is a backward step. The problem has been that both periods of interest kept creativity *marginal* to the main business of education in literacy: the first phase, because of its concentration on the fictional genres and not on the rest of the writing/composing curriculum; the second, because of its broad-based conception that was not implemented within the curriculum.

The model proposed above is inherently and potentially creative in that it emphasizes composition as well as interpretation – the putting together of elements to make something new – and does so through the four main modes of communication: the spoken, the written, the visual and the physical. Creativity inheres in the act of making and in the potential links and cross-overs between the four modes, as well as within the modes themselves.

The fourth element in the productive modes of communication is the *physical*. In its simplest state, physical and bodily communication takes place in a number of ways: again, so as not to encroach on the curriculum area of physical educa-tion, most obviously in sport. But also through bodily and facial gesture; through socio-spatial positioning (e.g. in the way we walk down a street in relation to others, or position ourselves in relation to a crowd); in dance; and so on. The connections with the other modes of communication are pervasive; only in telepathic communication can messages between people have a disembodied ethereal nature. In speech, for example, the difference between speech without bodily communication and speech with it is considerable. Renaissance manu-als of rhetoric are full of gestures that can operate independently of speech but also accompany it. Physicality manifests itself, too, in written composition in a number of ways: first, in the physical act of writing, either with a pen/pencil on paper, or in any medium, or via a keyboard. Second, through the *materiality* of literacy in paper, on screen, in print etc. (cf. Haas 1995). Third, where the visual is unavailable or impaired, through Braille and other means of link between the physical and the written. The body is also 'present' in the visual mode, through direct marking on the body (the body as work of art); through figurative art; through issues of proportion (the work's relationship to the size of the human body); and through physical imprint or impression on the work itself, both in the arts and crafts.

In partial summary, as far as the *productive* skills and capabilities are concerned, an emphasis on making and composition via the four modes of communication constitutes a re-framing of the English/literacy curriculum. It appears that the emphasis to date in literacy education has been on the recep-tive interpretational skills. Such an emphasis mirrors the dynamic of class-rooms, with teachers doing most of the talking and marshalling and directing most of the discourse; and students being, on the whole, in passive mode. What is being proposed here is a more proactive classroom, with making and composition (re-framing) at the centre of learning alongside interpretation. There are pedagogic and training implications in such a shift of emphasis. In effect, the suggestion is to make the learning space more like a studio or 'lab' and less like a formal conventional classroom where learning is conceived in terms of teaching and in talk and writing *about* knowledge.

The initial and continuing training implications for teachers of such a con-ception are that they must be able to practise what they preach. In other words, a teacher of writing must be able to write in as wide a range of forms and genres as they are hoping their students will learn. Similarly, if the argument of the previous few pages is accepted, they must be competent not only in speaking and writing (the verbal skills and capabilities) but also in the creation and use of images and in physical expression (e.g. through drama). The work of the National Writing Project in the USA (see Andrews 2008c for a research review of the case for a national writing project in the UK) has demonstrated over a period of 40 years the value of teachers' writing. The personal gains and insights into the writing process, as well as a confidence that develops in gaining command of the craft itself, pays dividends in the classroom through greater job satisfaction and professionalism on the part of the teacher, and beneficial effects on the students in terms of advancement in writing.

Exposition of the *interpretational* side of the model need not be so exhaustive, as for each of the productive modes of communication – speaking, writing, visual and physical communication – there is a corresponding interpretational dimension. The principle here is one of reciprocity: speaking implies listening, writing implies reading and so on. But there are specialist aspects of listening, reading, responding to images and to physical communication that need to be discussed.

Within the curriculum category of *listening* can be included listening to sounds, including music, as well as to the spoken voice. In a multimodal conception of communication, sounds and music are important. Their rise in importance is indicated by the increased facility and use of soundtrack on websites; the opportunity for oral and aural variation and experimentation in literacy lessons; and the ubiquity of personal listening devices like iPods and MP3 players, replacing the transistor radios of the 1960s and 1970s.

Reading is the most researched and most central (to date) aspect of literacy and of the English curriculum. Reading covers the decoding of print and especially, as far as English is concerned, of the phonemic/alphabetic code in the English language. But its wider definition embraces decoding and interpretation of visual and other modes as well as in the verbal code. The value of writing and other forms of composition are often underestimated in the process of learning to read, as the productive activities lay the ground for interpretation. In the conception that is being proposed here, reading would not have first place, or be a necessary precursor to making in written and other forms. It would simply take its place as a crucial interpretational activity alongside the others mentioned in this model, and would benefit from closer association with them.

Image-based interpretation is often found under the canopy of 'visual literacy', which has been discussed in Chapter 4. Elkins (2008) is a more recent collection of essays on the topic of visual literacy, spreading its net wide to include not only the reading of images in art history, but the application of visual literacy in the sciences and politics as well as the arts. Visual literacy, the hybrid term, needs to expanded to include the breadth of conception and interpretation posited in the present model, where the physical, written and visual can sit alongside each other in any social semiotic act of representation ('visual literacy' does not extend as far as interpreting the aural). In such multimodal creations, the links and relationships between the various modes are as important as the (seemingly) monomodal affordances. 'Visual literacy', from the perspective of a multimodal theory of interpretation, may be seen as an important hybrid breakthrough in thinking about the visual/verbal interface, but one that needs to be progressed further to take account of a wider range of modes, and of the application of multimodal analysis to the monomodal (where other modes are implied, suggested or brought to bear on the analysis).

Finally, in the list of interpretational modes, the understanding of bodily and physical presence in communication includes sensitivity to body language; sophisticated reading of facial and bodily gesture; an understanding of the materiality of communication and the effects of different degrees of materiality on the act of communication; and a sense of the choreographic in communication. The latter aspect of physical positioning and movement is a natural part of rhetorical thinking. In books on argument at school and university levels (e.g. Andrews 1995b and 2009c) I have accounted for choreographic moves in argument informed by an overarching theory of rhetoric (as opposed to logical moves). Choreography can be applied to other written, spoken and visual dimensions of communication, like narrative forms, because it provides a prosody/diction, as well as a metaphor, for how elements in a composition are articulated (joined together) within a particular frame.

Breaking Frames in English/Literacy Education: Conclusion

The above proposals map out a different conception of English/literacy in the curriculum to the one which has become the norm. The conventional model foregrounds and privileges the reading – decoding, comprehension and interpretation – of verbal text above and before all other modes of communication. It presupposes a particular form of study, in which knowledge is transmitted from teacher to learner. It also assumes that reading comes before writing, and that the English/literacy curriculum is concerned mostly with the reading/writing nexus.

The new conception embraces a wider range of modes. Within an overarching theory of the rhetoric of communication, it uses framing as a means to composition, on the one hand, and to interpretation, on the other. Between these two poles of the communicative curriculum, the modes of speaking, writing, visual communication and physical communication operate reciprocally, both in productive terms and in receptive terms. The old framework of a reading-based literacy curriculum in English is no longer appropriate, as English takes its place as one of a number of world and other languages and must therefore benefit from comparison with those languages. The division, too, between fiction and non-fiction, discussed in Chapter 8, becomes less distinctive in the field. 'English' is no longer a cultural entity based on a particular language celebrating a particular literature in a particular country. Indeed, the term itself is so laden with associations of these kinds that it can no longer be used to denote the curricular subject and university discipline that has been mooted and assumed during the present discussion. Rather, in a contemporary field of social semiotics, informed by rhetoric, 'discourse arts' is a better term because it embraces all languages, and all modes of communication.

Framing is the way to depict the new conception as well as the principal agent of rhetoric in helping students to shape the arts of discourse; but in its very shaping of the curricular field, it contains the possibility of its own re-framing according to social, political and communicative needs. It is into the territory beyond rhetoric and framing that we now turn.

Chapter 10

Panning Out
Beyond Rhetoric and Framing

The final chapter summarizes the argument of the book, explores its limitations and speculates as to the future relationship between verbal, visual and spatial languages and the business of 'getting the world's work done'. It revisits the question of the link between fiction and non-fiction, and considers other media in which this dichotomy provides a way of categorizing its modes of operation. Discussion includes theories of communication arts related to action; how language itself can be reified into action and provide the basis for further action; implications for the re-unification of rhetoric and the likely shape of future theories of communication arts; whether there is a tradition running from the Greeks to the present, and what lessons can be learnt from such a consideration; multimedia in the light of rhetoric; and advantages and limits of rhetorical theory.

Introduction

The last few chapters have moved from a consideration of how framing operates in practice in the classroom, and how rhetorical choices are made by teachers and learners to optimize learning; in the last chapter a curricular model was posited which re-configures English/literacy. Because the new configuration finds 'English' an inappropriate term to denote the breadth of communication demands that the new model covers; and because literacy (and its pluralistic version, 'literacies') still favours reading and writing (in that order), a new term will be used in this chapter in an attempt to re-define the territory: communication arts.

'Communication arts' may sound like art-school speak from the 1970s, but it is an attempt to cover the range of modes, functions and genres, as well as the twin pillars of composition and interpretation that were explored in the previous chapters. It could also be called 'contemporary rhetoric', thus distinguishing itself from classical rhetoric but locating itself within the tradition that runs continuously, if variously, from pre-Athenian times through the Renaissance to the present. Rhetoric, as the 'arts of discourse', is socially and politically embedded. Bringing that dimension to communication arts enables schools, colleges and universities to create an informed 'studio' approach to communication, integrating languages, visual arts (still and moving), spatial arts, print and computer interfaces under one department or faculty, and, if possible, under one roof. The addition of the historical, social and political context that rhetoric offers ensures that the communication arts approach does not fall into a 1970s studio art-school stereotype. At the same time, the studio is a concept to hold on to: it implies that works are *made*.

Beyond Framing

It has been the thesis of the present book that framing is a key act in the composition and interpretation of 'messages' between people, whether those are day-to-day spoken interactions or epic works in any one or a number of modes and media. The book has suggested that frames, deriving from genre theory and manifesting themselves as scaffolds for learning with quasi-Vygotskian justification, have helped improve composition to an extent, but have now reached the end of their usefulness, particularly because they have been appropriated for assessment purposes and also stultified the acts of composition and interpretation. Instead, it has proposed an approach that sees *framing* as the key creative and critical act in composition and interpretation. Such a shift puts the power for forming and shaping communication in the hands of the composer (the rhetor, speaker, writer, author) and, to a slightly lesser extent, in the hands of the interpreter (audience, listener, reader). The shift also implies precedence for composition over interpretation, as opposed to the conventional attitude towards literacy which tends to favour reading over writing.

But what if framing itself is superseded by another concept in a few years' time, thus requiring a whole new approach to the curriculum, to teaching and to learning in the language arts? Part of the value of moving the term to the verb form rather than letting it sit statically in its noun form, is that it can change with circumstances and with time. Because framing sits within a theory of rhetoric, and rhetoric is socially, historically and politically informed, framing itself will change according to the times. To give a concrete example: it could be the case that in 10 years' time schools and classrooms as we have known them for centuries will have disappeared, and the so-called school writing genres (highly simulated, often distilled into their own categories and styles) will go with them. We would be in a position where there is no more committing of text to paper and print, but one in which electronic/digital transfer of information is the only way in which communication can take place, other than through face-to-face oral communication. Framing approaches would have no problem with such a scenario. Framing is not committed to any particular medium or mode; it simply puts into place the boundaries of the act of communication that are required in a particular situation, so that both the composer and the interpreter understand the parameters of their mutual communication. The framing acts as an intermediary between what is outside the frame and what is inside it.

And yet it is possible to conceive of important issues in communication that are beyond framing. First it is stating the obvious to say that *frames* become redundant once the purpose of the communication is fulfilled. Like scaffolds, they are merely there to help put up the building, and are taken down as soon as the building is completed. They are a means to an end. With *framing* the situation is different. The act of framing that enables the composition to take place is an act that is determined by a number of factors: the composer's intentions, his/her available resources, the position and nature of the audience in relation to the composer and crucially the content of what he/she has to 'say'. Framing is often invisible, implied, intangible. It does not manifest as a concrete entity (though it can) in the same way as frames do, and so it is easier to dismantle and take down at the end of the communication process. It may subsume itself into the structure and fabric of the building. In a sense, then, framing remains present in any act of communication, even when it is complete.

At the same time, communication is not about framing: rather, its function is to move things on in the world (in terms of action); to change people's minds; to relay to others a sense of how the past informs the present and future, and vice versa; to express and understand experience; to engineer social relations; to consider the relationship between fictional worlds and real worlds. Framing, therefore, is a means to these ends. It is the focus of this book, and of curricular attention, because it operates in every act of communication, and it sits exactly where the various modes and media of communication operate theoretically and practically: between contemporary rhetoric/the communication arts at the theoretical/curricular design level, and the business of making/composing and interpreting communication at the everyday, practical and classroom level.

It is important in a book like this to ask: What is framing for in a world of discourses? What exactly is being framed? By asking such questions we move beyond framing itself to consider the function of framing. The short answer is that framing makes acts of communication possible. The phenomenon that is framed is unconscious (not always intangible) social action. As soon as consciousness of the act of communication is brought to bear, framing re-asserts itself as a key agent in making that communication possible. It presents or forges a mutually comprehensible framework for successful communication; and when the frames of composition and interpretation are not aligned, miscommunication ensues. The longer answer to what is being framed, and why framing helps to effect it, is that social action and experience that is *of the moment* are unaware, on the whole, of their frames. Even in a highly framed space like an art gallery, the moment and state of total absorption in a painting is a moment beyond the apparatus of framing.

Objections to Framing as a Principal Tool for Composition and Interpretation in the Communication Arts

In Toulminian rebuttal terms, let us deal with the objections to framing as a key tool for composition and interpretation in the communication arts.

First, there is the late-Romantic objection. MacLachlan and Reid (1994) capture the source of this first objection clearly: "A desire to escape framing, mixed with knowledge of the impossibility of satisfying this desire, is part of the post-Romantic condition that most of us now inhabit" (p.115). It is possible to see this late- or post-Romantic objection as related to the desire for absorption of the self in an artwork (mentioned in the previous paragraph) or in a wider sea of representation. If the core of experience is *being*, pure consciousness untrammelled by the world and by social constraint, framing looks like confinement, physical border-setting and entrapment. In answer to this objection, we can say that framing does not pretend to operate in a Romantic, late-Romantic or post-Romantic mode. Its commitment to structuration, to working at the interface of composition and interpretation and its impersonal nature make it more naturally affiliated to classical structuralist approaches than to Romanticism. It is, however, a more complex field than a simplistic division between form and content would suggest (i.e. a simple equation like framing = form and what is framed = content). Rather, the act of framing allows the composer to connect with the audience; and allows the audience to find the right approaches to connecting with the work/utterance itself. Ultimately, we can only escape framing in the realms of higher consciousness, ethereality and 'oneness'. Framing, therefore, is part of the human condition.

Another objection would be one of a more worldly, curricular kind. It would suggest that if framing is so ubiquitous, not only in English and the language arts, but in all aspects of the school curriculum at primary/elementary- and middle/high/senior- school levels, then why do we need a separate subject in the curriculum like 'English' that seems to dominate curricular design and assessment regimes? If what 'English' offers is an in-depth focus on the language arts (in a general sense), might that be 'delivered' in subjects that had a clearly identifiable content? This is a debate about the content of English that has been raging for 30 or 40 years, and which variously rests on claims about the content being literature, 'the self in society' or, slightly differently, personal and social development. Rather, if the arts of communication are the real core of English as a subject, it can be seen as a space in the curriculum where these arts are practised, honed and developed; as well as being practised/implemented in other subjects in the curriculum where 'content' is more settled, more foregrounded. Although 'English' may disappear from the curriculum as a misnomer for what actually goes on in that space, it is unlikely that a need for communication arts in education – or whatever they might be called – will disappear. Framing, as this book argues, is central to the compositional and interpretive dimensions of those arts.

A third objection is that the pitch of the present proposition is wrong; that 'framing' is an agent of rhetoric, and as such, is inappropriate for twenty-first century language arts; that it is part of an apparatus that is theoretically too top-heavy, too mired in Athenian/classical and sexist discourse; that rhetoric itself is too associated with sophistication, with both these latter terms used in the negative sense. We have dealt with objections to contemporary rhetoric elsewhere in the book, arguing that a high-level theory which distinguishes but does not discriminate between the various modes and media of communication is a *necessary* level of abstraction to reach in making sense of contemporary communication – and education in such communication, both inside and outside school. The objection to framing can be levelled at frames, at genre theory (as interpreted in recent derivative curriculum practice) but not at the act of framing itself, which escapes the fossilized world of frames and sets the whole approach *in verb*, linking it to social and political practices. As suggested throughout the book, framing operates at a mezzanine level in the world of discourse, mediating between the high theory of rhetoric and the actual practices of teaching and learning in the language arts. It is a transformative agent.

Lastly, an objection could be made that framing is acceptable as a way of helping to compose and interpret at the (whole) textual level, but that it ceases to have any relevance to sub-textual features like arrangement (internal structuration), sentence construction or grapho-phonemic relationships in the linguistic mode; or sub-textual features in other modes and hybrid multimodal forms. To an extent, this objection can be upheld and accepted. It would not be helpful to have a Goffman-like series of frames within frames that described, with ever-increasing miniaturism, the moves that determine the choice of one sentence construction over another, and (further down) the morphemic and grapho-phonemic choices that are made in composition. And yet such informing of the lower levels of language expression and construction *are* determined by a two-way relationship between top-down and bottom-up forces that operate in (verbal) language. Rather than devise a Chinese boxes approach to the pedagogies of English and the language arts, it is better to see framing as an informing principle that operates from the top downwards. It can be invoked whenever composition or interpretation is focusing on a particular level, and the relationships between frames at different levels can be revealed and discussed. There is no apology for a model that operates from the top downwards: such a model begins with the desire or need to communicate, incorporates and transforms meaning, then finds the large-scale forms via which to convey that meaning to that audience with a particular motivation from a speaker/writer/composer. Framing, then, is an unapologetic servant of the top-down approach.

Resolving the Relationship between Fictional and Real Worlds

A previous section in this chapter suggested that one of the functions of communication was to consider the relationship between fictional worlds and real worlds. This relationship has already been mentioned briefly apropos of English as a school subject in Chapter 7. Here we draw on Pavel's *Fictional Worlds* (1986) to resolve a matter that has been a problem for English studies in schools and, to a lesser extent, in colleges and universities. The problem is that English as a school subject has been split between a focus on literature, on the one hand, and language, on the other.

The problem is not just an intellectual or philosophical one. It is a social, political and curricular one too. In England, at the end of the first decade of the present century, proposals were put forward by the Qualifications and Curriculum Authority to separate 'English' as a subject into three qualifications at the end of schooling: English, English Literature and Functional English. The drive for functional English came from the need to make sure that all young people at 16 were equipped to operate in society; that they were, in effect, literate. The narrowness of the conception of what it means to be literate, and how to get there, was evident in the nature of the functional English agenda and curriculum, which focused on language at the expense of literature. This debate and the decisions to move towards a stripped-down language curriculum are not new; this is simply the latest version of a reactive curricular response to the demands of communication in the workplace. 'English' is seen to be a half-way house between language and literature study, with 'English Literature' focusing on literature and likely to be taken by those in the top sets of state schools and in independent schools. 'Literature', within this configuration of possibilities, becomes an élite subject of choice for those whose 'language' is already well developed. What is more, '*English literature*' continues to mean, at core, writing in the English tradition (which still includes American writing and some aspects of Commonwealth writing), even though writing by Black-British or Asian-British writers is characterized as 'writing from other cultures'. English Literature can also mean literature written in English, or, at its most extreme (and rarely) literature written in other languages and translated into English. The nationalistic narrow way in which English literature is seen to be core to the culture and the curriculum, but only available to those at the higher levels of language competence, is reason enough to decide that 'English', English Literature' and 'Functional English' are categories, terms and approaches that have outlived their usefulness.

Pavel solves the problem of the relationship between language and literature by suggesting that fiction creates possible worlds:

> Possible worlds can be understood as abstract collections of states of affairs, distinct from the statements describing those states ... in Alvin Plantinga's view, a possible world defines a "way things could have been ... a possible state of affairs of some kind" (1974, p.44). In our world, states of affairs may obtain, or be actual, but they may also not obtain.
>
> (1986, p.50)

Plantinga's philosophical position is that of modal logic: there is an actual world which acts as a base to "different conceptions of possibility: logical, metaphysical, psychological, and so on" (Pavel 1986, p.51). But as indicated in the longer quotation above, even in the actual world, states of affairs may obtain or not obtain. For example, we may miss a train and thus an interview and thus a potential job that could have taken our life down a particular path. On a grander scale, two heads of state may, through chance or the pressure of affairs, bring a particular nuance or angle to a meeting which leads to a decision that, in turn, affects tens of thousands of people; or they may not. Pavel's argument is that fiction works as parallel possible worlds, answering the question 'what if?' These worlds are at various distances from the actual world, and are of different sizes. So,

> With respect to scope, we can construct a scalar typology ranging between maximal fictional universes, such as the universe of the *Divine Comedy*, and minimal universes, such as the world of *Malone Dies*. The well-documented transition towards ever smaller universes that has accompanied the evolution of Western fictional writing may well be connected to the previously noted decrease in distance: closer views tend to be limited in scope.
>
> (ibid., p.101)

Whether or not we agree with the thesis that Western fictional writing has increasingly created worlds that are nearer and smaller than in the past is beside the point. Pavel's main point is that fictional worlds can be positioned in relation to the actual world in terms of distance and size. For example, *Lord of the Rings* would denote a far-off large world; the *Harry Potter* series has closer connections to the actual world but still retains elements of a far-off world, and its scale varies from the local to the universal; a gritty BBC drama, like 'Freefall', shown in 2009 and about the then contemporary issue of the global financial recession and its effect on three people's lives, is a possible world that is closer in distance (both in its setting and in time) and also more limited in scope (London, although related to the global recession through the financial markets). All these projections of possible worlds are based on a common-sense notion and perception of a shared 'actual world', which is in itself contentious.

The point, as far as the theme of the present book is concerned, is that fictional worlds created in novels, plays, films, TV dramas, poems and other genres are not a category of language use that is so far removed from that of the actual world as to need a separate curriculum category. The *language* of fiction is not that far removed from the language of the actual world, and they benefit from study along each other. In fact, some works of fiction use the languages and dictions of the actual world; and some do not. The range of dictions, registers, vocabularies, styles etc. of language in the actual world is as great as the use of these types of language in fiction. It is a category error to assume that these two worlds operate totally separately in terms of language use.

What is different about the possible worlds embodied in fiction is that they are framed differently from the actual world. They are more highly framed, suggesting a completeness of the created world itself; a separate world; and a world where the attention required from the reader is different from the attention afforded by the complexities of the actual world. These reasons explain why some readers see fiction as an 'escape' from the real world, and others as a reflection upon it.

Crucially, both fiction and actual world genres sit happily within a theory of rhetoric. Both can be designed by, and interpreted by, acts of framing. There is no need to separate them off from each other in curricular categories like 'English' and 'English Literature'; rather, they benefit from proximity and comparability. The relationship between fictional worlds and the real world is analogous to that between play and 'reality', play and the world of work. The strand of play that runs alongside operation in the real world in childhood continues through adolescence into adulthood, through the imagination, through 'escape' and through the generation of possible scenarios in advance of and in reflection on action in the real world.

The Limits of Rhetorical Theory

It is not classical rhetorical theory that we should consider as the overarching (or underpinning) structure at this point, but contemporary rhetoric. As indicated earlier in the book, and in Andrews (2009c), contemporary rhetoric moves beyond classical rhetoric and its derivatives by: i) situating rhetoric in contemporary social contexts; ii) accepting multimodality; iii) embracing changes in communication in the digital age; and iv) inhering in the 'dialogic'. But is contemporary rhetoric a suitable theory for the communication arts? Rather than counter the objections to it, this section will re-justify its centrality to English, literacy and wider communication arts in teaching and learning; and then go on to look beyond its boundaries. In other words, the framing of rhetoric itself will be considered.

Contemporary rhetoric (the qualifying adjective is necessary to distinguish it not only from classical and other historical phases of rhetoric, but also from the pejorative sense of rhetoric), in addition to the characteristics listed above, is politically and socially grounded. Its political grounding comes from an acute awareness of power relations in communication. Who is speaking/communicating to whom about what, and why, are fundamental considerations in rhetoric. The emphasis on power relations between the speaker/rhetor and the audience is crucial to the composition of the communication as well as to its reception and interpretation. *Power* as a major factor in the determination of language form and choice has been a preoccupation for many in sociolinguistics. From a rhetorical perspective, it is inevitable that power is taken into consideration. On a larger canvas, power relations in government and internationally are mediated by communication. When such communication breaks down – for example when the discourses of one nation cease to 'speak to' those of another nation – either a cold war or actual war can break out. To put such a problem another way, the frameworks and framing devices used in one set of discourses can be rejected by or incompatible with those used in another set. Such an impasse would require both parties to agree on some shared values and shared frameworks for communication before any progress is possible. In terms of conflict resolution, an understanding of rhetoric and a great deal of work on the infrastructure for open discussion via adjustment of frameworks and the framing of particular discourses is required.

The social grounding of rhetoric places contemporary rhetoric in line with (but above, in terms of abstraction) social theories of communication and language development/teaching, like Vygotskian theory and its implementation and derivatives; socially situated theories; social practices and their connection to communication; social semiotics; and sociolinguistics. For a rhetorician, all social situations are politically and economically determined (and thus explain Eagleton's characterization of rhetoric as related to Marxist literary criticism). In practice, to come down to a more everyday level, a (social) encounter between two people on a street, however brief, is a rhetorical act: it can be analysed in terms of their respective social standing; the demands of the moment (the economies of time and attention); the nature of the substance to be communicated, if any; and the purposes (if any) of the exchange. Such an approach to communication sees the school and its classrooms as extensions of social space, with their own discourses (conventions, practices, genres), with scope for comparison between the discourses of the classroom and those outside it; and scope for bridging any gaps that may have developed. Essentially, rhetoric allows us to see that the communities of learning represented by classrooms, on the one hand, and all other kinds of communities, on the other (including electronically linked communities), are all potentially communities for learning.

Furthermore, despite the differences between contemporary rhetoric and classical rhetoric listed at the head of this section, it is the *continuity* of the rhetorical tradition that is a strength of rhetoric as a field of study and as a theory. This does not mean that the same rhetorical theories apply throughout history; on the contrary, the flexibility of rhetoric (like the flexibility of framing as opposed to frames) enables it to adapt to changing political, economic and social patterns. From such a long perspective, the splitting of English Literature from English Language of the last 150 years, at least in England, would seem an aberration.

Finally, the characteristic of contemporary rhetoric that suits it to the composition and interpretation of communication in the twenty-first century is the fact that it is not linked to any particular language. Rhetoric can apply to any language, including mathematical, musical and architectural languages.

What is beyond rhetoric? It is important to consider what is beyond the boundaries of contemporary rhetoric itself so that: i) rhetoric can be put in perspective; ii) other fields of operation can be defined in relation to it; and iii) rhetoric can be critiqued. If contemporary rhetoric is the arts of discourse and communication, beyond it lie the substantial fields of knowledge, divided epistemologically into various categories and sub-categories. So chemistry, biology and their interdisciplinary or sub-category, biochemistry would be examples of such categories, variously termed subjects or disciplines according to their status and the particular stage at which they are studied. In such subjects as the sciences, arts, humanities and social sciences cover, there is an irreducible 'content' or area of interest that, despite all rhetorical analysis and filtering, lies at the core of that subject/discipline. Rhetoric may be said to have fought off logic and grammar by subsuming them; and even philosophy has recognized that its propositions, methods and discourses are inextricably tied up with the forms of communication in which those elements are expressed. Rhetoric therefore stands in relation to contemporary disciplines at a meta-level, thus justifying its centrality to the school curriculum, but is often seen as marginal when the substances of the various disciplines themselves comes to the fore at university and higher-education levels.

A second dimension, beyond rhetoric, can be represented by the terms *presence* and *resonance*. Presence is the moment of contemplation or realization that is beyond material couching in some form of communication. Spirituality and its manifestations in different religions/paths are examples of presence or an awareness of presence. They take on rhetorical identity as soon as they express themselves in words, images, sounds and other communicative modes, but at core they are built on silence and contemplation. Rhetorical combinations of words, images, sounds and/or physical expression can bring about presence, as, for example, some Noh plays in particular productions can engineer *sartori*. Resonance is the communication of such presence without recourse to verbal, musical or spatial languages. Its operation is outside the domain of rhetoric.

The danger of a contemporary rhetorical perspective to curriculum design and implementation in the language arts is that it might raise theory in the field to a level of abstraction that is hard to comprehend or is impractical. But first, one could counter by saying that, up to now, the field of English and language arts has been swept by a series of incompatible sub-theories that are not appropriate to the nature of the field. Second, that rhetoric is a simple theory (Who? To whom? What? When? Why? How?) that operates at a theoretical level but also at a practical level in the framing and design of communication. Third, that the fissure between literature and language, between fiction and non-fiction, can be closed by rhetoric.

Further justifications and exposition of contemporary rhetoric – its boundaries, lineaments, contours – in relation to multimodality, digitization, communication and education require another book. For now, with regard to the argument regarding framing and re-framing, rhetoric remains the overarching theoretical framework that best fits. From the high theoretical ground of contemporary rhetoric, the chapter and the book now return to the practicalities of framing and re-framing in terms of the curriculum and teaching/learning.

Curriculum Design

For the moment, the assumption of the book is that schools and universities as institutions that monitor and mediate learning for students will continue in their present form. The institutionalization of education requires curricula. What are the implications of framing and re-framing within a theory of rhetoric for curriculum design?

It is not so radical a shift from the present state of curricula worldwide to suggest that English (or its equivalent in other countries that do not use English as the lingua franca), language arts, modern foreign languages (or classical written languages like Latin or Arabic), mathematics, music, the visual and performing arts and physical education (sport, dance etc.) might be clustered in one third or one half of the timetable; and might also be clustered as departments under one overarching 'faculty' or 'school', both at school and university levels. Such a clustering would allow for more commerce between the various subjects and disciplines that make up the communication arts. In all these areas, it is the process and means of expression that is more important in education than the actual substance of that expression. What these subjects or disciplines have in common is that they are 'languages'; and have, over the past two decades, been described in terms of 'literacies': verbal, visual, mathematical, musical and even physical and spatial literacies. But the terms 'literacy' and 'literacies' – or even 'new literacies' – are inappropriate for contemporary practice and curriculum design because they are predicated on verbal language: words, in speech and print. If verbal literacy is only one of the modes in which communication takes place, it makes sense to move up one level of abstraction to denote the field: viz. to the term 'communication arts'.

The advantages of such a denotation are several. The various modes of communication are able to stand alongside each other, and specialist teachers of those different modes can collaborate. Instead of a situation where a language arts or English teacher elicits excellent written work from his/her students, then asks them to illustrate it with low-quality drawings; or, conversely, an art teacher who encourages his/her students to produce brilliant artwork, then has the students add fatuous, abstracted, verbal commentary ... instead of these, a multimodal rhetorical approach where framing is the creative critical act that brings about new communication would provide the conditions for excellent writing alongside excellent art. The same is true of the other communication modes: because it is normal for communication to be multimodal in the real world, such multimodality can and should be reproduced in the curriculum and in the classroom. Such contiguity of the 'languages' of expression can enhance and sharpen the awareness of the affordances of each mode; help teachers to see the strengths and boundaries of their own specialist arts; and make the classroom a more exciting place for students to work. Part of the advantage is that the particular languages are used more economically (there is an economy of use implied in multimodality) and with more focus. One 'language' is not used to do the work of another without conscious deployment to that end. What has been suggested about the verbal and visual arts can just as well – though differently – be applied to connections between mathematics and speech; dance, music and words; physical movement and listening.

The next advantage of such a curricular configuration is that the teaching of all languages can be brought under one roof. At present, the split between 'English', on the one hand, and 'modern foreign languages' and other languages (e.g. Latin, Ancient Greek), on the other, is an odd one. Learning a first or mother-tongue language, if that language is English (and probably any other language), is seen as having a separate research tradition and a separate pedagogy from 'second' or 'additional' or 'foreign' modern or classical language learning. To an extent, these different traditions are helpfully separate, as the differences between 'naturally' absorbing/acquiring a mother tongue and 'artificially' learning another language are marked. But there is much more in common between the two types of language learning, and these commonalities are lost or minimized by a curricular and pedagogic split. For example, French language teachers in a predominantly English-language speaking school often complain that the English teachers no longer teach formal sentence grammar to students, thereby making the job of the French teacher more difficult as the students do not have a meta-vocabulary for understanding and applying rules of syntax. In the curricular configuration that is being proposed here, such misunderstandings of: i) the way sentence construction is taught in English; ii) the possibilities for transfer between languages and the levels at which such knowledge is useful; and iii) pedagogic practice in the different subjects can be discussed, clarified and resolved. The discussion itself is valuable, and students can be included in such discussion, thus learning more about comparative language study. Further implications of a closer connection between the various verbal languages that are taught in a school or university are that English, Mandarin or Spanish (as the three current main world languages) are seen in a world context, not in a narrower nationalistic context. Such a wider perspective on language learning allows 'second and third tier' languages more status, as the limitations of the world languages are made clear. Just as, at the end of the previous paragraph, we suggested connections between differently coded languages, so too the clustering of curricular design to include all languages enriches further the possibilities of commerce between verbal languages and other modes of communication.

The emphasis is on a clustering of the communication *arts*. In the USA, elementary school linguistic teaching tends to be termed the language arts; and in the UK and elsewhere, visual and performing arts are common terms. These terms indicate that gaining command and exploring the different modes of communication is an art; that is to say, there is an aesthetic and formal dimension in the composition and appreciation/interpretation; that the various systems in themselves are worthy of study as well as the ends that they help to bring about; and that expression and communication through these arts can give pleasure. In all the arts, both individually and in multimodal and hybrid forms, composition and interpretation are common actions, with similarly common sub-categories: learning codes (both coding and de-coding); the rhetoric of design; comprehension, appreciation, argumentation; narrative and other structuring; and the relationship between components at the various levels of coding in each of the 'languages'.

It is at this general level of the communication arts that the cluster of subjects and disciplines can be distinguished from other clusters: the sciences and the humanities, for example. This is not the place to discuss the exact configuration of the rest of the curriculum, except to say that the inclusion of physical arts and mathematics under the umbrella of communication arts places the rest of the curriculum in a different light, implying new and different patterns of clustering.

Bulfin (2009) suggests further innovations on curriculum design in his thesis on literacies, new technologies and young people, offering a combination of Kress's (2003) notions of design with rhetorical models for the English/literacy curriculum which give attention to the production (composition, in the present book) and reception (interpretation) of texts "and the development of an attitude of civic engagement" (ibid., p.265). He suggests that a rhetorical approach, along with a critical-historical perspective, would enable not only better focus on production and reception of texts in and outside school, but also teaching *about* technologies and their relationship with new literacies.

Finally, in this section on the curricular implications of the concept and implementation of communication arts, what are the implications for teacher education? As has already been implied, it is likely that each of the arts will require specialized training in the subject knowledge and pedagogical knowledge required to teach them well. At the same time, beginning and continuing teachers need to at least be aware, but preferably to have further knowledge of at least one of the other communication arts so that they can make connections, professionally as well as intellectually. These connections are not just made for their own sake: their function is to sharpen and enhance knowledge of the initial subject or discipline area and to maximize the possibilities for communication so that rhetorical (ultimately, social, political) choices can be made by both teachers and students.

Panning Out: The Case of Film

Hardly addressed in Chapter 2 on framing in the visual arts is the case of the moving image and particularly that of film. In important papers published by the British Film Institute (1999, 2008, 2009) the case for including film within a wider conception of literacy is made. At the same time, the integrity of film as a medium and art form in itself is made. The dilemma for film education appears to be that, on the one hand, it needs to be part of the core of cultural education and thus subsumes itself within the wider conception of literacy (as well as finding ways to enhance verbal literacies through motivation, pedagogical approaches and accessibility, especially, for example, through short films used in in-service work with teachers and with students at primary and secondary levels). On the other hand, it needs to protect its integrity as a specialized art form and as a popular medium.

Framing is central to the making of film, from the decision-making about how the whole narrative of a film will be composed to the decisions about how individual scenes and shots are framed. The polyptical principle, discussed in Chapter 2, is central to the composition of film, as is the practice of editing once the filming has been completed: films are composed of individual frames. Framing is also essential to the viewing, 'reading' and interpretation of film in terms of which critical frames are brought to bear on the experience.

At a higher theoretical level, rhetoric allows a solution to the dilemma described above about the place of film in the curriculum. A rhetorical perspective sees film as one medium for the expression of narrative, lyrical, documentary and/or argumentational content. It sees it as a naturally multimodal medium in itself, with further possibilities of composition and interpretation alongside other 'purer' and hybrid modes. It is therefore not necessary to either separate film as a separate art form for educational and pedagogic purposes; nor to see it, at the other extreme, as being subsumed under canopies like 'English', 'literacy', 'literacies' or even 'new literacies'. Literacy itself, as a term, is – as has been suggested – passing its sell-by date as a term that is of value in the twenty-first century. Whether in the narrow sense of being able to read and write at a 'functional' level, or in the wider sense of a range of cultural literacies that can be both social and/or technological in nature, the term has been over-used and has become flaccid.

What Advantages will Re-framing Literacy Bring?

Re-framing literacy teaching and learning is important now because the social practices in schools and universities are getting further away from the social practices in the world outside school and higher education. Although states of alienation like these can go on for decades and centuries, becoming legitimate areas of intellectual enquiry and scholarship, it is also necessary for the discourses of the everyday world to be reflected in the discourses of schooling – both to motivate students and to keep communication about social, cultural, scientific, economic and other matters clear, engaging and relevant.

Using the concept of framing as the key agent in bringing about such change is deliberate. The act of framing provides flexibility to change the nature of the frame (the relationship between what is inside and outside a communicative framework) according to circumstances and need; a rhetorical device that is culturally and linguistically neutral; at the same time, a means by which power relations can be understood and mediated; a means by which modes may be considered alongside each other, individually and in combination; and a way of both limiting the prevalence of verbal language as a predicate for other languages and, at the same time, valuing its affordances and place alongside other modes of communication.

Crucially, framing and re-framing allow creative action with regard to composition and interpretation. Such action is in the hands of the student as well as the teacher, and part of what framing affords is the possibility of negotiation between student and teacher on the shape and development of discourse. Hence, learning is enhanced because the student is no longer the recipient of a tradition of a finite set of genres – or even more limitingly, school genres. He/she is empowered to shape communication, to frame and re-frame it according to need and according to the particular demands of the situation.

In practice, teachers are also empowered by a framing/re-framing approach. The emphasis on re-framing means that creativity in composition can come from re-working an old theme or an existing piece of literature (cf. Bakhtin 1981) on dialogic principles, not just from a quasi-Romantic notion of expressing the thoughts and feelings of a single self. Framing is a social act as well as a linguistic and literary one: it can involve other teachers in workshops, and even if a teacher is inclined not to compose themselves, it can aid the process of understanding how reception and interpretation of words, sentences, paragraphs and whole texts (including multimodal texts) operate.

Framing and re-framing are the focus of the present book. They represent the missing level between, on the one hand, a high theory of communication with a long history and with relevance to contemporary communication arts – rhetoric – that operates in society. On the other hand there is the more practical and specific level of curriculum design in school and university systems, design pedagogies and the business of teaching writing and reading well. The present approach also includes the productive arts of composition and the reciprocal arts of interpretation. This level has been missing for some time, resulting in practice without theory (the notion of 'best practice') or too big a gap between practice and theory. Such a gap, in itself, results in tenuous connections between practice and theory so that neither seems connected or relevant to the other. The problem with such a gap is that there is no clear framework for research, practice or policy to gauge whether they are effective or even clearly related to each other. Into such gaps quasi-theories and solutions present themselves, but they have limited life and usually fail when scaled up to national level. The short-termism of governments which fall upon one solution or another to address critical problems in educational provision only adds to the confusion about whether high-stakes testing regimes or more deeply embedded pedagogies are the best way to enhance students' compositional and interpretive skills.

It is the argument of this book that we need a model of communication in education that is clear, accessible and powerful enough to serve the needs of students and teachers in the twenty-first century. Framing and re-framing are proposed as operating at a level that provides such a model for the communication arts: they sit at a level that is practical enough for deployment in and beyond the classroom, but also is informed by higher levels of theory. These higher levels are to be the subject of another book, on contemporary rhetoric.

Notes

1 What's in a Frame?

1 Lanham notes (1993, p.94) "I don't come by this quotation from Susanne Langer's *Philosophy in a New Key*, honestly; Stewart Brand quotes a report from the MITY Architecture Machine Group (the forebear of the Media Lab) which quotes the passage in Brand, S. (1987) *Bab: Inventing the Future at MIT*, New York: Viking.

2 Tillers' piece was exhibited at the SoHo Guggenheim, New York, as part of a celebration of Contemporary Australian Art in July 1995. *Polyptiques* was the title of an exhibition at the Louvre in 1990.

3 *The Silence*, photographs by Gilles Peress at the Museum of Modern Art, New York City, July 1995. In the exhibition notes, Peress explains his shift to photography after studying political science and philosophy as a result of his conviction that "words were no longer adequate to deal with and describe reality".

4 There is a paragraph in the report that reveals the significance of punctuation. Clause 6(c) of the Nuremberg Charter reads "murder, extermination, enslavement, deportation and other inhuman acts committed against any civilian population before or during the [Second World] War, or persecutions on political, racial or religious grounds ...". Clause 111 of the 1994 document, in referring to the Nuremberg Charter, states "The original version [of the Charter] contains a semi-colon which followed the word 'war' which seemed to imply that murder etc could be considered as crimes against humanity ... However, the semi-colon was replaced with a comma by the Protocol. The result was to imply that crimes against humanity were to be interpreted to import liability only for acts connected to the war".

4 Visual and Verbal Frames

1 There still seems to be a prevalent Leavisite attitude towards the media that we need to *protect* ourselves against it rather than enjoy and appreciate it, as we do literature.

2 Literacy is being used in a number of fields to describe both the semiotic systems used in those fields and the language used to talk about them. See, for example, Barnett (1994) on technological literacy. There is, of course, nothing wrong with using the term literacy in a metaphorical way.

3 Syntaxes don't work outside language and computer programmes because they imply fixed units (words) with relatively tightly defined meanings. One of the shortcomings of Chomskian syntactic linguistics was that it tried to account for language through syntactic structures, when meaning in fact derives from the whole composition within a social context. There is a danger that a visual literacy based on a syntax of art will look only within the frame, not at the nature of the frame and what that suggests about the relationship of signs within the frame to those without it.

4 Most galleries are full of words as well as images. Galleries like Kettle's Yard in Cambridge or the Frick collection in New York are exceptions in that they resist the temptation to mediate artworks through language.

5 Artists like Ian Hamilton Finlay deliberately place 'words' and other linguistic icons in landscape to debunk the conception of a pure uninscribed landscape.

6 See for example Barr (1986) and Greatrex (1992).

7 Like all category lists, this is an oversimplification. Conventions can be subverted, and there is plenty of overlap or combination possible between these categories. The *function* of this map, however, is to reinforce the predominant presence of the visual/written in printed communication.

8 *Word & Image*, a quarterly journal of verbal/visual enquiry, published by Taylor & Francis, 4 John Street, London WC1N 2ET.

9 Typography strongly conveys significance through its shape and layout on the page. The presence of sub-headings, right justification, spacing; the use of sérif and sans-sérif faces; the boldness of type – all these, and other non-linguistic features, have an effect on our response to texts. Word-processing has increased the ability of creators of texts to design their writing.

10 I am grateful to Alison Sealey for the perception that the visual and written aren't entirely analogous. As a category, the visual embraces the written more readily than the written embraces the visual.

11 Buchanan refers to Vygotsky, whose writing on symbolic systems such as drawing and writing serves as the basis for reflections on socio-cognitive development in children (Vygotsky 1971, 1978, 1986). In *The Psychology of Art*, Vygotsky in turn refers to Potebnia's notion of the analogy between the activity and evolution of language and art:

> The psychological system of philology has shown that the word is divided in to three basic elements: the sound, or external form; the image, or inner form; and the meaning, or significance. The inner form is understood to be the etymological form that expresses the content. Frequently this inner form is forgotten, or is displaced by the expanded meaning of the word. In other cases, however, this inner form can be readily determined. Etymological investigation reveals that where only the outward form and meaning were retained, the inner form existed but was forgotten as the language evolved.
>
> (1971, p.30)

Elsewhere, Vygotsky talks about speech and drawing as primary symbolic systems; that is to say, they are direct representations or framings of meaning in social contexts. Writing is different, because it represents speech. It is therefore classed as a *secondary* symbolic system. Where writing overlays drawing/painting, as it does in much Dadaist and Surrealist art, it perhaps has the function of a secondary layer of meaning. In Russian Formalism (to various extents) writing plays a more primary role, brought about by its political significance. For an illuminating discussion of speaking, writing and drawing in relation to *architectural* practice, see Medway (1995).

12 I have elsewhere suggested that in the post-colonial world, 'English' is no longer the appropriate term for the subject that is studied under that name in Australia and in other parts of the world. It is merely the historical accident that the language they use was shaped and developed in England. A better term might be 'Language Arts' or 'Discourse Arts'. See Andrews (1993).

13 Howard Hollands has suggested to me the following in relation to the role of computers in art education: "Communicating in front of a screen and manipulating images and texts must be about something. What is it about? Colour on a TV monitor is not the same as colour in the visually experienced world, although clearly,

it is part of that world. The complexities of reflected colour and all those qualities of the outside world can only be recreated on the screen. Chance itself has to be programmed. Perhaps we now enter the spiritual domain of IT. The monitor is just a box of tricks and a valid art form, but the form is running way ahead of development in content".

14 See Bazerman (1994).

15 Rhetoric can cope with a challenging art installation like Camerawork's 'A-baa', in which, on 18 November 1995, a live audio transmission of a sheep grazing in a field in Devon was relayed to a 'white gallery' in London "for the listener to ruminate over". The audience was also invited to graze on written thoughts related to the installation on the World Wide Web.

5 Frames of Reference: Framing in Relation to a Theory of Multimodality

1 The discussions of punctuation (pp.122ff.), on the one hand, and the difference between reading a page and reading a screen (pp.136–9), on the other, in *Literacy in the New Media Age* (Kress 2003) are well worth re-visiting, though they are not dealt with in the present book. See Agarwal-Hollands and Andrews (2001) for a discussion of reading on screen. I return to the different framings of speech and writing later in the book.

2 I am grateful to Brian Street for introduction to the notion at a seminar at the Institute of Education, London, in May 2009.

6 Pre-school Writing and Drawing: Before Framing

1 Kress's second and third 'value judgements' on p.29 – that all modes and forms of representation present both potentials and limitations to meaningful action and to imagination, and that "if the limitation to one mode of representation *is* a limitation, then we should do everything we can to overcome that limitation" – shed interesting light on the distinctions between the visual and verbal made in Raney (1997). Raney describes the practice of an artist/teacher who deliberately asks his students to take the verbal – and then the visual – to the limits of their expressive ability in order to explore, or at least become aware of, the space in between.

2 Here I agree with Kress that the reader determines the size and nature of the frame that is brought to the interpretation of the text.

3 The number of works created per month differs significantly. While the average per month is 44 works, November and December – the most intense months of the move and its build-up – totalled 16 and 12 works respectively; whereas March – perhaps a period of relative stability – totalled 92 works.

4 Goodnow (1977) in a study of the development of children's drawings, poses the 'answerable question' (i.e. answerable by research) of whether the "tendency to proceed from top to bottom and left to right ... appears to apply as well to the way we construct letters of the alphabet and geometric shapes" as to drawings of people (p.81). She cites interesting research by Bernbaum (1974) who suggests that familiarity with shape and familiarity with the medium are critical factors in the development of children's drawings. There are implications in her research for writing development too:"[The] teacher should recognize that most ... students ... come to school equipped with several basic skills necessary for learning to write ... [they] should seek media and figures with which the children are already familiar and use them as a stepping stone to the relatively unfamiliar writing situation" (p.79). Perhaps children who do not take easily to learning to write with a pencil or pen in the early months of

schooling should be given the opportunity to write using a variety of media: painting, collage, and – as Bernbaum's research suggests – writing in sand with a finger.

9 Breaking the Frame: New Horizons for English

1 The findings of this report are mirrored in a recent report by the US-based Alliance for Excellent Education – see Graham and Perin (2006) – which, based on a meta-analysis of research studies, concludes there are 11 strategies for improving writing in middle and high schools, including writing strategies, summarizing, collaborative writing, specific product goals (audiences), word-processing, sentence combining (cf. grammar review by Andrews et al., 2006a), pre-writing (planning), inquiry activities (research) and a process writing approach.
2 See DfEE 2001a, c; 2002a, b and c; and DfES 2003b, for example.
3 The Ofsted Annual Report for 2005/06 states "In English [imaginative and enjoyable learning] was achieved through a range of teaching styles … For some pupils, however, the experience of English had become narrower in certain years as teachers focused on tests and examinations; this affected pupils' achievements in speaking and listening in particular" (2006, p.57).

Bibliography

Ackerman, J. and Oates, S. (1996). Image, text and power in architectural design and workplace writing. In Duin, A.H. and Hansen, C.J. (eds) *Nonacademic writing: social theory and technology*. Mahwah, NJ: Erlbaum.

Agarwal-Hollands, U. and Andrews, R. (2001). From scroll ... to codex ... and back again. *Education, Communication, Information*, 1:1, Spring 2001, 59–73.

Alexander, R. (2006). *Towards dialogic teaching* (3rd edition). Thirsk, Yorks: Dialogos.

Allen, D. (1994). Teaching visual literacy – some reflections on the term. *Journal of Art and Design Education*, 13:2, 133–43.

Allen, D. (1995). Is it possible to be visually literate? *NFAE Newsletter*, January 1995, 6–7.

Ananth, D. (1996). Frames within frames: on Matisse and *The Orient*. In Duro (ed.), 153–77.

Andrews, R. (1981). Telling stories. *The English Magazine*, 7, Summer 1981, 21–5.

Andrews, R. (ed.) (1992). *Rebirth of rhetoric: essays in language, culture and education*. London: Routledge.

Andrews, R. (1993). The future of English: reclaiming the territory. *English in Australia*, 106, December 1993, 41–54. (Also published in *English in Aotearoa*, 22, May 1994, 34–45.)

Andrews, R. (1995a). Framing: a visual metaphor for education in the language arts. Inaugural professorial lecture, Middlesex University, 11 October 1995.

Andrews, R. (1995b). *Teaching and learning argument*. London: Cassell.

Andrews, R. (1996a). Visual literacy in question. *20:20*, 4.

Andrews, R. (1996b). The visual/verbal interface: questions for research. Paper presented to the Linguistics Circle, Lancaster University, 10 October 1996.

Andrews, R. (1998a). The nature of 'visual literacy': problems and possibilities for the classroom. *Literacy Learning: Secondary Thoughts*, 6:2, June 1998, 8–16.

Andrews, R. (1998b). The base of a small iceberg: mark-making in the work of a four year old. In Woods, C. (ed.) *Image Text Persuasion*. Adelaide: University of South Australia, 5–22.

Andrews, R. (ed.) (2004). *The impact of ICT on literacy education*. London: RoutledgeFalmer.

Andrews, R. (2000). 'Framing and design in ICT in English: towards a new subject and new practices in the classroom. In Goodwyn, A. (ed.) *English in the digital age*. London: Cassell, 22–33.

Andrews, R. (2008a). Ten years of strategies. *Changing English*, 15:1, 77–85.

Andrews, R. (2008b). Shifting writing practice: focusing on the productive skills to improve quality and standards. In *Getting going: generating, shaping and developing ideas in writing*. London: Department for Children, Schools and Families, 4–21. Also available at www.teachernet.gov.uk/publications, accessed 9 February 2010.

Andrews, R. (2008c). *The case for a National Writing Project for teachers*. Reading: Centre for British Teachers (CfBT) Educational Trust.

Andrews, R. (2009a). *The importance of argument in education*. Inaugural professorial lecture, University of London, Institute of Education. London: IOE Publications.

Andrews, R. (2009b). English at school in England. In Maybin, J. and Swann, J. (2009). *The Routledge companion to English language studies*. London: Routledge, 171–80.

Andrews, R. (2009c). *Argumentation in higher education: improving practice through theory and research*. New York: Routledge.

Andrews, R. and Gibson, H. (1993). A critique of the 'chronological/non-chronological' distinction in the National Curriculum for English. *Educational Review*, 45:3, 239–50.

Andrews, R. and Gibson, R. (2009). *As You Like It* (Cambridge Schools Shakespeare, 2nd edition). Cambridge: Cambridge University Press.

Andrews, R. and Haythornthwaite, C. (eds). (2007). *The handbook of e-learning research*. London: Sage.

Andrews, R. and Smith, A. (forthcoming). *Writing development: teaching and learning in the digital age*. Maidenhead: Open University Press/McGraw-Hill.

Andrews, R., Torgerson, C., Beverton, S., Freeman, A., Locke, T., Low, G., Robinson, A. and Zhu, D. (2006a). The effect of grammar teaching on writing development. *British Educational Research Journal*, 32:1, 39–56.

Andrews, R., Torgerson, C., Low, G., McGuinn, N. and Robinson, A. (2006b). *Teaching argumentative non-fiction writing to 7–14 year olds: a systematic review of the evidence of successful practice*. In *Research evidence in education library*. London: EPPI-Centre, Social Science Research Unit, Institute of Education, University of London. Also available at http://eppi.ioe.ac.uk/reel, accessed 29 January 2010.

Andrews, R. with Morgan, W. (1999). City of text? Metaphors for hypertext in literary education. *Changing English* 6:1, March 1999, 81–92.

Andrews, R. with Simons, M. (1996). The electronic word: multimedia, rhetoric and English teaching. *The English and Media Magazine*, 35, November 1996, 40–3.

Anning, A. (1997). Drawing out ideas. Paper given at Media, Arts and Representation in Education and the Community Colloquium, Carleton University, Ottawa, April 1997, 17–20.

Auping, M. (1995). A long view. In Auping, M. et al., 9–32.

Auping, M., Elderfield, J., Sontag, S. and Price, M. (1995). *Howard Hodgkin paintings*. London: Thames & Hudson.

Bakhtin, M.M. (1981). *The dialogic imagination* (trans. Holqvist, M.). Austin, TX: University of Texas Press.

Barnes, D., Britton, J. and Rosen, H. (1969). *Language, the learner and the school*. Harmondsworth: Pelican.

Barnett, M. (1994). Paper on technological literacy given at 2nd 'Domains of Literacy' conference, Institute of Education, London, September 1994.

Barr, J. (1986). *Illustrated children's books*. London: British Library.

Barrs, M. (1988). Drawing a story: transitions between drawing and writing. In Lightfoot, M. and Martin, N. (eds). *The word for teaching is learning*. Portsmouth, NH: Heinemann/Boynton-Cook, 51–69.

Barthes, R. (1988). The old rhetoric: an aide-mémoire. In *The Semiotic Challenge*, (trans. Howard, R.). Oxford: Blackwell, 11–94.

Bartlett, F.C. (1932). *Remembering: a study in experimental and social psychology.* Cambridge: Cambridge University Press.

Barton, D. and Hamilton, M. (1998). *Local literacies: reading and writing in one community.* London: Routledge.

Bateson, G. (1954). *A theory of play and fantasy: steps to an ecology of mind.* New York: Ballantine.

Bauers, A. and Boyd, E. (1989). *Early mark-making by Jacqueline and Christopher.* London: Middlesex Polytechnic and London Borough of Enfield.

Bazerman, C. (1994). Where is the classroom? In Freedman, A. and Medway, P. (eds). *Learning and teaching genre.* Portsmouth, NH: Heinemann/Boynton-Cook.

Beckett, S. (1970). *Breath* in *Gambit*, 4:16. Reproduced in Beckett, S. (1986) *The complete dramatic works.* London: Faber and Faber.

Beckett, S. (1980). *Company.* London: Calder.

Berger, J. (1972). *Ways of seeing.* Harmondsworth: Pelican/BBC.

Bereiter, C. and Scardamalia, M. (1987). *The psychology of written composition.* Hillsdale, NJ: Lawrence Erlbaum Associates.

Bergonzi, B. (1990). *Exploding English: criticism, theory, culture.* Oxford: Oxford University Press.

Bernbaum, M. (1974). Accuracy in children's copying: the role of different stroke sequences and school experience. Unpublished PhD dissertation, George Washington University.

Bissex, G. (1980). *Gnys at work: a child learns to read and write.* Cambridge, MA: Harvard University Press.

Black, P. and Muecke, S. (1992). The power of a dress: the rhetoric of a moment in fashion. In Andrews (ed.) (1992), 212–27.

Bolter, J. (1991). *Writing space: the computer, hypertext and the history of writing.* Hove and London: Lawrence Erlbaum.

Brand, S. (1986). *Bab: inventing the future at MIT.* New York: Viking.

British Film Institute (1999). *Making movies matter.* Report of the Film Education Working Group. London: BFI Education.

British Film Institute (2008). Reframing literacy: film education for all? London: BFI Education. Also available at http://www.bfi.org.uk/education/research/teachlearn/pdf/reframing_literacy.pdf, accessed 11 August 2009.

British Film Institute (2009). Film: 21st century literacy – a strategy for film education across the UK. London: UK Film Council. Also available at www.21stcenturyliteracy.org.uk, accessed 11 August 2009.

Britton, J. (1987). Vygotsky's contribution to pedagogical theory. *English in Education*, 21:3, 22–6.

Brook, P. (1972). *The empty space.* London: Pelican.

Brown, J., Clarke, S., Medway, P., Stibbs, A. with Andrews, R. (1991). *Developing English for TVEI.* Leeds: University of Leeds, School of Education.

Brunner, D.D. (1994). *Inquiry and reflection: framing narrative practice in education.* Albany: State University of New York Press.

Brutt-Griffler, J. (2002). *World English: a study of its development.* Clevedon, Berks: Multilingual Matters.

Bryson, B. (2007). *Shakespeare: the world as a stage.* London: HarperPress.

Buchanan, M. (1995). Making art and critical literacy: a reciprocal relationship. Prentice, R. (ed.). *Teaching art and design: addressing issues and identifying directions.* London: Cassell, 24–9.

Buckham, J. (1994). Teachers' understanding of children's drawing. In Aubrey, C. (ed.). *The role of subject knowledge in the early years of schooling.* London: The Falmer Press, 133–67.

Bulfin, S. (2009). Literacies, new technologies and young people: negotiating the interface in secondary school. Unpublished PhD thesis, Melbourne: Monash University, Faculty of Education,

Cameron, D. (2002). Schooling spoken language: beyond 'communication'. In *New perspectives on spoken English in the classroom: conference papers.* London: Qualifications and Curriculum Authority.

Carroll, D. (1987). *Paraesthetics: Foucault, Lyotard, Derrida.* New York: Methuen.

Cazden, C. (2001). *Classroom discourse: the language of teaching and learning* (2nd edition). Portsmouth, NH: Heinemann.

Cazden, C., Cope, B., Fairclough, N., Gee, J., Kress, G. and Kalantzis, M. (1996). A pedagogy of multiliteracies: designing social futures. *Harvard Educational Review,* 66:1, Spring 1996, 60–92.

Chaplin, E. (1994). *Sociology and visual representation.* London: Routledge.

Chomsky, N. (1964). *Syntactic structures.* Cambridge, MA: The MIT Press.

Clarke, S. and Andrews, R. (1996). A pile of iron filings: information, information technology and the English curriculum. *The English and Media Magazine,* November 1996.

Coles, R. and Harris, A. (1996). *Double Take,* 6, Fall 1996.

Conceison, C. (2001). Review article on Gao Xingjiang. *The China Quarterly,* 167: 749–53.

Cope, B. and Kalantzis, M. (eds) (2000). *Multiliteracies.* London: RoutledgeFalmer.

Cox, M. (1997). *Drawings of people by the under 5s.* London: The Falmer Press.

Davie, D. (1952). *The purity of diction in English verse.* London: Chatto and Windus.

Davis, S. (1993). Hypertext and multimedia. *English Today,* 9:1, 17–24.

Department for Education and Employment (1995). *English in the National Curriculum.* London: Her Majesty's Stationery Office.

Department for Education and Employment (2001a). *A framework for teaching English: years 7, 8 and 9.* London: DfEE.

Department for Education and Employment (2001b). *English department training 2001.* London: DfEE.

Department for Education and Employment (2001c). *Year 7 speaking and listening bank.* London: DfEE.

Department for Education and Employment (2002a). *English department training Year 7 2002/03.* London: DfEE.

Department for Education and Employment (2002b). *English department training Year 8 2002/03.* London: DfEE.

Department for Education and Employment (2002c). *Key objectives banks (for Years 7, 8 and 9).* London: DfEE.

Department for Education and Employment/Qualifications and Curriculum Authority (1999a). *The National Curriculum: handbook for primary teachers in England.* London: DfEE/QCA.

Department for Education and Employment/Qualifications and Curriculum Authority (1999b). *The National Curriculum: handbook for secondary teachers in England*. London: DfEE/QCA.

Department for Education and Employment/Qualifications and Curriculum Authority (2000). *All our futures: creativity, culture and education*. Report of the National Advisory Committee on Creativity, Culture and Education. London: DfEE/QCA.

Department for Education and Science (2003b). *Drama objectives bank*. London: DfES.

Department for Education and Science (2007). *Teaching speaking and listening* (DVD). London: DfES.

Dickson, P., Bazalgette, C. and Bowker, J. (1996). *A survey of media education: a BFI Education research report*. London: BFI.

Dixon, J. (1991). *A schooling in 'English': critical episodes in the struggle to shape literary and cultural studies*. Milton Keynes: Open University Press.

Dupuy, M-A. (1990). Exhibition notes to *Polyptiques: le tableau multiple du Moyen-Age au vingtième siècle*. Paris: Musée du Louvre, 30 March–23 July 1990.

Durant, A. (1995). Literacy and literature: priorities in English studies towards 2000. In Korte, B. and Müller, K.P. *Anglistische lehre aktuel: probleme, perspektiven, praxis*. Berlin: Wissenschaftlicher Verlag Trier.

Duro, Paul (ed.) (1996). *The rhetoric of the frame: essays on the boundaries of the artwork*. Cambridge: Cambridge University Press.

Dusinberre, J. (2006). *As You Like It* (Arden edition). London: Thomson Learning.

Eagleton, T. (1983). *Literary theory: an introduction*. Minneapolis: University of Minnesota Press.

Edwards, C., Gandini, L. and Forman, G. (eds) (1993). *The hundred languages of children: the Reggio Emilia approach to early childhood education*. Norwood, NJ: Ablex.

Eisner, E. (1989). Structure and magic in discipline-based art education. In Thistlewood, D. (ed.) *Critical studies in art and design education*. Harlow: Longman, 14–26.

Elkins, J. (ed.) (2008). *Visual literacy*. New York: Routledge.

Fairclough, N. (1991). *Language and power*. Harlow: Longman.

Frake, C.O. (1977). Plying frames can be dangerous: some reflections on methodology in cognitive anthropology. *The Quarterly Newsletter of the Institute for Comparative Human Development*, The Rockefeller University, 1:1–7.

Franses, R. (1996). Postmonumentality: frame, grid, space, quilt. In Duro (ed.), 258–73.

Freeman, J. (1989) *The Dada & Surrealist word-image*. Cambridge, MA: The MIT Press.

Frow, J. (1986). *Marxism and literary history*. Oxford: Basil Blackwell.

Gardner, H. (1985). *Frames of mind: the theory of multiple intelligences*. London: Heinemann.

Gardner, H. (1993). *The unschooled mind: how children think and how schools should teach*. London: Fontana.

Gee, J.P. (1999). *An introduction to discourse analysis: theory and method*. London: Routledge.

Goffman, E. (1974). *Frame analysis*. New York: Harper & Row.

Goodnow, J. (1977). *Children's drawing*. London: Fontana/Open Books.

Goodson, I. and Medway, P. (eds) (1990). *Bringing English to order: the history and politics of a school subject*. London: Falmer.

Graham, S. and Perin, D. (2006). *Writing next: effective strategies to improve writing of adolescents in middle and high schools*. Washington, DC: Alliance for Excellent Education.

Graham-Dixon, A. (1994). *Howard Hodgkin*. London: Thames & Hudson.

Graves, D. (1982). *Writing: teachers and children at work*. Portsmouth, NH: Heinemann.

Greatrex, P. (1992). How much more does a picture say? Beyond theprinted page – reading and interpreting the narrative power of children'spicture book illustration. Unpublished BEd dissertation, Middlesex University, School of Education.

Green, B. (1988). Literature as curriculum frame: a critical perspective. In Hart (1988), 46–71.

Green, B. (1995). On compos(IT)ing: writing differently in the post-age. Paper presented at the Annual National Conference of the Australian Association for the Teaching of English, Sydney, 13–16 January 1995.

Gumperz, J.J. (1977). Sociocultural knowledge in conversational inference. In Saville-Troike, M. (ed.) *Georgetown University round table on languages and linguistics 1977*. Washington, DC: Georgetown University Press, 191–211.

Gumperz, J.J. (1982). *Discourse strategies*. Cambridge: Cambridge University Press.

Haas, C. (1995). *Writing technology: studies in the materiality of literacy*. Mahwah, NJ: Lawrence Erlbaum.

Hardcastle, J., Medway, P., Andrews, R. and Crook, D. (2008). *Final bid to the Leverhulme Trust, Social change and English, 1945–65: a study of three London schools*. London: Institute of Education, University of London.

Hart, K. (ed.) (1988). *Shifting frames: English/literature/writing* (Typereader Publications No. 2). Melbourne: Deakin University, Centre for Studies in Literary Education.

Haythornthwaite, C. and Andrews, R. (forthcoming). *E-learning: theory and practice*. London: Sage.

Herrnstein Smith, B. (1968). *Poetic closure*. Chicago: Chicago University Press.

Heseltine, M. (1996). The heritage and the superhighway: a new golden age of patronage and opportunity. Speech at the Royal Society of Arts, London, 16 May 1996.

Hill, G. (1995). Exhibition at Guggenheim Museum, SoHo, New York City, 11 May–20 August 1995.

Hodgkin, H. (1996). *Paintings 1975–1996*. Exhibition at Hayward Gallery, London, 5 December 1996–23 February 1997.

Hodgkin, H. (2008). *Paintings*. Exhibition at Gagosian Gallery, Brittania Street, London, 3 April–17 May 2008.

Hoggart, R. (1957). *The uses of literacy*. Harmondsworth: Penguin.

Honderich, T. (ed.) (1995). *The Oxford companion to philosophy*. Oxford: Oxford University Press.

Horner, W.B. (ed.) (1990). *The present state of scholarship in historical and contemporary rhetoric*. Columbia: University of Missouri Press.

Howatson, M.C. (ed.) (1989). *The Oxford companion to classical literature*. Oxford: Oxford University Press.

Illeris, K. (2007). *How we learn: learning and non-learning in school and beyond* (2nd edition). London: Routledge.

Illeris, K. (ed.) (2008). *Contemporary theories of learning*. London: Routledge.

Isherwood, S. and Stanley, N. (1994). *Creating vision: photography and the National Curriculum*. London: The Arts Council.

Jones, N. (1991). A map of reading. In Dougill, P. (ed.) *Developing English*. Buckingham: Open University Press, 81–97.

Kammler, B. (1984). Punch writes again: a child at play. *Australian Journal of Reading*, 7:2, 61–70.

Kellogg, R. (1969). *Analyzing children's art*. Palo Alto, CA: National Press Books.

Kemp, W. (1996). The narrativity of the frame. In Duro (1996), 11–23.

Kinmouth, P. (1984). Howard Hodgkin. In *Vogue* [UK] 141, June 1984.

Kinneavy, J. (1971). *A theory of discourse: the aims of discourse*. Austin, TX: University of Texas Press.

Kress, G. (1995). *Writing the future: English and the making of a culture of innovation*. Sheffield: National Association for the Teaching of English.

Kress, G. (1996). The place of writing in the light of the turn to the visual. Paper presented at School of Education research seminar, Middlesex University, London, 27 June 1996.

Kress, G. (1997). *Before writing: rethinking the paths to literacy*. London: Routledge.

Kress, G. (2003). *Literacy in the new media age*. London: Routledge.

Kress, G. (2004). A theory of children's meaning making. In Grainger, T. *The RoutledgeFalmer Reader in Language and Literacy*. London: RoutledgeFalmer, 81.

Kress, G. and van Leeuwen, T. (1996/2006). *Reading images: the grammar of visual design*. London: Routledge.

Kress, G. and van Leeuwen, T. (2001). *Multimodal discourse: the modes and media of contemporary communication*. London: Edward Arnold.

Kuhn, D. (1996). The view from giants' shoulders. Paper presented at the April 1996 Piaget/Vygotsky Centenary, Brighton.

Lanham, R. (1993). *The electronic word*. Chicago: University of Chicago Press.

Lanham, R. (1995). Digital literacy. *Scientific American*, September 1995, 160–1.

Li, L. (2005). My language autobiography: a critical view. *English in Education*, 39:3, 93–108.

Lucquet, G.H. (1927). *Le dessin infantin*. Paris: Alcan.

MacLachlan, G. and Reid, I. (1994). *Framing and interpretation*. Melbourne: Melbourne University Press.

MacLure, M., Phillips, T. and Wilkinson, A. (1988). *Oracy matters: the development of talking and listening in education*. Milton Keynes: Open University Press.

Markle, S.M. (1969). *Good frames and bad: a grammar of frame writing*. New York: Wiley.

Matisse, H. (1943). Temoingnage. In Fourcade, D. (ed.) *Ecrits et propos sur l'art*. Paris: Hermann (1972), 196.

Matthews, J. (1988). The young child's early representation and drawing. In Cohen, A. and Cohen, L. (eds). *Early education: the pre-school years*. London: PCP Education Series.

Matthews, J. (1994). *Helping young children to paint and draw: children and visual representation*. London: Hodder and Stoughton.

Medway, P. (1988). Response to Ian Reid. In Hart (1988), 90–3.

Medway, P. (1990). Into the sixties: English and English society at a time of change. In Goodson, and Medway (1990), 1–46.

Medway, P. (1996). Writing, speaking, drawing: the distribution of meaning in architects' communication. In van der Geest, T. and Sharples, M. *The new writing environment: writers at work in a world of technology*. Berlin: Springer-Verlag, 25–42.

Meek, M. (1991). *On being literate*. London: Bodley Head.

Miller, C.R. (1984). Genre as social action. *Quarterly Journal of Speech*, 70, 151–67.

Mitchell, S. (1992). *The teaching and learning of argument in sixth forms and higher education: interim report*. Hull: University of Hull, Centre for Studies in Rhetoric.

Mitchell, S. (1994). *The teaching and learning of argument in sixth forms and higher education: final report*. Hull: University of Hull, Centre for Studies in Rhetoric.

Mitchell, S. and Riddle, M. (2000). *Improving the quality of argument in higher education: final report*. London: Middlesex University, School of Lifelong Learning and Education.

Mitchell, W.J.T. (1986). *Iconology: image, text, ideology*. Chicago: University of Chicago Press.

Mitchell, W.J.T. (1994). *Picture theory*. Chicago: University of Chicago Press.

Mitchell, W.J.T. (1995). What is visual culture? In Lavin, I. (ed.) *Meaning in the visual arts: essays in commemoration of Edwin Panofsky* (1892–1968). Princeton, NJ: Institute of Advanced Studies.

Mitchell, W.J.T. (2002). Showing seeing: a critique of visual culture. In Mirzoeff, N. (ed.) *The visual culture reader* (2nd edition). London: Routledge, 86–101.

Moffett, J. (1968/1987). *Teaching the universe of discourse*. Portsmouth, NH: Boynton-Cook.

Myhill, D. and Fisher, R. (2005). *Informing practice in English: a review of recent research in literacy and the teaching of English*. London: Ofsted.

National Portrait Gallery (1996). *The art of the picture frame*. Exhibition at National Portrait Gallery, London, 8 November 1996–9 February 1997.

Nelson, R.S. and Shiff, R. (eds.) (1996). *Critical terms for art history*. Chicago: University of Chicago Press.

Newbolt, H. (1921/2005). *The Teaching of English in England*. London: Phaidon.

New Zealand Ministry of Education (1993). *English in the New Zealand curriculum*. Wellington: Ministry of Education.

Nicholson, A. (2008). *Sissinghurst*. Swindon: The National Trust.

Ofsted (2005). *English 2000–2005: a review of inspection evidence*. London: Office for Standards in Education.

Ofsted (2006). *The annual report of Her Majesty's Chief Inspector of Schools*. London: The Stationery Office.

Pavel, T. (1986). *Fictional worlds*. Cambridge, MA: Harvard University Press.

Plantinga, A. (1974). *The nature of necessity*. Oxford: Clarendon Press.

Poole, C. (1995). *Framing the child: photography in the classroom*. Stoke-on-Trent: Trentham Books.

Pound, E. (1964). *The Cantos*. London: Faber and Faber.

Pound, E. (1970). *Drafts and fragments of cantos CX–CXVII*. London: Faber and Faber.

Queneau, R. (1947). *Exercises de style*. Paris: Editions Gallimard.

Queneau, R. (1979). *Exercises in style*. London: John Calder.

Raney, K. (1997). *Visual literacy: issues and debates*. London: Middlesex University School of Education (Reports and Evaluations series) and the Arts Council.

Reid, I. (1988). Genre as frame: redesigning for English/literature/writing. In Hart, K. (1988), 77–89.

Reid, I. (1996). *Higher education or education for hire? Language and values in Australian universities.* Rockhampton: Central Queensland University Press.

Richards, I.A. (1929). *Practical criticism: a study of literary judgement.* London: Kegan Paul.

Roberts, J. (2005). *Guide to scripts used in English writings up to 1500.* London: British Library.

Rogoff, B. (1991). *Apprenticeship in thinking: cognitive development in social context.* New York: Oxford University Press.

Russell, J. (1967). Hodgkin colour locals. *ARTnews* 66, May 1967.

Scholes, R. (1985). *Textual power: literary theory and the teaching of English.* New Haven: Yale University Press.

Sheeran, Y. and Barnes, D. (1991). *School writing: discovering the ground rules.* Milton Keynes: Open University Press.

Simon, J. (1996). *The art of the picture frame.* London: National Portrait Gallery.

Solzhenitsyn, A. (1973). *Stories and prose poems.* London: Penguin.

Smith, A. and Andrews, R. (2009). Towards a comprehensive, contemporary model: writing development. Paper given at Symposium on Hybridity, Multimodality and New Forms of Composing, American Educational Research Association Convention, San Diego, 13–17 April 2009.

Smith, B.H. (1968). *Poetic closure: a study of how poems end.* Chicago: Chicago University Press.

Smith, N.R. (1972). The origins of graphic symbolization in children 3–5. Unpublished PhD dissertation, Harvard University.

Sontag, S. (1995). About Hodgkin. In Auping et al. (1995), 105–12.

Staniszewski, M.A. (1995). *Believing is seeing: creating the culture of art.* London: Penguin.

Stoneman, P. (1992). Reading across media: the case of *Wuthering Heights.* In Andrews (ed.) (1992), 172–96.

Street, B.V. (1985). *Literacy in theory and practice.* Cambridge: Cambridge University Press.

Street, B.V. (1996). Academic literacies. In *Challenging ways of knowing: in English, mathematics and science.* London: Falmer Press, 101–13.

Summerfield, G. (1965). *Topics in English for the secondary school.* London: Batsford.

Summerfield, G. (ed.) (1968). *Voices.* Harmondsworth: Penguin Education.

Summerfield, G. (ed.) (1970). *Junior voices.* Harmondsworth: Penguin Education.

Summerfield, G. (ed.) (1979). *Worlds.* Harmondsworth: Penguin Education.

Tannen, D. (ed.) (1993). *Framing in discourse.* New York: Oxford University Press.

Tonfoni, G. (1994). *Writing as a visual art.* Oxford: Intellect Books.

Toulmin, S. (1958/2003) *The uses of argument.* Cambridge: Cambridge University Press.

Tweddle, S. et al. (1994). *The future curriculum with IT: implementing English for the 21st century.* Coventry: National Council for Educational Technology.

Vickers, B. (1988). *In defence of rhetoric.* Oxford: Clarendon Press.

Vieler-Porter, C.G. (1984). On the classification and framing of the documentary text, unpublished dissertation, University of London.

Vygotsky, L. (1971). *The psychology of art.* Cambridge, MA: The MIT Press.

Vygotsky, L. (1978). The prehistory of written language. In *Mind in society.* Cambridge, MA: Harvard University Press.

Vygotsky, L. (1962/1986). *Language and thought*. Cambridge, MA: The MIT Press.

Walton, K. (1995). *Picture my world*. London: The Arts Council.

Wolf, D.P. (1989). Artistic learning as conversation. In Hargreaves, D. (ed.) *Children and the arts*. Milton Keynes: Open University Press.

Wray, D. (2004). *Teaching literacy: using texts to enhance learning*. London: David Fulton.

Zhao, H.Y.H. (2000). *Towards a modern Zen theatre: Gao Xingjian and Chinese theatre experimentalism*. London: University of London, School of Oriental and African Studies.

Index